# A Guide to Castles & Moated Sites in Herefordshire

Monuments in the Landscape

Volume II

# A Guide to Castles & Moated Sites in Herefordshire

by
**Ron Shoesmith**

**Logaston Press**

LOGASTON PRESS
Little Logaston Woonton Almeley
Herefordshire HR3 6QH


First published by Logaston Press 1996
Copyright © Ron Shoesmith 1996

ISBN 1 873827 59 8


Set in Times 11/13 pt by Logaston Press
and printed in Great Britain by The Cromwell Press, Melksham

# Contents

|  |  | Page |
|---|---|---|
| Acknowledgments | | vii |
| Introduction | | viii |

**Part One - Herefordshire, a county of castles**

| I | Herefordshire's origins as a Border County | 1 |
| II | The Domesday Evidence | 11 |
| III | Early Castles - Siting and Design | 21 |
| IV | Building in Stone | 29 |
| V | Decline and Decay | 37 |

**Part Two - The Sites**

| The Gazetteer | | 41 |
| *including a Parish Map* | | 44 |
| Index of Site Names, giving Parishes | | 243 |
| Select Bibliography | | 245 |

# Please Note

Whilst many of the sites mentioned in this book are situated alongside roads and public paths, most are on private land and permission from the owner must, therefore, be obtained before visiting them. Access arrangements are given for what are considered to be the main sites which are often, fortunately, fairly accessible.

The following points must always be observed:

1. Always follow the Countryside Code.

2. On all sites, extreme care should be taken.

3. Any artefacts found within the county should be reported to the County Archaeological Officer or at any local museum.

4. Under no circumstances should visitors dig around or on any site. Any damage could result in prosecution.

5. It is an offence under the 1979 Ancient Monuments and Archaeological Areas Act to use metal detectors on or near scheduled ancient monuments. In addition, simple 'treasure hunting' near ancient monuments can well damage evidence to such an extent that archaeologists are unable to interpret it fully in the future.

# Acknowledgments

The author of almost any book that contains a gazetteer is dependent on many other people who have gathered information together and recorded it in one form or another. In Herefordshire, much of this stirling work has been undertaken during the last twenty years or so by members of the Archaeological Research Section of the Woolhope Naturalists Field Club, amongst whom several stand out and have been of particular help—Paul Remfry, who in addition read the drafts of this volume; Roger Stirling-Brown, who allowed me to use the results of his researches; Bruce Coplestone-Crow, who can always be relied on to produce additional early historical information; and the late Richard Kay, whose careful and meticulous drawings of historic sites throughout the area should be an inspiration to us all.

Several castles in the county have been surveyed in detail by present and past members of the City of Hereford Archaeology Unit including Richard Morriss, Alan Thomas, Richard Stone, Nic Appleton-Fox, Robert Williams, Tim Hoverd and Steve Macklin. The history of Goodrich Castle has been researched by Bruce Coplestone-Crow and Dr Pat Hughes in preparation for an English Heritage Research Report—I am grateful to them for allowing me to use a précis of their material. Special thanks must also go to Brian Byron for the last minute rush of work on maps and plans and for the reconstruction drawings used in this book. Photographs have been obtained from many sources and once again I am full of gratitude to Ken Hoverd who has been responsible for several of those included, notably of Bronsil, Goodrich and Wigmore.

This book has taken much longer in preparation that was anticipated and throughout that period my wife, Ruth, and our children, Ben and Katy, have had to tolerate my moods when the work seemed never-ending. To them my love and thanks for their understanding. Finally Andy Johnson of Logaston Press has been a shoulder to lean on as publication dates came closer and closer.

# Introduction

A book such as this can be several years in the writing and can often change its form and character during the writing process. Originally this book was designed to present the results of over a decade of work that has been undertaken by the City of Hereford Archaeology Unit on castles in Herefordshire. After several chapters had been produced in a first draft state, Logaston Press went to press with its first volume in the 'Monuments in the Landscape' series—*Prehistoric Sites of Herefordshire*.

It was then suggested that the proposed book on Herefordshire castles could become a second volume in that series, presenting information about the many castles in the county in addition to the new information about the few that had originally been proposed. The book was redesigned with the main section becoming a gazetteer and reference work to all possible sites. The introductory chapters from the original work were retained and the chapters on individual castles were subsumed into the gazetteer. As the work progressed, it became increasingly difficult to establish any conclusive arguments to separate simple castles and ringworks from moated sites. As a result, it was decided that all moated sites should be included in the gazetteer. In addition three new chapters describing the growth, design and decline of the castle in Herefordshire have been written.

There are several hundred sites mentioned in this volume. Whilst many have been visited personally, descriptions of others will be out-of-date and there will be some inevitable mistakes. Suggestions and amendments for any future edition will always be welcomed.

Ron Shoesmith,
October 1996

# CHAPTER I

## Herefordshire's origins as a Border County

Throughout recorded history Herefordshire has always been one of the counties, along with Shropshire and Cheshire to the north and the Forest of Dean section of Gloucestershire to the south, that separated the main part of England from the ancient principality of Wales. Here are the Welsh Marches, lowland areas as compared with the mountains and hills of Wales to the west, but areas that are, in their own right, effectively separated from the rest of England by natural features. In the south, the long curve of the River Severn forms an impressive barrier from its wide estuary, sweeping around the whole southern coast of Wales, northwards through Gloucester and Worcester to Shrewsbury and beyond. Further north, the River Dee forms a similar barrier between the main part of Cheshire to the east and the coastal regions of north Wales to the west. The other great river of the Marches is the Wye, which separates south-western Herefordshire from the rest of the county.

Herefordshire is a well-contained county with most of its borders due to natural features. On the east, separating the county very firmly from the rest of England, are the Malvern Hills, ancient rocks that grow steeply out of the clay lowlands of the Midland plain further east. South of Ross-on-Wye is the Forest of Dean, still well-wooded and probably as difficult to penetrate in earlier times as it is now. The Wye valley provides a route from Herefordshire through Monmouth to Chepstow on the Severn Estuary and separates the Forest on the east from the uplands around Trelleck to the west, where once again large areas remain afforested. The modern boundary between England and Wales, between Herefordshire and the Welsh county of Brecknock, follows a ridge of the Black Mountains running to the west and high above the Olchon valley. The boundary then drops down to Hay where the River Wye flows out of Wales. The river valley is quite narrow here, and the encircling hills continue to the north-west with Hergest Ridge and Rushock Hill just to the west of Kington. Here the main road from Leominster passes through Kington on its way to Aberystwyth. Further north, the Lugg valley leads through Presteigne into the Radnorshire uplands, whilst the narrow valley of the Teme provides a third route into Wales. These routes were often the scene of conflict between the English and the Welsh and provide the sites of many castles, complementing the natural defences further to the south.

In the north of the county, the wooded areas around Bringewood Chase separate the two natural routes leading into Shropshire; one through Leintwardine, following the River Clun and the route of the Roman road along the Welsh border, and the other through Ludlow, Bromfield and Craven Arms along the River Onny, the route followed by the modern A49 Welsh border road. Finally, there is the north-eastern part of the county, an area with a collection of small valleys and sudden rises that has proved to be an effective barrier to any principal through route apart from the winding A44 from Leominster through Bromyard to Worcester.

The predominant surface rocks of the county are associated with the Devonian Old Red Sandstone with Dittonian sandstones, grits and marls forming the lower parts of the Black Mountains and the capping of most hills in the west of the county. These soft sandstones provide the familiar red colour of many Herefordshire castles. The limestone exposures are often associated with springs and lead to the creation of tufa, a limestone growth on sphagnum moss, that can be cut into blocks with a spade and then dried and used as a light-weight building material. It was used particularly in the twelfth and thirteenth centuries for vaulting and as quoins. Found particularly in the Moccas and Downton areas, it was used in castles and churches throughout the county.

To the south-east of Hereford folding and erosion has brought the limestones and shales of the Silurian period to the surface in what is known as the Woolhope Dome. These rocks are rich in fossils from the shallow sea that then covered the whole of Herefordshire as far east as the Malvern Hills. This complex series of deposits is now deeply buried over the whole county except for the Woolhope exposure and areas in the north of the county around Aymestrey and Wigmore. The stone from these deposits provides a completely different building material to that in the rest of the county—it is easy to quarry and shape, but weathers badly if not protected as is evident at Wigmore Castle.

The geological event that finally shaped Herefordshire was the drift, or debris, left by the Wye glacier. In the west of the county the glacier just about covered Merbach Hill (318m above sea level). In this area the drift is of no great thickness, the underlying sandstone being often exposed. Further down the Wye towards Hereford there are terminal moraines at Staunton-on-Wye (Oakers Hill) and, close to the city, a great band that runs from Three Elms through Stretton Sugwas to Kingstone and Whitfield. The thickness is well shown at the gravel quarry at Stretton Sugwas which is over 30m deep. A short distance to the east, the city of Hereford is well founded, being built on some 350 hectares of best quality gravel! The northern branch of the Wye glacier followed the valleys of the Arrow, Lugg and Teme, where other, smaller moraines are apparent. In the lower lying parts of the county that are covered with this glacial debris, stone was not readily available as a building material and the use of timber was prevalent. This has left many of the large castles in central Herefordshire appearing just as earthworks. Although in later years stone may have been imported for defensive works, most of the internal buildings in these castles would have continued to be made of timber. In addition, once a castle in an area where stone was scarce became deserted, it was much more likely to become the prey of stone-robbers than would be the case with an equivalent building in an area where stone was readily available.

The earliest human occupation in the county dates to the Upper Palaeolithic period (35,000 to 10,000 BC) with a few scattered finds, but it is only in the rock shelters on the Doward that any definite evidence of occupation has been found. This was followed by the 5,000 or so years of the Mesolithic period which flourished as the temperature rose and woodlands thrived. It is only in the south and west of the county that there is evidence of occupation during this period, and this is mainly towards the end of the Mesolithic. Once again, it is mainly on the Doward, but there is an increasing amount of evidence in and around the Golden Valley and the Black Mountains.

The Neolithic period heralded a gradual change from hunting to farming and brought with it a progressive increase in the more settled population of the county. Direct evidence for Neolithic settlement is still limited to the south-western part of the county, where there is also a concentration of chambered tombs and finds of flints and stone axes. A lack of settlement evidence also characterises the Bronze Age, although barrows, cist burials and standing stones provide evidence for the continuation of human occupation throughout most of the county.

It is with the Iron Age, starting around 800 BC, that the population of Herefordshire grew to the extent that each clan had its own settlement, usually located on the top of a hill with massive earthen defences and complex entrances. Some of the hillforts were the size of small towns—the largest, Credenhill, some 8km north-west of Hereford, covered 20 hectares and could have supported a population of some 3 to 4,000. Indeed, Credenhill can well be seen as the natural predecessor of Hereford as the capital of an area roughly synonymous with the modern county. Towards the end of the Iron Age the total population of the county could well have been as high as 25,000, a figure not to be reached again until the late Middle Ages. In the lowland areas farms were established and the land was gradually cleared to grow the grain that was needed to feed the increasing population (Children & Nash, 1994; Stanford, 1991).

The Roman invasion of Britain began in AD 43, but it was several years later that Ostorius Scapula led a campaign against the tribes occupying the Herefordshire hillforts. He took the frontier westwards to a line that ran through Usk, Clyro and Leintwardine. Eventually, by the mid-to-late 70s the whole area had been subdued and legionary fortresses were built at Caerleon in the south and Chester in the north. Although the whole of Wales was nominally under Roman control, the frontier was preserved between the military area in Wales and the rest of the province which was under civilian rule. The Romans maintained garrisons at many strategic points, including Leintwardine in the north of Herefordshire, whilst the civilian population was rapidly dispersed, some to work on farms and others to be sent abroad. At the same time most of the hillforts were slighted and almost all were abandoned. The effects of the warfare, coupled with the changes in culture as a result of the gradual Roman settlement of the county were probably jointly responsible for the reduction of the native population of Herefordshire throughout the three hundred year period after the birth of Christ.

Although only a few Roman villas have been found in Herefordshire, it is significant that most are in the area around the only Roman town in the county, at Kenchester, just below the deserted hillfort at Credenhill. This was *Magnis*, well-defended, but in size small by Roman standards. In the east of the county there was a village at Canon Frome, presumably acting as a centre for agricultural activities in the fertile Frome valley, whilst in the south-east of the county was Herefordshire's other major Roman community at Weston-under-Penyard. This was *Ariconium*, an industrial settlement, making use of iron ore, timber, and charcoal from the Forest of Dean. The more hilly areas in the south-west and north of the county would probably have continued under military control (Stanford, 1991).

When the Roman legions withdrew from Britain at the beginning of the fifth century, attempts were made to defend the towns and villages. It was perhaps inevitable that this was not to be, and within a relatively short length of time all the major Roman settlements had been abandoned, their buildings in ruins. Within a couple of generations at the most, the population had probably been further decimated and war lords such as Vortigern, Ambrosius Aurelianus and the semi-legendary King Arthur, all of whom may well have been associated with Herefordshire, came to the fore (Andere, 1996). Roman settlements soon disappeared, gradually becoming buried in their own debris.

But the Roman legionnaires left the whole of the British Isles with a monument in the landscape that is still with us today—the Roman road system that joined their military establishments with straight lines, irrespective of the contours of the ground. In Herefordshire there were two principal roads; the main north-south road that followed the whole of the Welsh border, joining Chester in the north with Caerleon in south Wales, and passing through Wroxeter, Leintwardine and Kenchester; and the west-east road leading from Clyro, again through Kenchester and thence to Canon Frome and Gloucester (Margary, 1967, 342). It was these roads, neglected for several generations but still usable, that formed the basic routes from the more civilised central areas of England into and through the Welsh border area at the time of the Norman Conquest.

Virtually nothing is known about the area that is now Herefordshire during the two to three hundred years after the Roman troops abandoned the country. The few people who were left probably held on to small farms of which few traces can be expected to survive. Slowly, a measure of order came out of the chaos and small kingdoms began to emerge. The Saxon kingdom of Mercia was formed in the Midlands and under the rule of King Penda its boundaries extended westwards with the incorporation, probably by agreement, of south Shropshire and north Herefordshire at some time between 630 and 650. By the time that Penda died, in 655, the kingdom of Mercia extended from the Welsh border to the North Sea.

This huge midland state was basically a federation of several peoples and, with Penda's death, it appears to have been split into several parts. Certainly by the late seventh century there was a sub-kingdom of the Hwicce which was based on the newly-created bishopric of Worcester; and the land belonging to the Magonsæte[1], which included the parts of north Herefordshire and south Shropshire that had been taken out of the vast diocese of Lichfield to form the new diocese of Hereford. Merewald or Merewalh, considered to be the third son of Penda, apparently became the king of the Magonsæte. He had several daughters, all of whom became saints, including St Mildburg founder of the monastery at Much Wenlock.

The Mercia of Penda was a pagan country, but Merewalh and the Magonsæte were converted to Christianity some time after 660. The diocese of Hereford, which was formed about 676 with Putta as the

---

1. The Magonsæte were long supposed to be the people associated with the Roman town of *Magnis* at Kenchester. It has now been shown that this is probably erroneous and a more likely derivation is from one of the many place names containing *Maund* to the north-east of Hereford (Gelling, 1992, 82).

first bishop, had its borders almost as far north as Shrewsbury and, not surprisingly considering Mildburg's association, included Much Wenlock to the north-east. Although there has been much discussion about the seat of administration of Merewalh and, indeed, the original seat of the bishop, it would seem reasonable, on the whole, to accept that it was at Hereford rather than the often-quoted alternative of Leominster.

The southern part of Herefordshire was following a completely different path to that of the north. By the middle of the sixth century it had become a small independent kingdom in its own right—the Welsh kingdom of Ergyng (Davies, 1979, 74f.). It included lands on both sides of the Wye and was named after the Roman settlement of *Ariconium*, in the south-east of the county near Ross. A glance at a map of the county shows a massive concentration of Celtic and British place-names in the southern part of Herefordshire as compared with the the rest of the county and the neighbouring counties to the north and east (Gelling, 1992, 69-70 & Fig 34)[2]. It is now considered likely that Christianity continued in the Ergyng area right through from the Roman period. The last king of Ergyng, Gwrfoddw, set up religious foundations at Bellimoor and Garway in 610 and 615, and probably others at Welsh Bicknor and Llandinabo (Davies, 1979, 74f.).

With the death of Gwrfoddw, it appears that Ergyng came under the control of the kings of Gwent, but part of it at least, continued to preserve its own identity. It gained a new name, Archenfield, and was still sufficiently independent to have its own bishop, Cyfeiliog, in 914.

The boundaries of the kingdom of Mercia continued to alter and the Magonsæte once again became part of that kingdom. Welsh raids over the border in the early eighth century demonstrated that the agreed borders were not respected. This was to change with the arrival of Offa on the throne of Mercia in 757.

Although Offa (757-96) attempted to define the boundary between Wales and Mercia by the construction of the great earthwork that still

2. Indeed Gelling comments 'in the greater part of Herefordshire, Welsh speech cannot have been exceptional.' This language tradition continued in the county and even in Hereford city well into the seventeenth century (Shoesmith, 1995, 39).

bears his name, it did not remain a stable frontier line. For several centuries, up to and well beyond the Norman Conquest of England, there were regular periods of border warfare and the frontier inevitably suffered many changes. Indeed, the modern boundary bears little resemblance to the line of the earthwork over much of its length. It is only the walkers, following the Offa's Dyke footpath, that can dimly appreciate the logic behind the various alignments and the sheer effort that went into its construction.

The line of Offa's Dyke runs from the estuary of the Dee near Prestatyn to a point close to the confluence of the Wye and Severn near Chepstow, a distance as the crow flies of almost 200kms. It was described in detail some 40 years ago (Fox, 1955). There are stretches where its alignment is uncertain and other places where the Dyke probably never existed, but even so it was a massive undertaking, both in terms of men and organisation. In its most prominent stretches the ditch is some 2m deep with the embankment rising up 7m on the inside. It could represent many things, from a negotiated frontier to a complex patrol line. Was this the answer to the border raids that culminated in the battle of Hereford in 760?

The Dyke is not continuous throughout the county—there is a 7.5km long gap south of Lyonshall and a total lack of any trace from Bridge Sollars, 8km west of Hereford, to Redbrook in Gloucestershire. The northern gap could possibly have been defended by a strong timber palisade—the area was well wooded—but the long southern gap requires a more pragmatic solution. Rather than accepting the suggestion that this massive embankment and its associated ditch has mysteriously been totally flattened throughout much of Herefordshire, it would seem far more likely that the reason for the lack of a marked out frontier was associated with the presence of the semi-independent and privileged buffer state that had earlier been called Ergyng and was then known as Archenfield.

The older kingdom of Ergyng had extended some distance east of the Wye, perhaps as far as the Severn. During Offa's reign, and indeed for some considerable time afterwards, this eastern area was still apparently considered to be part of Archenfield, although it would appear that the two halves had been gradually growing apart. During the sixth and seventh centuries, according to the *Book of Llandaff*, the then kingdom of Ergyng had also incorporated the

Dore valley and had a northern frontier following the Wye as far as Hay. To the west of Erging, and north of the kingdom of Gwent, was the Welsh commote of Ewyas, apparently centred on the area around Clodock and Longtown in the Olchon valley. By Offa's time then, there were two parts of this miniature state, separated by the Wye from a point near Monmouth in the south to Holme Lacy in the north.

If it is accepted that the Wye was the eastern and northern boundary of the western part of Archenfield at the time of Offa, then the lack of any demarcation in this area would suggest that the Welsh of this buffer state had come to an arrangement with the king that the Wye would act as a frontier. This would have accelerated the break-up of Archenfield into its two component parts, for it can be assumed that from that time onwards Welsh law and customs were accepted on one side of the river, whilst on the other side Mercian law began. Although it has been suggested that the river would be a poor barrier because of low summer levels and frequent crossing places (Gelling, 1983, 14), it would surely have been as good as the embankment and dry ditch of the main part of the Dyke. If it was a patrolled boundary, the main problem would be the length—the Wye from Ross to Fownhope follows a tortuous 29km course whilst the direct line is a mere 11km. As a boundary it is acceptable, but as a line that was regularly patrolled, it would have had obvious difficulties.

Although Offa had fixed the border between England and Wales in Shropshire and the northern part of Herefordshire, and Archenfield filled the gap in the southern part of the county, this did not mean that there was peace throughout the 300 or so years between the Dyke being built and the Norman Conquest. It does appear that there were some lengthy intervals when peace prevailed, but they were interspersed with periods of border raiding and open warfare. Indeed, Mercian expansion into Wales followed shortly after the end of Offa's reign and by 816 they had apparently penetrated into the area around Snowdon.

The attacks by the Danes did not really have much effect on Herefordshire, although, in 893, Aethelred of Mercia called out the king's thegns 'from every fortress (?burh) east of the Parret both west and east of Selwood, and also north of the Thames and west of the Severn together with a section of the Welsh' in order to defeat the Danes at Buttington in Montgomeryshire. Hereford at that time was almost certainly the only Saxon 'burh' west of the Severn and was obviously an important part of the West Saxon defensive system (Whitehead, 1982, 14).

The independent state of Archenfield seems to have continued to exist well into the tenth century, but only to the west of the Wye, and probably with the loss of its northern territories. For several generations the people of Archenfield on the east of the Wye had gone their own way taking up the English laws and customs. The situation was apparently regularised when the 'Ordinance concerning the Dunsæte' was drawn up, probably by King Athelstan in consultation with the Welsh around 926. It is suggested that the Dunsæte included the people of both parts of Archenfield and possibly those of other surrounding areas. The Ordinance was a set of laws providing regulations and penalties to be observed between the Welsh section of the Dunsæte on the one side of an unnamed river and the English section on the other. It is assumed that the Wye was the unnamed river. The presence of such a document infers that the separation of the Dunsæte into two distinct parts was of long standing. The rules may have lasted for a short while, but the elaborate procedures concerning the tracking of cattle thieves outlined in the Ordinance may well have fallen into disuse once the Wye ceased to be considered as a boundary and the division of the area into 'Hundreds' became of more importance. To a certain extent the medieval Deanery of Archenfield reflects the Welsh Dunsæte, whilst the Deanery of Ross may provide a similar indication of the extent of the English Dunsæte (Coplestone-Crow, 1989, 5; Gelling, 1983).

Changes came to the whole of the country, but especially to the Welsh Marches, with the Norman Conquest. The invaders not only brought their own laws and regulations, they also encouraged colonisation, with French knights, monks and tradesmen dominating and exploiting the local populace.

# CHAPTER II

## The Domesday Evidence

When William, Duke of Normandy, became king of England following the Norman Conquest of 1066, he took land from the English owners that showed themselves disloyal to the new rule and shared it out amongst his followers. It was subsequently appreciated that, as a result of these rapid changes, there was no proper record to show who owned what throughout the country. This was a situation that, with taxation in mind, could not be allowed to continue and the *Anglo-Saxon Chronicle* records that in 1085 'the king had deep speech with his counsellors ... and sent men all over England to each shire ... to find out ... what or how much each landholder held ... in land and livestock, and what it was worth.' Some 12 months later, when the information had been gathered together, it was copied into two books which at a later date became known as the Domesday Book. 'Domesday' refers to the 'day of judgment' and the book was so called because the facts within it were not able to be disputed.

In each district, the Commissioners took evidence on oath and then made use of a local body of men known as a 'jury' to verify the facts. They had to determine:

The name of the place; who owned it before 1066, and who owned it at present

The size of the holding (usually in hides, each of which is considered to be sufficient to support one family. It varied from 60 to 120 acres depending upon agricultural conditions.)

The number of freemen, serfs and slaves

The extent of woodland, meadowland and pasture
The number of mills and fishponds
The number of plough teams (oxen at eight to a team)
What the value was before 1066, after 1066, and at the
time of survey
Any other information that they thought relevant such as
customs and local taxes

There was no requirement to name anyone apart from the chief landowners and those who held land from them; the rest were merely counted. Nor was there any requirement to mention, list or count buildings of any description. Individual mentions of castles, houses and churches are therefore very much the exception rather than the rule and are nearly always included only because of a connection with taxation and income.

The Herefordshire section of the Domesday Survey also covers several villages that are now in Radnorshire. The Domesday hundreds are not the same as the medieval ones that survived into the nineteenth century. The Herefordshire section also contains two areas that were still considered to be Welsh—Ewyas and Archenfield. They had a different treatment to the rest for they were still subject to Welsh law although by 1086 they were beginning to be accepted as part of England.

The Domesday Survey clearly suggests that the large areas to the north of the River Wye and west of Offa's Dyke, that had once been part of the kingdom of the Magonsæte, had been part of Herefordshire for many years. This is indicated by the method of assessment. In the survey, long-standing English settlements are reckoned in terms of hides and virgates, whilst the 'new lands' are assessed as plough-lands or carucates. The whole area north of the Wye and west of the Dyke is hidated, as is much of the area to the south of the Wye that was once, according to the *Book of Llandaff*, part of Ergyng. Archenfield and Ewyas, by comparison, are shown separately and both typically contain plough lands. Ewyas and the kingdom of Gwent, according to the *Book of Llandaff*, only came under Anglo-Norman influence shortly after the Conquest. Indeed they continued to keep their Welsh connections for many years thereafter, for both areas remained in a Welsh diocese, originally Llandaff and then St David's, until 1852.

The Survey starts off by describing the customs that applied in Hereford before 1066 and then goes on to describe those that applied in Archenfield. It is evident that that area was still a semi-autonomous Welsh district with its own laws. The major part is not surveyed in any detail at all—the entry simply reads: 'In Archenfield the King has 100 men less 4, who have 73 ploughs, with their men. In customary dues they give 41 sesters of honey, 20s. in place of the sheep that they used to give, and 10s. for hearth tax. They do not pay tax or other customary dues, except that they march in the King's army if they have been ordered. If a free man dies there, the King has his horse with his arms. The King has one ox from a villager when he dies. King Gruffydd and Bleddyn[1] laid this land waste before 1066; therefore what it was like at that time is not known.'[2] The only place in the southern part of Archenfield mentioned by name is Garway. The survey does list some lands in Archenfield—those where Norman lords had succeeded their English predecessors—mainly in the centre and north of the area.

About 1046, Edward the Confessor had allowed several Norman settlers into the area including Ralph, the son of Count Drogo of Vexin, Osbern Pentecost and Richard Scrope. Ralph was made Earl of Hereford and is accredited with the construction of the first castle at Hereford (Lobel, 1969, 2). The town, and possibly the castle, were overrun and destroyed by the Welsh in 1055 (Garmondsway, 1953, 184-7) and the castle may not have been rebuilt until after the Conquest.

Shortly after the Norman Conquest the most important person in the southern part of the Welsh border was William fitz Osbern. He came from Breteuil in Normandy and was made earl of Hereford. Just after the Conquest the border areas were still under the control of the Saxon, Edric the Wild. Although Earl William may have paid

---

1. Gruffydd ap Llywelyn was the ruler of Powys and Gwynedd from about 1039. He was responsible for several raids into England including the one in 1055 when he defeated Earl Ralph of Hereford and his army sacked the city and plundered the cathedral. Archenfield probably suffered during this major raid. Gruffydd died in 1063.
2. The quotes from the Domesday Survey are taken from Thorn & Thorn, 1983. Some of the additional information in this book is from the same source—a valuable reference work for anyone carrying out research on this period in the history of the county.

a short visit to his new territories in 1068, it was not until the autumn of 1069 that he finally quelled Edric at the battle of Stafford and found an area that had been ravaged by the Welsh several times during the previous 20 years.

As earl of Hereford, fitz Osbern had palatinate powers throughout Herefordshire and probably similar powers in Gloucestershire and Worcestershire. A palatine earldom, such as Roger of Montgomery had in Shropshire a few years later, meant that 'the earl wielded all the king's powers as his deputy, not only administratively, but even to the extent of holding all the royal demense land that in any other county would have been managed for the king by the sheriff' (Wighton, 1962). He was also responsible for defence (or attack) along the whole of the southern border with Wales. His first and principal objective was to secure that border area from any future incursions of the Welsh.

In the first instance Earl William secured the southern part of his realm by building a castle at Chepstow and by carrying out raids into Gwent and establishing a firm foothold on the western side of the Wye. It was during these attacks that he probably established castles at Caerleon[3] and at Monmouth. He followed this up with a mixture of treaties and new settlements with the aim of establishing a region which had a consolidated frontier and was fully colonised by people he could trust—settlers from his own lands in Normandy.

Fitz Osbern appreciated that his new territory could not be fully secure unless it was defended by a series of castles on the borders. How far he progressed with this work is uncertain, but the Domesday Book mentions four castles in Herefordshire: Wigmore, Richard's Castle, Clifford and Ewyas Harold. In addition to these castles Domesday records two 'domus defensabiles' or fortified houses, one at Eardisley and the other at Walelege[4]. There could well have been more—the obvious case is the complete lack of any mention in the Survey of the castle of Hereford that had been built by Earl Ralph some years before the Conquest. Although it had

3. It existed in 1086, but there is no evidence for the foundation.
4. Once thought to be at Ailey in Kinnersley Parish, Walelege means 'wood of the Welshmen' and is now thought to be in Brilley Parish, in the region of Welshwood Farm (SO 277 492) although there no trace on the ground (Coplestone-Crow, 1989, 46).

been destroyed in 1055, it was in existence in 1067 when it was 'harassed' by Edric the Wild (Garmondsway, 1953, 200). Fitz Osbern, as Earl of Hereford, would appear to be the most likely contender for the reconstruction of this castle, especially as he was in the process of designing and building a vast new marketplace at Hereford outside the Saxon town defences and encouraging Norman settlers to move there by offering them tax advantages.

Earl William was a loyal follower of the king who was active in several fields. In addition to his many possessions and varied enterprises in Herefordshire he was responsible for Gloucestershire and Worcestershire and had control of the Isle of Wight. He only had a little time to carry out his grand schemes along the southern Welsh border, for shortly after his return to France he was killed at the battle of Cassel on 20 February, 1071. His son, Roger, who was heir to his estates, became involved in an unsuccessful attempt to depose King William in 1074. Because of this Roger forfeited all his English lands to the crown, and his father's uncompleted projects were taken over by others who were to become the dominant families in Herefordshire in the early Middle Ages. Even so, William fitz Osbern's short rule in Herefordshire affected the whole of the subsequent history of the county.

The position of the early castles mentioned in the Domesday Survey relative to the southern part of the Welsh border is of considerable interest. Several reflect the boundary of the country as it was in 1086: Caerleon in the south, replacing the Roman 'Fortress of the Legions', was the limit of expansion from Gloucestershire into the southern part of Gwent. Chepstow controlled the crossing of the River Wye on the line of the important Roman road that had led from Caerleon to Gloucester, and in addition guarded the port of fitz Osbern's realm. Monmouth, also near the border, was at the strategically important junction of the rivers Wye and Monnow. These three castles reflected the conquest of Gwent and the consolidation of the whole of that area following alliances with the local Welsh.

Further to the north, Ewyas Harold Castle was built on land that had been taken from the Welsh before the Conquest. It is in the lower part of the Golden Valley near the confluence of the Dore and Monnow and was well-placed to control both the land of

15

Ewyas and the kingdom of Archenfield. The customs of the land 'in the castlery of Ewyas' are Welsh in origin—rents being paid in sesters of honey and land being measured in carucates. The Domesday Survey records that William fitz Osbern had re-fortified the castle at Ewyas Harold, indicating that it was there before the Conquest. It was probably the 'Pentecost Castle' originally built by Osbern Pentecost, for the Survey records that, in 1086, it belonged to Alfred of Marlborough, a nephew of Pentecost. 'Harold', after whom the castle was eventually named, could have been the son of Ralph, the first Norman earl of Hereford. As with Hereford, this castle could have been destroyed in the 1050s by Gruffydd ap Llewelyn.

The gradual Norman conquest of this remote part of the English border is well shown in the Domesday Survey with Roger de Lacy, the son of Walter, holding land both within the castlery of Ewyas Harold and at Ewyas Lacy (Longtown). The Lacy land did 'not belong to the castlery nor to the Hundred' and it would appear that Roger had only a tenuous hold over it, although he administered justice there. At the time of the Survey he was the greatest of the local tenants in chief being based on the Honour of Weobley.

Clifford Castle, another of those mentioned in the Domesday Survey, overlooks the River Wye where it now forms the boundary between England and Wales. It is also at the opposite end of the Golden Valley to Ewyas Harold. The Survey describes the castle as being built on waste land by Earl William, and goes on to say that at the time of the Survey it was held by his brother-in-law, Ralph de Tosny. Before the Conquest the land had been held by one Browning. The survey records that the castle 'is in the kingdom of England and not subject to any Hundred or customary dues.' It was well situated, being in a position to dominate any movement on the southern side of the Wye and, together with Ewyas Harold, to control the Golden Valley.

There is little evidence in the Survey of any significant attempt to control the area to the north of the Wye. The fortified house at Eardisley may well have been the predecessor of Eardisley Castle. Eardisley, described as being in the middle of a wood, was held by Robert de Baskerville from Roger de Lacy. In the Survey it is treated as a small castle, possibly involving a moat and defensive

*The exterior of the fourteenth century south tower, Wigmore Castle*

wall, and, in a similar fashion to Clifford 'does not pay tax, nor give any customary dues, nor lies in any Hundred.' The other *domus defensabilis* is described as 'a fortified house; a large wood for hunting.'

Further to the north and east, the castles at Wigmore and Richard's Castle were both built on land that had long been part of

England—land that was measured in hides and was within the Hundred system. Wigmore Castle was built by Earl William on waste land called '*Merestun*' that had been held by Gunfrid before 1066. It was forfeited by Earl William's son, Roger, following his rebellion, and at the time of the Survey was held by Ralph de Mortimer. Although the castle was some distance from the Welsh border, it was in the area that had suffered from Gruffydd ap Llywelyn in 1052 and Edric the Wild in 1067. It was midway between the valleys of the Teme and Lugg and close to the line of the main Roman road that followed the Welsh border from Chester in the north to Caerleon in Gwent.

Richard's Castle was in many ways the odd man out. It is some 8km to the east of Wigmore and almost half way between Leominster and Ludlow. Any strategic value that it may have had in a pre-Conquest context would have been replaced by the castle at Wigmore. At the time of the Domesday Survey it was held by Osbern the son of Richard Scrope, a Norman who had settled in Herefordshire well before the Conquest. It is some distance from both the Teme and the Lugg and did not control either valley. In defensive terms it can only be seen as a general stabilising influence in the area following the Welsh raid into north Herefordshire in 1052.

The Domesday Survey provides another interesting viewpoint on these early castles—the potential for the growth of an adjacent settlement. The most impressive example is at Chepstow. One of fitz Osbern's titles was Lord of Striguil, the early name for Chepstow (a corruption of the Welsh '*ystraigyl*'—'the bend') (Delaney & Soulsby, 1975). However this 'bend' in the River Wye should not be thought of as a peninsular town site, but instead as the carefully chosen site for a Norman castle, designed to protect the southern boundary of William's palatinate earldom and to control shipping on the River Wye. The site for the castle was well chosen—a narrow promontory with cliffs plunging some 100m to the river on one side and a dry ravine, separating it from the main peninsula, on the other. It is apparent that Earl William intended that Chepstow Castle would provide him with a secure base for further advances into Wales and would also ensure that supplies could arrive safely from across the River Severn or from further afield. Fitz Osbern's Great Tower still survives as one of the best preserved of the early castle halls of Europe. The use of stone and the enormous size of the building (27.5m long by 9m wide), is an indication of the importance that fitz Osbern attached to his one castle next to the sea.

But Earl William was responsible for far more than the castle at Chepstow as the Domesday Survey shows: 'Earl William made the castle of Estrighoiel and it paid in his time only for vessels going to the forest, forty shillings. But in the time of Earl Roger, his son, this town paid sixteen pounds, and Ralph de Lumesi had half of it. The king has now twelve pounds from thence.'

Before he returned to France and his eventual death, fitz Osbern had founded a priory at Chepstow, as a dependent cell to his abbey at Cormeilles. It had to be sufficiently far away from the castle so as not to affect the defensive potential of the site, but sufficiently close to benefit from the mantle of protection that the castle offered. The site chosen, almost central to the spur of the peninsula and some 250m from the castle, fulfilled both these criteria. The Survey makes it evident that, within a few years of the Conquest, a small settlement had grown, or been planted, between the castle and the priory. Burgages were formed on either side of Upper Church Street, the road that still runs across the spine of the peninsula from the west door of the church towards the castle. As the pressure of development increased, the series of parallel streets which now run down the central part of the peninsula towards the river were built at right angles to Upper Church Street, creating an embryo grid pattern which is commensurate in size with the town described in the Domesday Survey (Shoesmith, 1991).

Chepstow was the most successful of the embryo-boroughs described in the Domesday Survey as being attached to castles in the southern part of the Welsh border area. Burgesses are mentioned at Clifford where the value increased from waste land at the time of the Conquest to £8 5s. at the time of the survey. Similarly at Wigmore, where the castle was built on waste land, the value increased to £7. At Ewyas Harold there is mention of two dwellings implying the beginning of a settlement.

The Domesday Survey describes the Honours of Kilpeck and Weobley in addition to those of Richard's Castle, Ewyas Harold,

Wigmore and Monmouth. It has been suggested that each of these honours was based on, and took its name from a castle and that the omission of any reference to these honours is probably due to nothing more than the indifference of the compilers (V.C.H., 1905). Thus, at Kilpeck, one of the few places described in the Survey as being in Archenfield and where William son of Norman, described as 'the forester of Herefordshire' had his caput, the importance would indicate an early castle site. Similarly Roger de Lacy, the son of Walter de Lacy, had his caput at Weobley, where there was also a park. It would seem inconceivable that there was not also a castle there.

# CHAPTER III

## Early Castles - Siting and Design

Once the Norman Conquest had become an established fact, each major landowner was allowed to have a castle as his principal seat which he held on behalf of the king. Apart from rare exceptions such as Chepstow, where there is a long, narrow, stone-built hall with simple loops and pilaster buttresses, such Norman castles were almost all of timber as shown by the illustrations of Dinan and Hastings castles in the Bayeux Tapestry. On the Tapestry these and other castles are all shown with mounds each presumably with its associated bailey, and this would appear to be the common design. In addition, it has been shown that ditched enclosures commonly called ringworks, where the small internal area is only slightly raised above the surrounding ground, can also be of an early date. Without excavation, it can be very difficult to establish the difference between a Norman ringwork castle and a later moated dwelling. Even traces of outer enclosures can be common to both. As a whole it would appear that ringworks are relatively uncommon in Herefordshire, but this theory has not been tested to any great extent.

The earliest castles of Herefordshire demonstrate the design and style that had been brought into the country by earlier French settlers and by the followers of William the Conqueror. Although there were exceptions, the typical Norman stronghold included a great moated mound—the motte—designed to carry on its crest a wooden palisade and probably a timber tower, and one or more attached courts—the bailey(s), also defended by palisades and ditches, in which were the residential buildings of the 'castle'.

A glance at the ground plans provides every indication that Ewyas Harold and Richard's Castle, both almost certainly of pre-Conquest date, followed this straightforward design and, in addition, took advantage of the natural features by defending the end of a promontory. Leland emphasised this by pointing out that Ewyas Harold 'stondythe on a mene hill' and described Richard's Castle as being 'on the tope of a very rokky hill'. In addition, the mounds of these two castles are typically large—this is especially so at Ewyas Harold where the mound is 32m across at the top and stands an impressive 15m above the bailey. The size of the motte at Richard's Castle is rather uncertain due to the construction of the later stone keep, but it must have been of the order of 20m or more across the top. At Richard's Castle the motte was separated from the bailey by a ditch, later infilled. The plan of Hereford, the other castle in Herefordshire known to have been built before the Conquest, was dictated by the confines of the defended Saxon city, but even so the standard design seems to have been followed with Hogg's Mount, the mound at the north-eastern corner of Castle Green, acting as the motte and the northern part of St Guthlac's monastic grounds becoming the bailey. Later defensive works associated with the royal castle, followed by eighteenth century landscaping, have made it impossible to establish the original size of the mound and bailey, but both were probably considerable.

Following the Conquest, fitz Osbern was charged to build new castles along the border with Wales, and in Herefordshire he is specially connected with those at Clifford and Wigmore which he is said to have founded.

There is some uncertainty about the site of fitz Osbern's castle at Clifford. Was it at Old Castleton, some 4km to the east of Clifford village, where there is a reasonably well-preserved motte and bailey castle standing on a slight rise overlooking a bend in the Wye, or is it represented by the site of the present Clifford Castle? Although the Old Castleton site includes a large motte and a kidney-shaped bailey, it is relatively low lying and little attempt seems to have been made to make use of natural features to add to the defensive capability. As a result the site appears relatively poorly defended.

By comparison, the site of the present Clifford Castle is far more promising. The castle stands on the top of a cliff above 'the Island' where there was an important ford across the river (Lamont, 1922, 76). The earthworks of Clifford Castle consist of a circular motte, strategically positioned some 26m above the river. The site was chosen to make best use of natural features, for there is a natural scarp on the north-west towards the river whilst the steep slope on the south-east is also more or less a natural feature. All that was needed to make the site impregnable was to cut deep ditches on the north-eastern and south-western sides. The top of the motte is now about 10m above the bottom of these dry ditches. As at Ewyas Harold and also probably at Richard's Castle and Hereford, the Clifford motte was large, being some 30m across, easily large enough to contain a substantial timber building as well as an encircling palisade. It has another similarity to Richard's Castle, for the motte was also separated from its bailey by a ditch, now crossed by a causeway, but that feature could well be of Victorian date. The mound now includes the remains of the twelfth century stone castle described in the Gazetteer. To the south-west of the motte is a small triangular-shaped bailey, but the main bailey is to the east and was of considerable size. Once again, the defences are mainly natural, the bailey being surrounded by scarp slopes, but it was probably originally enclosed with a timber palisade, possibly replaced with stone at a later date. It is evident that the design and siting of the castle at Clifford is of similar standard to the other castles erected around the time of the Conquest.

Once again there are two possibilities for the site of fitz Osbern's original castle at Wigmore, both on the same ridge. The present stone castle sits astride a spur with a deep valley on the south and the 'Wig-moor' on the north. It is separated from the main part of the ridge by a deep, apparently man-made ravine. The stone castle is largely a fourteenth century creation of the powerful Mortimer family, and it is only the underlying earthworks that can provide the clues about the nature of fitz Osbern's scheme.

One of the possible sites for the early castle is well to the south-east of the masonry castle, but still on the ridge and not far from the church. Here the ridge is narrow and steep on the north side, but unfortunately much of the remainder of this area has been developed for housing making interpretation difficult. This castle, if such it is, would have consisted of a small motte with an equally small bailey running along the ridge on each side of the mound. An alternative suggestion for its presence, if it is not part of the early Norman work, is that it is part of the works that were built by the attackers during the siege by royalist forces in 1155.

An alternative site for fitz Osbern's work could be part of the present castle—the part that is presently described as the shell keep. On the western side this overlooks the man-made ravine, and observers in the nineteenth century recorded that it included 'a mound of earth, in form conical, and about 30ft high, above its rocky base, though 100ft or more above the bottom of the ravine. The mound is about 30ft diameter at its flat top' (GTC, 1874). Since that description was written the mound has almost disappeared, having collapsed into the ravine. It is quite possible that the mound had once been larger and that other parts have disappeared into the ravine at an earlier date. However, if it is accepted that there was a mound with a keep upon it at the western edge of the present shell keep, then it can be postulated that the whole of the uppermost levels could represent a motte and bailey castle in its own right, with the present shell keep simply reflecting the bailey. Both potential sites have natural defensive capabilities and either could well be the original eleventh century Wigmore Castle. However, the balance of probability would appear to favour the second site, being on the higher part of the ridge with the steep drop to the present bailey providing a natural defence to the east, even though the choice of such a site would have involved the excavation of the great ravine on the west, or perhaps an eleventh century lesser ditch that has since been totally lost in the thirteenth or fourteenth century works.

Earthwork castles of this nature, making the best use of naturally defensive sites and built on a relatively massive scale, seem to be a feature of the early Norman period. At that time the choice of site could be based entirely on military needs; the question of the land's ownership would have been very much a secondary consideration. Accepting this, it can be suggested that where similar well-chosen castle sites occur, then they could be of an early date. Within the county the promontory site of Goodrich Castle overlooking an early ford across the Wye, the well-defended castle at Kilpeck with its large (30m across) motte, and the impressive Snodhill Castle in Peterchurch parish all have characteristics of this nature and could well be of the early Norman period.

By comparison, there are many examples of lesser mottes and baileys that are built on low lying ground or on sites where the natural defences are limited to the availability of water to fill the moat. It would seem that such castles were built by the lesser lords and placed on the most practical site available within their limited landholdings in order to properly govern their lands. Perhaps Eardisley, which was not dignified with the description of 'castle' in the Domesday Survey being simply a *domus defensibalis* (fortified house), was an establishment of this nature. As they expanded in size and strength, many such sites may well have grown to become fully fledged castles. Originally, such motte and bailey castles could have been built at any time up to, during, and possibly even after the period of the Anarchy (1136-54). Many were associated with embryo boroughs that gradually grew outside the bailey. Typical examples which included a settlement and where there are still substantial earthworks surviving include Almeley, Dorstone, Eardisland, Huntington, Kingsland, Llancillo, Longtown (Ewyas Lacy), Lyonshall, Stapleton, and Staunton-on-Arrow. Some of the motte and bailey castles apparently without settlements include Brampton Bryan (Upper Pedwardine), Clifford (Old Castleton and Newton Tump), Huntington (Turret Castle), Lingen, Longtown (Pont Hendre), Peterchurch (Urishay Castle) and Walterstone. Most of these are of reasonable size and have mottes that vary from 15m to 33m across at the top and are between 5m and 10m above the encircling ditch. In many cases a nearby stream could have been diverted to fill the moat, and in several cases, such as Lyonshall and Walterstone, the motte is completely surrounded by a ditch.

There are many examples where there is little apart from a mound and, perhaps, a surrounding ditch, but without any sign of a defended bailey, although there may be slight signs of an attached enclosure not sufficiently strong to be accepted as a proper castle bailey. Such sites are variously described as castle mounds, tumps, or occasionally twts. They vary in size and were presumably designed to be used as a final defensive point, once the undefended house and outbuildings had been lost. As a whole they are smaller than those mottes that include good evidence for an attached and defended bailey, and in almost every case there is little sign of any stonework. Many must have been built around the time of the Anarchy and abandoned shortly afterwards. A typical one with a mixed history is the Tump at St Weonard's. Here, excavation has shown that a Bronze Age burial mound was enlarged to become a castle mound. In its final form the top was some 23m in diameter and 5m high above the encircling ditch. This is somewhat larger than most and in use was presumably defended with a timber palisade around the summit and contained some form of tower or other building. Other mounds are as little as 6m across the top.

It has been shown that there is a tremendous variation in shape and size, from massive mottes, such as those at Dorstone, Ewyas Harold and Kilpeck, with tops well in excess of 30m across, to the smallest ones that have tops considerably less than 10m across. There have been no excavations of Herefordshire mottes which give any indication of the original structures built upon them, though investigations elsewhere give an impression of what is likely. One of the best examples is the small motte at Abinger in Surrey (Hope-Taylor, 1956). The mound was a bare 11m across at the top and around the edge archaeologists found a line of postholes representing a palisade, with two larger posts indicating the entry. A line of smaller postholes to the rear of the main palisade is interpreted as the supports for a fighting platform. In the centre of the flat top of the mound postholes indicated that there had been a timber tower, only some 3.5m square, but possibly more than one storey high. The tower is so small that it is unlikely that it was ever permanently occupied and it must be seen as a watchtower or a place of last retreat during a siege. Access was by steps up the side of the mound. The tower and palisade were dated to the mid-twelfth century and replaced an earlier ill-defined structure. It was suggested that the reconstruction works could well have been associated with the Anarchy—the 'nineteen long winters' of Stephen's reign. There may have been a bailey associated with the motte, but if so it had been totally destroyed many years previously.

It was the bailey of a castle and not the motte that contained the main buildings. Here would have been the great hall, the chapel and all the buildings associated with a small self-sufficient community—in effect a large family and retainers—that appreciated that it was their own responsibility to defend themselves from attack. In the initial stages these buildings would have been of timber to be gradually replaced in stone during the latter part of the twelfth century when conditions were more stable. In many ways the bailey of a castle can be equated with a ringwork, or alternatively a ringwork can be seen as a castle but without the motte. There has been little excavation in the baileys of Herefordshire castles, but one site that could well be described as a ringwork was examined in the late 1950s and early 1960s (Heys, 1963). This is the 'camp' at Breinton some 3km west of Hereford and standing on a bluff above the left bank of the Wye. The excavations established that the site consisted of an irregular-shaped enclosure, about 36m by 25m, surrounded by a low perimeter bank and thin curtain wall, with a dry ditch up to 2m deep and 5.5m wide on all sides except the south, where the ground falls steeply away to the river bank. There was no trace of any mound, but the pottery evidence indicated that it was occupied by c.1150. In the initial phase there may well have been timber buildings, but during the main occupation phase there was a stone gateway to the north and the stone footings of a building interpreted as an upper hall and including a cellared portion, to the south-east. The site was probably abandoned by the mid-thirteenth century.

There is little difference between a ringwork and a moated site. Both were designed to contain the buildings of a household within a moat or ditch that could, dependent on the circumstances of the site, have contained water. Both would have had a palisade or a stone wall around the perimeter of the enclosed area. Both would have had some form of defensible entry, either a bridge with a gatehouse and a drawbridge, or a timber structure that was totally removable in times of trouble. In the initial stages the great hall would have stood alone, but as fortunes improved a solar range would have been added to one end to provide some privacy for the owner, and a service range would have been built at the other. In many cases the moated sites must have been very restrictive in terms of size and possibly very damp and uncomfortable. With the new-found peace that followed the Edwardian Conquest of Wales, many of the minor gentry built new houses a short distance from their original moated defences which were then abandoned. In other cases the moated site was kept, buildings were replaced from time to time, so that in places like Brockhampton Court, near Bromyard, the manor house and gatehouse, both built of timber, still survive.

# CHAPTER IV

## Building in Stone

It has been shown that there is a reasonable probability that, at the time of the Domesday Survey, there would have been a few more castles in Herefordshire than the seven (accepting Hereford and the two defended houses) mentioned in that work. But the Survey took place only twenty years after the Conquest and the idea that 'the Englishman's home was his castle' had not become fully apparent. In addition, castles were sources of expenditure rather than income and the lack of any mention of a site in the Survey is no proof that it was not fortified by 1086. In any case, within a few generations the whole of the county was to become full of castles, from small mounds with a slight ditch, through the standard picture-book motte and bailey castle, all possible variations of ringworks without mottes, leading to complex stone castles surrounded by curtain walls and massive ditches and containing keeps, great halls and many other ancillary buildings. In addition there were fortified houses—built on an island and surrounded with a water-filled moat—not dignified with the name of a castle until the owner procured a licence to crenellate.

In historical terms the Norman period ended with the death of Stephen in 1154. Previous to the commencement of his reign there had been some seventy years of strong rule under the Conqueror and his two sons William Rufus and Henry Beauclerk. Although castles were built as defensible structures throughout the period following the Conquest, they were designed as much to deter any attempt at local rebellion as to make the country safe from invasion. The number grew throughout the eleventh century as new towns were planted and the benefits of firm government were appreciated. In Herefordshire and the border counties, the ravages of the Welsh were repaired and new settlements were founded in the areas described in the Domesday Survey as being 'waste.'

The loss of Henry's legitimate son William the Atheling in 1120 in the 'White Ship' tragedy caused a predicament. When Henry died should his daughter, Matilda, or his nephew, Stephen of Blois, take the throne? In 1135, following Henry's death, Stephen hurried to England and was crowned on 22 December. By 1138 many towns throughout England had closed their gates and declared for the Empress Matilda. The nobility, during the decade or so of what was effectively civil war that followed Matilda's invasion, threw their hand in with one side or the other and, using forced labour, disinherited barons rapidly built newer and stronger castles from which they could ravage the surrounding countryside. Throughout the country villages were razed, farms were burnt and crops were left untended to rot on the ground. Famine and the inevitable rape and plunder followed and thousands died of starvation and murder. Throughout Herefordshire small defensive castles were built to protect individual families—castles that were to have a life of less than a decade. Many of the attacks involved sieges, and the two small mottes adjacent to the castle at Wigmore could well be siege castles. Many church towers were used for defence, and, on occasion for attack, as was the case with the cathedral at Hereford. There, towards the end of 1139, catapults were mounted on the tower in order to assault the nearby castle.

For eight years or more parts of England, including the border areas, were ravaged by war. Eventually a compromise was reached allowing Matilda's son, Henry of Anjou, to become king as Henry II on the death of Stephen. He was the first of the Plantagenet kings from which grew the Houses of Lancaster and York. His first concern was to restore order to his devastated land. He demolished many of the castles built by rebellious nobles and took others into the possession of the crown. Throughout the second half of the twelfth century the Pipe Rolls—the annual accounts made by the sheriff of each county—indicate a vast expenditure by the Crown on castles and particularly on keeps. Gradually law and order prevailed as these strong points were developed and as justice was once again administered by judges and the newly formed juries, as opposed to the former trials by ordeal.

In addition to those that had been deliberately demolished, well before the end of the twelfth century many of the minor castles— the simple mounds, the isolated mottes and baileys and the defensive ringworks—had already been abandoned. The ones that survived were mainly those that were designed to be residential; often those associated with a town or village. In most cases they had been built of timber, often rapidly and with little care, and many were due for renewal. There was no great change in the design of castles following the end of the Norman period, rather it was a gradual shift to more permanent structures, a change that was eventually to produce the massive Edwardian castles of the latter part of the thirteenth century.

There is a great difference between the construction of a defensive mound, or even a motte and bailey and its associated timber buildings, with the building of a major stone castle. The former could be built from materials that were immediately to hand and using labour from the estate. A stone castle was a totally different matter. It required a considerable amount of money and needed specialists in the growing complex art of castle planning and construction. Half the cost could well be spent on getting the materials and transporting them to the chosen site. As with the building of cathedrals and major churches, this work was well outside the experience of local tradesmen.

The earliest stone buildings in most castles tended to be square or rectangular keeps constructed towards the end of the eleventh century and into the twelfth. The role model on the Welsh border should be the enormous long hall of Chepstow Castle built of well-squared sandstone blocks separated by narrow courses of Roman tiles and supported with pilaster buttresses. The hall had two main floors, each 26m long and 9m wide. It has been suggested that there was a similar, but smaller, long narrow hall at Clifford Castle (Remfry, 1995a, 27) in addition to the foundations of a square keep found in the centre of the motte (Marshall, 1938, 153).

By comparison with the narrow Norman halls, the keep at Goodrich Castle is small, but it is also built of sandstone ashlar, has clasping pilaster buttresses in the Norman style and stands three stories high. The entrance doorway was at first-floor level and could have been approached by a ladder or wooden steps. However, the relatively poor quality of the present ground floor walling has led to the suggestion that the lower part of the keep was enclosed within a mound for some time after it was built. The only access to the basement was by an internal ladder, but the upper floor and roof were approached by a spiral stair in the north-west angle. The rooms were small—a mere 4.3m square. The date of this keep is uncertain but is likely to be in the second half of the twelfth century. Square stone keeps are rare in Herefordshire. Apart from Goodrich and Clifford there is one shown on a 1655 plan of Weobley Castle and an indication of a possible one at Dilwyn No. 1.

Such keeps may well have been associated with stone curtain walls, but once again the evidence is slight. At Goodrich, there is a short section of the eastern curtain wall that contains two arrow slits that appear to be of twelfth century date and are now below the level of the present courtyard.

In an attempt to improve the design, several keeps were built on a polygonal plan. In Herefordshire, the stone keep built on the motte at Richard's Castle is of this style. The excavations in the 1960s exposed the lower part of an octagonal tower which has been dated to about 1175. An apsidal projection built on the eastern side about 1200 could have contained some form of defended entry. The internal rooms would have been almost circular and about 7m across. The keep on top of the motte at Snodhill in Peterchurch parish is a variant on this design being an irregular ten-sided polygon with internal measurements 7m by 11.5m. It was probably built late in the twelfth century. The remains are sufficient to indicate that the almost buried basement was octagonal in shape whilst the ground floor apparently had ten sides. The entrance, which was in one of the narrow facets facing west, had circular flanking towers added at a slightly later date.

Two other keeps, now lost, may also have been of this transitional form—Wigmore and Hereford. A nineteenth century antiquarian recorded that at Wigmore: 'Upon the summit of the mound he built, as the foundations still shew, a circular or polygonal tower as a keep. From thence a curtain-wall sprang from its opposite sides and encircled the small eastern area, forming the inner ward' (GTC, 1874). It has been suggested that this keep was at least 14m in diameter, with unequal sides. If it was associated with the surviving remnant of a stair tower then it must have been three stories in height. In addition it could well be related to sections of the wall of the so-called shell keep which are also of twelfth century character. In the centre of the county, the motte and keep at Hereford were described by Leland in the early sixteenth century as being 'highe and very stronge, havynge in the utter waull or ward 10 towres *forma semicirculari*, and one great towre in the inner ward.' This could well have been a polygonal tower built around 1200.

Circular keeps were an improvement on the square and polygonal varieties. They did not require as much stone to build, whilst missiles hurled at them tended to glance off rather than cause damage. The most complete example in Herefordshire is at Ewyas Lacy Castle in Longtown. It is one of a group of nineteen such keeps that have been recognised in what is defined as the Brecon region, three of which—Longtown, Lyonshall and Lower Ashton 'Camp' (Eye, Moreton & Ashton parish)—are in England. To these could be added the traces of possible round keeps at Bacton and Wacton, and the circular tower at the western angle of Pembridge Castle (Welsh Newton).

The keep at Longtown stands on top of a high mound and consists of two stories above an unlit basement or undercroft. It is built of the local shaly sandstone with ashlared dressings. On the outside are three semi-circular projections; one containing the flue for the fireplace on the main floor, a second associated with a garderobe on the upper floor and the third, which mainly collapsed at the end of the eighteenth century, contained the spiral stair that linked the main floor with the upper one and the roof. The keep would have been entered by a door at first-floor level. The fragments of twelfth century moulding in the window on the north side are clearly reused and do not provide any reliable dating evidence. If this keep was indeed the *Novi Castelli* of 1187, it would be the earliest of the round keeps in the Brecon region. It is perhaps more likely that it was built in the early thirteenth century, a date between 1213 and 1223 having been suggested (Hillaby, 1985, 223-6).

At Pembridge Castle there is a circular keep tower that stands four stories high and has a typical battered plinth. It is smaller in diameter than Longtown being only 7.5m externally as compared with Longtown's 14m. However, the walls are thinner giving an internal diameter of 5m, Longtown being 8.5m. The upper floors were residential—even the third floor contains a fireplace and a corbelled-out latrine. However, Pembridge Castle has had extensive restoration work and it can only be suggested that the round tower is of early thirteenth century date, perhaps associated with fragments of the adjoining sandstone curtain wall.

Lyonshall contains the remains of a circular keep standing on a slight rise in the northern part of the inner bailey. The sandstone wall stands less than 2m high, but includes roll-moulding above a battered plinth. It is 11m in external diameter with the rooms 6m across. The surviving walling includes the jambs of three splayed loops to the north and a possible entry to the south. The date of the keep is uncertain, but on stylistic grounds is unlikely to be earlier than the beginning of the thirteenth century.

With stone keeps came encircling walls to replace the timber palisades and stone gateways. Initially the walls were built with sharp angles, often including rectangular towers such as those at Ludlow Castle. As the castles grew in importance the gateway—not just potentially the weak point in the defence, but also the first impression that an eminent visitor would gain—had to be improved. Initially a simple entrance through a curtain wall, this developed into a passage running through a tower attached to the wall. The more sophisticated castles of the later thirteenth century had elaborate gatehouses flanked with twin towers for additional strength.

Gate passages are apparent at several castles in Herefordshire. An early example is at Richard's Castle, where the entrance was through a two-storey tower some 7m square. This could well have been built in the latter part of the twelfth century at the same time as the octagonal keep. Like many others, it was extended forwards towards the ditch in the thirteenth century. At Wigmore the central portion of the gatehouse, astride the line of the curtain wall,

34

remains and stands two storeys high. The fourteenth century segmental-pointed outer arch is buried in debris to about half its height. There was an external gate passage, apparent on early prints, but this is now also buried in debris. At Longtown, the remains of the gateway leading from the outer bailey to the inner bailey survive. Probably of early thirteenth century date, it consists of a semi-circular arched opening flanked by two solid semi-circular towers. Grooves for a portcullis would suggest that there was a room above.

The earliest phase of the gatehouse at Brampton Bryan, built in the late thirteenth century, was contained completely within the line of the curtain wall. Even so, it would have been relatively impressive for it extended two floors above the gatehouse passage. In the fourteenth century a long narrow passage was added to the outside and a new outer gatehouse was built with the new entrance flanked by round towers, one of which contained a well. This relatively simple example of an extended gatehouse was to develop even further into the formidable gatehouses and barbicans such as the one at Goodrich. There, the defenders were not content with the long passage containing a double portcullis fronted with a draw-bridge that was built around 1300. During the fourteenth century the passageway was continued over the moat to an outer gatehouse or barbican. The passageway over the moat was effectively designed as a killing-ground being overlooked by the main gate, the curtain wall on each side, and the rear of the upper floor of the outer gate.

As gateways improved so did the curtain walls, with semi-circular towers being built to protect the corners and to enfilade the curtains. Initially small, and sometimes solid such as those at Pembridge (Welsh Newton), later ones were sufficiently large to contain residential chambers. Excellent late thirteenth century examples survive at the Edwardian castle at Goodrich and others are incorporated into later houses such as those at Croft Castle. In the final stages of castle building, during the fourteenth and fifteenth centuries, defence often took second place to comfort and design. At Wigmore, where only one thirteenth century semi-circular tower survives, large rectangular residential towers were built into the curtain walls in the fourteenth century. At Bronsil

(Eastnor), built in the mid-fifteenth century, a symmetrical design and an impressive double moat were as important as the octagonal towers that flanked the entry and ornamented the corners and mid-points of this regular design.

In many cases the last part of the castle to be improved was the residential quarters. It was not until after the Edwardian conquest of Wales between 1277 and 1282 that the residential parts of the castles along the Welsh border became of more importance that the defensive aspects.

# CHAPTER V

## Decline and Decay

Castles which had survived the demolition programme conducted by Henry II after the Anarchy and the various wars with the Welsh and the barons, most notably in the 1260s, were redesigned to become large houses. In some cases luxurious solar wings and extensive service ranges were added to existing great halls. In others, such as Goodrich, the whole castle was replanned around 1300. Alterations continued as needs grew and the old draughty large halls had first floors inserted and were converted into smaller chambers. At the same time estates were being amalgamated into larger units and the smaller castles then became redundant. It can only be suggested that many of the early castles in the county had a relatively short life especially as maintenance became a more costly and demanding problem.

Some castles were pressed into service at the time of the Owain Glyn Dwr crisis in the early fifteenth century, including Ewyas Harold, Goodrich, Eardisley, Ewyas Lacy (Longtown), Huntington, Lyonshall, Dorstone, Stapleton, Brampton Bryan, and Snodhill (Hodges, 1995). For those which were already semi-derelict, it is likely that the repairs effected were of a temporary nature and only served to marginally lengthen the castle's life.

By the time of Leland's visit in the early sixteenth century, not only had some of these fallen further into ruin, so had Hereford Castle, often the base for Prince Henry's (later Henry V) campaigns against Glyn Dwr. Leland described several castles in Herefordshire including:

Ewyas Harold—'it hath beene a notable thinge'
Hereford—'the hole castle tendithe toward ruine'
Kilpeck—'sum ruines of the waulls yet stonde'
Kingsland—'a castle ... the diches wherof and a parte of the
     kepe be yet sene'
Richard's Castle—'The kepe, the waulls, and towres of yt yet
     stond but goynge to ruyn'
Snodhill—'The castle is somewhat in ruine'
Weobley—'a goodly castell, but somewhat in decay'

(Smith, 1964)

Several of these abandonments, such as the one at Richard's
Castle, were due to the lack of a male heir. By Leland's time there
was even a timber-framed farmhouse situated in the bailey of the
redundant castle. Another case was Kilpeck which became a small
part of the larger holding of the Earl of Ormond in 1325. The castle
was probably abandoned and, within a period of some 13 years, the
village decreased in value by two-thirds. In many cases such as
these what had been fairly prosperous settlements dependent on
strong castles rapidly declined and, with the Black Death in the
mid-fourteenth century, abandonment was inevitable.

Even so, many castles survived these problems, gradually
becoming converted into houses until the advent of the Civil War in
1641. Suddenly the walls and gates had to be renewed and the
buildings made defensible. Others, notably Wigmore, were made
incapable of any defensive use by destroying the walls and gates.
Many suffered from attack, siege and fire, but this was not all. After
the war was over, parliament made great efforts to ensure that never
again should the castles of England be able to hold out against their
troops and many were slighted. The list of Herefordshire castles
that suffered during this period of strife is some indication of how
much the whole county had to endure:

Brampton Bryan—totally destroyed apart from the gatehouse
     and the porch to the hall which still survive as ruins
Canon Frome—under siege several times and ordered to be
     abandoned and slighted

Eardisley—'Roysters from Hereford burnt Sir Robert Welch's house.'

Eastnor, Bronsil—possibly burnt during the Civil War, certainly abandoned thereafter

Kilpeck—already in ruins but garrisoned during the War and slighted thereafter

Longtown, Ewyas Lacy—probably abandoned. Its use during the Civil War is doubtful

Goodrich—under siege during the War and the castle and 'the new works' slighted thereafter

Hereford—repaired and under siege during the War. Garrison maintained there afterwards but 'new works' slighted

Peterchurch, Snodhill—said to have been bombarded during the War

Stapleton—slighted in 1645

Welsh Newton, Pembridge—suffered a siege, was captured, garrisoned and eventually slighted

Wigmore—slighted at the beginning of the Civil War to ensure that it could not be used

The abandonment and slighting of a castle left it in ruins but still standing. At a later date the efforts of the stone robbers, especially in areas where good building stone was scarce, could reduce a mighty castle to little more than earthworks in a few years. Such was the case of Hereford where the stone was used to build the Tolsey and a new hall for the Vicars' Choral College. Eventually even the gravel of the mound was sold for road metalling. The stone from Snodhill was used to build Snodhill Court and that from Bronsil was used to construct the nearby house. In other cases the stone removal was not a regular event, but occurred when new buildings were needed on the local farm. Such a gradual loss coupled with the collapse and gradual burial of the remainder has left many Herefordshire castles with just the vestiges of stonework showing above the grass or through the undergrowth.

Other ruined castles suffered different fates. Goodrich, together with the ruins of Tintern Abbey, became recognised stopping points on the Wye Tour and the ruins were carefully protected from the stone robber. Wigmore, at the other end of the county, was in an area where stone was plentiful and does not appear to have suffered to any great extent from stone removal. Indeed, it now seems to be buried in its own debris to at least first-floor level.

Finally there was the gothic revival of the nineteenth century, when vast castles were built in the Herefordshire countryside. Foremost amongst them were Eastnor Castle and Goodrich Court. The former survives, but the latter has suffered the fate of many of its medieval predecessors and was demolished in the 1950s.

# Gazetteer

This section comprises a gazetteer and index to castles and moated sites within the limits of the pre-1974 county of Herefordshire. Initially, an attempt was made to separate castles from moated sites, but it was then appreciated that there were many sites that could only be described as 'possible castles' or 'possible motte and bailey' sites, even 'ringworks' or 'simple mounds', with or without encircling ditches. The only logical solution was to include all sites that could be described as 'private defensive works' as different from communal defensive works such as Offa's Dyke, and the various city and town defences. Even then, there is potential for an element of confusion, with flattened mounds, also with or without ditches, that could equally be either Bronze Age tumuli or ringworks. In such cases, the generally accepted identification has been followed unless it has recently been queried.

The earlier chapters have shown that the main period of castle building was from the Norman Conquest up to the beginning of the reign of Henry III (1216). Although a few were built, and many improved, during the thirteenth century, the need for castles as defensive features against the Welsh had effectively ceased by 1282. Even so, new castles were being built, and older castles were being 'modernised' for several centuries afterwards. A few castles had improvements made to their defences and, indeed, experienced 'their finest hour' in the mid-seventeenth century during the Civil War. Several medieval castles and fortified houses were substantially altered in the nineteenth century to bring the accommodation up-to-date, often changing their character substantially. And finally, during the early part of that same century there was the period of the Norman Revival, when castles were built simply for show, but included in their designs many medieval defensive features. The best example to survive in Herefordshire is Eastnor Castle, near Ledbury, but the oft quoted and perhaps best remembered one was the castellated and tower-bedecked Goodrich Court, designed by Blore as a home for Samuel Meyrick and his world famous collection of arms and armour, which sadly was demolished in the 1950s. To many people such extravaganza were the last examples of buildings typifying the idea that 'the Englishman's home is his castle' and because of this feeling the surviving examples are included in this gazetteer.

Each entry is listed under the parish, followed, as appropriate, either by the name of the site (if it has one) or the name of the nearest building. The remainder of the heading describes the type of site (castle, motte & bailey, mound, moat, moated site, etc,) and, if applicable, an indication of the certainty of the interpretation (possible, probable). A six-figure grid reference enables the site to be pin-pointed on Ordnance Survey maps (the central part of the county is on sheet 149 of the 1:50,000 Landranger series, but sheets 137, 148, 150, 161 and 162 are needed to cover the whole of Herefordshire). A map showing the position of all the sites would be impracticable, but a map of parishes (pages 44-5) has been included to reduce the need for complex directions for each site. Most sites are related to parish churchs or other local features.

Some sites that are of particular interest, and often those that are easily accessible, have more detailed entries. The entries for such sites are included in the gazetteer in parish order, but to bring them to the attention of the reader there is a box of information giving an outline of what there is to see, their location and information about access. Plans, at scales of 1:500 to 1:4000 are also included where appropriate. At index at the rear of the book gives the parish for each named site.

It has to be appreciated that not all of the sites mentioned in this gazetteer have been visited by the author, and in many cases the report is dependent on descriptions provided by others in a variety of publications. In each case, the references consulted are given in abbreviated form at the end of the section. There is a complete bibliography at the end of the volume, but for convenience the ones most commonly used in the Gazetteer are given opposite.

# Abbreviated References used in the Gazetteer

HAN *Herefordshire Archaeological News*, First published in December 1966. Woolhope Naturalists Field Club Archaeological Research Section. The issue number and page number(s) are given.

HAS *Hereford Archaeology Series*, A series of internal reports published by the City of Hereford Archaeology Unit and available in Hereford Library. The report number is given.

Pevsner N. Pevsner, *The Buildings of England, Herefordshire*, 1963

RCHM *An Inventory of the Historical Monuments in Herefordshire*, in 3 volumes (Vol 1 - 1931; Vol 2 - 1932, Vol 3 - 1934), Royal Commission on Historical Monuments - England.

Remfry P. Remfry, various reports published on Herefordshire Castles - see bibliography, and comments on reading a draft copy of the Gazetteer

Robinson Cas. C.J. Robinson, *A History of the Castles of Herefordshire and their Lords*, 1869

Robinson Man. C.J. Robinson, *A History of the Mansions and Manors of Herefordshire*, 1872

RSB R. Stirling-Brown, *Herefordshire Castles*, Privately published, 1989

Salter M. Salter, *The Castles of Herefordshire and Worcestershire*, 1989

Treasures *Herefordshire Countryside Treasures*, 1981, Hereford & Worcester County Council

TWNFC *Transactions of the Woolhope Naturalists Field Club*, Yearly parts since 1852. The year and page number(s) are given.

VCH *The Victoria History of the Counties of England - Herefordshire*, 1908, (Vol. 1 only issued)

| | | | | | | |
|---|---|---|---|---|---|---|
| 177 | Abbey Dore | 36 | Eye, Moreton & | 219 | Orcop | |
| 6 | Adforton | | Ashton | 31 | Pembridge | |
| 179 | Allensmore | 99 | Felton | 151 | Peterchurch | |
| 67 | Almeley | 228 | Foy | 8 | Pipe Aston | |
| 162 | Ashperton | 218 | Garway | 117 | Pipe & Lyde | |
| 18 | Aymestrey | 238 | Goodrich | 164 | Pixley | |
| 175 | Bacton | 183 | Grafton | 39 | Pudleston | |
| 71 | Birley | 224 | Harewood | 14 | Richard's Castle | |
| 124 | Bishop's Frome | 226 | Hentland | 197 | Rowlestone | |
| 113 | Bishopstone | 247 | Hope Mansell | 203 | St Devereux | |
| 74 | Bodenham | 72 | Hope-under- | 172 | St Margarets | |
| 208 | Bolstone | | Dinmore | 220 | St Weonards | |
| 147 | Bosbury | 214 | How Capel | 68 | Sarnesfield | |
| 4 | Brampton Bryan | 63 | Huntington | 25 | Shobdon | |
| 78 | Bredenbury | 200 | Kenderchurch | 215 | Sollars Hope | |
| 105 | Bredwardine | 201 | Kentchurch | 15 | Stapleton | |
| 155 | Breinton | 202 | Kilpeck | 28 | Staunton-on-Arrow | |
| 132 | Bridge Sollars | 212 | King's Capel | 102 | Stoke Lacy | |
| 239 | Bridstow | 33 | Kingsland | 45 | Stretford | |
| 86 | Brilley | 70 | Kings Pyon | 143 | Stretton Grandison | |
| 94 | Brinsop | 41 | Kington Rural | 136 | Stretton Sugwas | |
| 84 | Brockhampton-by- | 90 | Kinnersley | 118 | Sutton | |
| | Bromyard | 16 | Kinsham | 161 | Tarrington | |
| 213 | Brockhampton-by- | 1 | Leintwardine | 54 | Thornbury | |
| | Ross | 49 | Leominster Out | 137 | Thruxton | |
| 2 | Buckton & Coxall | 38 | Leysters | 225 | Tretire | |
| 115 | Burghill | 62 | Lingen | 173 | Turnastone | |
| 24 | Byton | 245 | Linton-by-Ross | 100 | Ullingswick | |
| 145 | Canon Frome | 22 | Little Hereford | 58 | Upper Sapey | |
| 95 | Canon Pyon | 196 | Llancillo | 229 | Upton Bishop | |
| 146 | Castle Frome | 232 | Llangarron | 174 | Vowchurch | |
| 104 | Clifford | 230 | Llanrothal | 77 | Wacton | |
| 55 | Collington | 170 | Longtown | 243 | Walford | |
| 168 | Colwall | 138 | Lugwardine | 5 | Walford, Letton & | |
| 23 | Combe | 43 | Lyonshall | | Newton | |
| 126 | Cradley | 153 | Madley | 195 | Walterstone | |
| 19 | Croft | 110 | Mansell Lacy | 231 | Welsh Newton | |
| 127 | Cusop | 148 | Mathon | 69 | Weobley | |
| 44 | Dilwyn | 150 | Michaelchurch | 140 | Westhide | |
| 73 | Dinmore | | Escley | 141 | Weston Beggard | |
| 194 | Donnington | 37 | Middleton-on-the- | 244 | Weston-u-Penyard | |
| 128 | Dorstone | | Hill | 85 | Whitbourne | |
| 3 | Downton | 129 | Moccas | 236 | Whitchurch | |
| 32 | Eardisland | 158 | Mordiford | 87 | Whitney | |
| 66 | Eardisley | 116 | Moreton-on-Lugg | 11 | Wigmore | |
| 193 | Eastnor | 123 | Much Cowarne | 9 | Willey | |
| 154 | Eaton Bishop | 204 | Much Dewchurch | 82 | Winslow | |
| 59 | Edvin Loach | 217 | Much Marcle | 142 | Yarkhill | |
| 81 | Edwin Ralph | 163 | Munsley | | | |
| 198 | Ewyas Harold | 121 | Ocle Pychard | | | |

LEOMINSTER

KINGTON

BROMYARD

LEDBURY

HEREFORD

ROSS

# Abbey Dore

**Morehampton Park Farm moated site** (SO 377 341)
This moated site is some 4km north-north-west of the abbey and south-west of Morehampton Park farmhouse. It is now dry and the north-east and south-west arms have been filled in. (RCHM, **1**, 9; Treasures, 46)

# Adforton

**Possible castle** (SO 404 711)
A castle site has been suggested, on the basis of aerial photographs, on the ridge just to the east of the village of Adforton and about 2km north of Wigmore. Adforton was a demense manor of the Mortimers in 1086 and remained one afterwards, so is an unlikely site. However, the position is strategically good and it could have controlled the passage of the road running north from Wigmore. (HAN, **60**, 7 & 59-60)

# Allensmore

**Meer Court moated site** (SO 438 363)
Allensmore is some 6.5km south-west of Hereford on the A465, and Meer Court is almost 3km to the west of the village church. The fragmentary moat is to the south-west of the house. In the 1930s only the south-west and a part of the south-east sections of the moat were wet, but at the beginning of the century the VCH recorded three-quarters of a rectangular moat of considerable size. There is a suggestion of a possible castle site at the adjoining Arkstone Court (SO 436 361), but this has not been demonstrated. (VCH, 249; RCHM, **1**, 16; HAN, **65**, 26-7 and plan on 27)

# Almeley

**Motte & bailey** (SO 332 514)

A large motte with traces of adjoining earthworks and fishponds
Location: Immediately south-west of the churchyard
Access: A public footpath runs through the site

Almeley, some 6km south-east of Kington, is described in the Domesday Survey as belonging to the priory of St Guthlac in Hereford. By 1086 it was held by Roger de Lacy. The castle was presumably one of the many built during the unsettled state of the country during the reign of Stephen, and appears as a 'castellum' in the Patent Rolls of John and Henry II. William Cantilupe was constable of the castle in 1216, and Henry III received the homage of Simon de Montfort when passing through there on 22 September 1231. This was one of the estates of the de Lacy Honour of Weobley and as such was occupied by Roger Pychard in 1242.

The roughly circular motte is about 11m in diameter and 7m high from the ditch bottom. Stonework, possibly representing a round tower some 10m in diameter, is said to have been exposed on the south side of the motte when a tree fell some years ago. There was

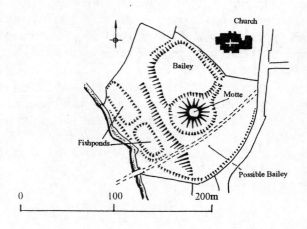

Church
Bailey
Motte
Fishponds
Possible Bailey

0    100    200m

a bailey on the north-western side of the motte, but the north-eastern part of the ditch has been infilled and is now part of the graveyard. There may have been a curtain wall, but there is no trace on the surface. There are slight traces of a possible second bailey on the eastern side. To the south-west of the motte are the remains of two rectangular fishponds. (Robinson Cas., 3-5; VCH, 232 + plan; RCHM, **3**, 6 + plan - xxviii; Salter, 10; RSB, 1; Treasures, 19; TWNFC, **1904**, 235-7; HAN, **50**, 43; **64**, 26-7 + plan)

## Oldcastle Twt or Batch Twt motte & bailey  (SO 328 520)

An overgrown but impressive motte, with a bailey to its north
Location: In Batch Dingle, 0.5km north-west of the church
Access: A public path runs past the foot of the motte

This motte and bailey castle is well-placed at the end of a spur of ground with steep slopes to the east, west and south down to the junction of two streams. The roughly-circular motte is impressively situated on the southernmost point of the spur and rises some 5m above the bottom of the ditch between it and the bailey to the north. The summit is now only 8.5m across at the widest point, but there is some damage from modern paths and there may have been a collapse on the eastern side. The rectangular bailey includes a ditch cut across the base of the spur with an internal rampart. A cottage, built in a gap in the bank, may be on the site of an entrance. A slight platform, in the eastern part of the bailey, may be the site of the former hall. Traces of a possible large outer bailey are visible further to the north.

Almeley is connected with the Lollard leader and rebel, Sir John Oldcastle (otherwise known as the 'good Lord Cobham'), who was condemned as a heretic and 'hanged and burnt hanging' on Christmas Day, 1417. Tradition has it that this was his castle. (Robinson Cas., 3-5; VCH, 232-3 + plan; RCHM, **3**, 6; RSB, 1; Treasures, 18; HAN, **64**, 28 + plan)

# Ashperton

### Ashperton Castle (SO 642 415)
Ashperton is on the A417, 2.5km north-west of 'The Trumpet' junction with the A438. The site is just to the west of the church and consists of an oval platform within an almost square wet moat. The platform, which is about 45m by 55m, is approached by a causeway on the east. There are traces of a roughly rectangular enclosure in the field to the east with traces of a possible hall block. This was a stone castle that William de Grandison had a licence to crenellate in 1292, but the walls were all grubbed out when trees were planted at the end of the eighteenth century. Fine ashlar foundations have been noted. (Robinson Cas., 6-7; VCH, 252; RCHM, **2**, 3; Salter, 10, RSB, 1; Treasures, 53; HAN, **13**, 6 + plan)

### Freetown moated site (SO 625 421)
1.6km west-north-west of the church is this formerly-moated seventeenth century house. There are now only fragmentary traces, but there is also an outer enclosure to the north. (VCH, 249; Treasures, 52)

### Walsopthorne moated site (SO 651 424)
About 1.3km north-west of Ashperton Church, Walsopthorne has fragmentary remains of a moat. (VCH, 249; Treasures, 52)

# Aymestrey

### Camp Wood mound (SO 396 654)
Aymestrey is on the A4110, 4km south of Wigmore. The mound stands on a small spur on the north bank of the River Lugg, some 3km west of Aymestrey Church. It is circular, 37m across at the base and stands 5m high. The top is embanked and the mound is surrounded by a ditch up to 3m deep except on the scarp side. Slight traces remain of a largely ploughed-out bailey. The castle was founded by Hugh Mortimer c.1144-54. (RCHM, **3**, 15 + plan - xxix; Treasures, 6; RSB, 1)

### Gatley Farm moated house (SO 449 686)
The VCH notes that Gatley Farmhouse, standing on lofty ground, retains a moat. This is presumably the early seventeenth century Gatley Park, 4km north-east of Aymestrey Church, but the RCHM makes no mention of a moat. (VCH, 249; RCHM, **3**, 11-12)

# Bacton

### Newcourt Farm possible castle (SO 371 335)
In the Golden Valley, 0.1km south-west of Newcourt Farm, this site has been described in the past as a fortified triangular enclosure with a small mound with a sunken top to the east. However, a recent, more detailed examination has led to the suggestion that this could represent the ground plan of a small castle. The mound has been described as containing the remains of a round keep, some 10m in diameter, with an apsidal buttress on the east and a fore-building on the west. In addition, it is suggested that the triangular bailey, also on the west, was surrounded by a curtain wall that included corner towers, and that the site of a possible hall, 10m by 17m, is apparent in the western corner. The whole enclosure covers about 0.13 hectares and is protected on the north and south by natural scarps and on the western side by a ditch. There is a possible entrance with gatehouse just south of the hall.

In 1086, Bacton was held by one Gilbert from Roger de Lacy. One of his descendants, probably William de Bacton or Richard de

Hampton, could have built this small castle. (VCH, 233 + plan; RCHM, **1**, 20-1 + plan - xxxiv; Treasures, 47; RSB, 1 + plan - opp.2; HAN, **50**, 43; **53**, 18-19 + plan-20)

# Birley

**Moated site** (SO 455 534)
Birley is about 5km north of Canon Pyon. The moated site is just opposite the church. Much of the ditch had been infilled by 1992. (HAN, **54**, 32; **57**, 5)

# Bishop's Frome

**Hopton moated site** (SO 668 471)
About 1.3km south of Bishop's Frome, and just north-east of the junction of the A4103 Worcester road and the B4214, is an incomplete moated site, just to the north of Hopton Farm. There is an outer enclosure on the north-east. (VCH, 249; RCHM, **2**, 11; Salter, 52)

**Cheyney Court moated site** (SO 669 477)
The VCH records that Cheyney Court retained a portion of the original moating, but there is no later description and the building has since been demolished. The only remaining feature is a sixteenth century barn, said to have once been a chapel. (Robinson Man., 24-27; VCH, 249)

# Bishopstone

**Bishopstone Court moated house** (SO 416 440)
10km west-north-west of Hereford, Bishopstone Court is 0.1km north of the church and is mainly of sixteenth century date. It is surrounded by a rectangular stone-lined moat of considerable size. The remains of a late sixteenth century gateway stand on the outer edge of the moat, east of the house. (VCH, 249; RCHM, **3**, 18; Treasures, 23)

# Bodenham

**Moat House** (SO 529 510)
Bodenham is 9km south-south-east of Leominster. The original building on this site, a short distance north-west of the church, was probably the home of Sir Walter Devereux, sheriff in the late fourteenth century. The name alone indicates that there was once a moat around this fifteenth century building, formerly known as Devereux Court, but no trace survives. (Robinson Man., 30-1; RCHM, **2**, 15)

# Bolstone

**Moated site** (SO 547 323)
Bolstone is 8km south-east of Hereford. This moated site lies in the middle of Trilloes Court Wood, some 0.6km south-west of the church. (RCHM, **3**, 25; Treasures, 64)

# Bosbury

**Old Court Farm possible moated site** (SO 695 436)

Late thirteenth/early fourteenth century gatehouse
and parts of walls of Bishop's Palace
Location: On the roadside to the east of the church
Access: Can be viewed from the road

Old Court Farm at Bosbury, 6km north of Ledbury, one-time palace of the bishop of Hereford, may well have been moated. There are traditions of a 'fayre palace' belonging to the bishop in the time of Offa in the eighth century. It was here that Bishop Athelstan died and the Domesday Survey records a prosperous well-established settlement with six hides paying tax, two ploughs in lordship, 17 villagers, 16 smallholders, two slaves, a priest (with one hide and one plough), a mill, and a 'buru' with 22 ploughs. Before 1066 and in 1086, it was worth £6. This was one of the more popular of the country 'palaces' with many of the bishops, and Bishop Swinfield died there in 1316. There was extensive rebuilding in 1572 when John Harford, the steward of the manor, undertook 'to newe build another house upon the same ground,' but the work was later considered to be poor and little more than extensions to 'an old tenement standing in that place before.' Although it was restored to the bishop after the Civil War, having been bought by Silas Taylor for £778 10s. 6d., it became a tenanted farmhouse and no bishop has resided there since.

A stream, a tributary of the River Leadon, which bounded the enclosure on the north and west, appears to have been straightened at some time. The late thirteenth or early fourteenth century gatehouse faces the road on the eastern side of the site. It is a composite of stone and timber-framing that has been considerably altered during the years. In the centre, flanked by flat buttresses, are the main gateway and, immediately to its south, the now-blocked wicket gate. It was probably built free-standing with a timber palisade guarding the palace grounds. Defences of this nature are often associated with water-filled defences such as probably existed here. The farmhouse incorporates some fifteenth century work and the palace once included extensive cellarage and may have been the main wine store for the bishop. (RCHM, **2**, 19-20; Treasures, 38; HAS, **231**)

### Temple Court moated house (SO 690 433)
Temple Court Farm, some 0.5km south-west of Bosbury Church, was originally a preceptory of the Knights Templar, but when the Order was dissolved in 1312 it was given to the Knights Hospitallers. The present building is mainly of eighteenth century date although the north range may be of medieval origin. The rounded moat formerly surrounded the house and there are traces of other outer enclosures. (Robinson Man., 33; VCH, 249; RCHM, **2**, 19; Treasures, 38)

### Upleadon Court moated site (SO 668 419)
There are slight traces of a moat in an orchard some 0.3km south-east of Upleadon Court, 4km west-south-west of Bosbury. (RCHM, **2**, 19; Salter, 52)

# Brampton Bryan

**Brampton Bryan Castle** (SO 369 726)

The gatehouse and parts of the great hall and curtain wall remain
Location: In the grounds of Brampton Bryan Hall
Access: On private land; glimpses can be had from the entrance to
the drive and over the wall near the church

Brampton Bryan is a rather pretty and now peaceful village in the
extreme north-western corner of Herefordshire, close to the borders
of Shropshire and the old Welsh county of Radnor. The castle,
central to the village, guarded the important route which led from
Ludlow along the Teme valley to Knighton and central Wales. The
castle was built at a point where the valley narrowed between the
heights of Brampton Bryan Park on the south and Coxall Knoll
with its Iron Age hillfort to the north. The importance and relative
ease of this route from Wales into England was confirmed as
recently as the end of the nineteenth century when the valley was
chosen for the Elan Aqueduct which carries water from mid-Wales
to Birmingham.

Although Brampton Bryan is mentioned in the Domesday Survey as part of the holding of Ralph de Mortimer, the date of the foundation of the castle is uncertain and may well have been some years later than the Conquest.

However, the de Bramptons must have been well settled in the area by 1172 when they were involved with Hugh de Mortimer in the foundation of the Abbey at Wigmore. Apparently the second stone was 'laid by Bryan de Brampton and he promised a hundred sols, but he gave nothing in money, though he granted them all easements in his lands in wood and field everywhere, which easements aided them greatly in their work'. The third stone was laid by Bryan's son John who eventually gave the monks the living of the church of Kinlet in Shropshire. By 1252, John's son, another Bryan, had obtained the king's charter for a weekly market on Tuesdays at Brampton and an annual fair associated with the Festival of St Barnabas. He was possibly the most energetic and successful of the five Bramptons of Brampton Bryan.

The earliest reference to any building at Brampton Bryan is in 1295 when the castle was described as having a tower with curtilage, garden and vivary (or fishpond) which was worth £8 7s. 8d. per annum. It was held under the Mortimers, there being a yearly rent charge of 13s. 4d. and guard duty which was due at Wigmore Castle for 40 days in wartime. This valuation followed the death in 1294 of yet another Bryan de Brampton, but this time without male issue. It was some fifteen years later, in 1309, that Margaret, the eldest daughter, married Robert Harley, the son of Sir Richard Harley. Since that time, for almost 700 years, the castle has belonged to one branch or another of the Harley family.

The castle was almost entirely destroyed during the Civil War, but the gatehouse and other fragments have been maintained for over three hundred years as a rather grand garden ornament in the gardens of the Georgian hall, the present residence of the Harley family.

The surviving masonry, of various dates between the thirteenth and seventeenth centuries, is somewhat difficult to interpret due to later garden landscaping. However, it is apparent that the castle was still very much a defensive structure at the beginning of the Civil War, for it was surrounded by a moat which could be filled with

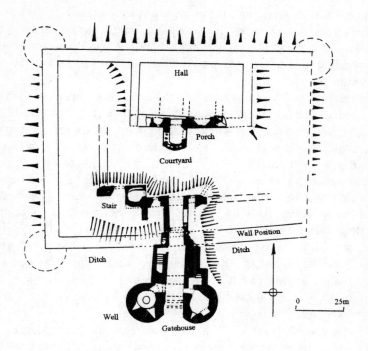

*Plan of the castle showing possible reconstruction*

water and was approached by a drawbridge on the south. Like many of the later castles, it was probably designed to have several ranges of buildings surrounding a central courtyard.

At the front of what was this courtyard is the most impressive surviving part of the castle—a complex gatehouse of two distinct periods. The earlier phase—the inner gatehouse passage—could well have been the work of Bryan de Brampton in the 1280s and, if so, may well have been the tower mentioned in 1295. This gatehouse was contained completely within the line of the curtain wall but would have been relatively impressive as it included two floors above the gatehouse passage. There was a single room or chamber on each of these floors, presumably for the gate-keeper. He would have lived directly above the entrance passage in the first-floor room with its fireplace, which would also have included the works for the portcullis. The inner of the arches in the passage includes some ballflower ornament. If this arch was indeed built by Bryan de Brampton it would be a very early use of this decorative form. Traces of the original curtain wall are evident on each side of the outer archway and there were evidently other buildings attached on each side.

In the fourteenth century major improvements were made which changed dramatically the whole external aspect of the castle. A long narrow passage was added to the outside of the original gatehouse and a new outer gatehouse was built onto the southern end of this passage with the new entrance flanked by round towers. This is an early example of an extended gatehouse and passage, the design of which was to evolve into formidable gatehouses and barbicans such as those at Alnwick Castle in Northumberland, Warwick Castle and locally at Goodrich. In all these, presumably later examples, the passageway crossed over the moat with the outer gatehouse or barbican on the landward side. The passageway, effectively a killing-ground, was overlooked by the main gate, the curtain wall-heads on each side, and the rear of the upper floor of the outer gate.

At the ground-floor level, a doorway from the passage leads to the eastern tower where there was a small guardroom with a fireplace and a garderobe cubicle. An opposing doorway leads into the west tower which contained a well, now backfilled. There was a portcullis at the southern end of the passage, reinforcing the earlier one in the inner gatehouse. A little further along the western side of the passage is a doorway which leads to stairs, built within the thickness of the wall, providing access to the upper chamber. This a poor defensive feature; for maximum security, and to protect the gatehouse as a whole, the upper works in the outer gatehouse should only have been accessible from the inner gatehouse.

The upper chamber is large but irregularly-shaped. It is lit only by the small windows in the two towers and contains a fireplace and separate garderobe. The fine, octagonal chimney, which still towers above the gatehouse, is of sixteenth century date. The first-floor window openings in the towers and the label course above the outer arch all include ballflower decoration. The passage and outer gatehouse are unlikely to be much later than the inner gatehouse and could well have been the work of Sir Robert Harley or his son Bryan.

The elaborate gatehouse and passage is now separated from the only other substantial part of the castle to survive, the great hall, by what looks like a ditch and is so interpreted in several descriptions. This 'ditch' can add to the interpretative confusion for it had a rather more prosaic purpose. It was dug about a hundred years ago as a path for the convenience of tennis players using the neighbouring court!

The remains of the great hall were separated from the gatehouse by a courtyard some 10m wide—the area which now contains the 'ditch'. Enough of the fourteenth century south wall of the building survives to indicate that the main room—the hall itself—was at first-floor level. It was set above a basement that was lit by single-light windows. The external steps were replaced in the late sixteenth or early seventeenth century by a large porch, containing a staircase that led up to the hall doorway, which still survives. The ashlar faces and square-headed mullioned and transomed windows are in striking contrast to the fourteenth century work in the main wall. This porch, and the second staircase in the south-western corner of the courtyard adjoining the gatehouse, were probably part of a comprehensive refurbishment programme which was designed to bring the castle up to the standards of comfort expected at that time. The work was probably started during the lifetime of Thomas Harley who died in 1631, but it would appear that it was incomplete when his son, Robert, succeeded to the estate and the whole project may have been curtailed by the start of the Civil War and never completed.

The Harley family have been involved in many of the significant events in the history of the British Isles, but it was during the war between king and parliament that their mettle was tested to its limits and their castle was totally devastated. Throughout the Civil War, Herefordshire was essentially a royalist county, but amongst the landed gentry there were one or two notable exceptions. The most prominent amongst these was Sir Robert Harley whose third wife was Brilliana, the second daughter of Viscount Conway. She was some twenty years younger than her husband when they were married in 1623. Even so, they had seven children, the eldest being Edward, born in 1624.

Sir Robert, who was described as a man of wit, learning and piety, but of an austere and decided character, was very much a

Puritan. In 1603 he was made a Knight of the Bath and shortly afterwards represented the borough of Radnor, and, at a later date, the county of Herefordshire, in the various parliaments of James and Charles. Due to his parliamentary duties, Sir Robert had to reside in London and left his wife, Lady Brilliana, to deal with their growing family, the domestic matters of the estate and the rapidly escalating problems associated with being of a puritan family living in a royalist part of the country.

In the first instance, arrangements were made to fill the moat with water and the garrison, mainly servants and local retainers, was strengthened by the appearance of a veteran sergeant called Hackluyt. In total there were about a hundred men, women and children in the castle when the siege finally began.

Sir William Vavasour, who was the royalist governor for the area, attempted to persuade Lady Brilliana to surrender but she refused— he had then no choice but to 'make an attempt upon Brompton Castle ... it is a strong place, but I am lodged very neare itt (three pikes lengths from the portes)'. So, on 26 July, 1643, he, Henry Lingen, Sir Walter Pye and William Smallman together with a body of horse and foot, surrounded the castle. By 30 July, the defenders had lost control of the church, which stood directly in front of the gatehouse, and as a result had to block up the double portcullises. The attackers placed a 'great gun' in the steeple and used it to fire on the roofs and battlements of the castle, eventually bringing down a stack of chimneys. As time went on, further such guns were used against the castle, but to little avail. The royalists were then occupied in burning most of the village including the castle mills, some 40 houses, the parsonage, and eventually the church itself.

For quite a while the defenders had no casualties at all, whilst apparently having considerable success against the enemy, killing some sixty of their attackers and supporters including the castle mason who, 'as he was pointing with his hand to show the enemy the weakest part of the castle was shot through that hand into his belly and died'. By the end of August it was apparent that the castle would not be easily taken and several days of parleying followed. Eventually, on 9 September, Colonel Lingen withdrew to Gloucester, leaving a castle of which 'the roof ... was so bayttered that there was not one dry room in it'.

THE SOUTH EAST VIEW OF BROMPTON BRIIN CASTLE, IN THE COUNTY OF HEREFORD.

To the R<sup>t</sup> Hon<sup>ble</sup> EDWARD Earl of Oxford and Mortimer, and Baron Harley of Wigmore, Owner of these Remains. This Prospect is humbly Inscrib'd, by May Lord Y<sup>r</sup> Lord<sup>ps</sup> most Obed<sup>t</sup> Serv<sup>ts</sup> Sam<sup>l</sup> & Nath<sup>l</sup> Buck.

THIS CASTLE belonged for some Ages to a Family of Distinction call'd Brian de Brompton. In the days of K. Edw. III. Robert de Harley married the Daughter & Heir of Brian de Brompton, by which means it came unto that Noble Family.

61

It is apparent from the contents of the many letters Lady Brilliana wrote to her son that she was of a delicate disposition and had suffered repeated attacks of illness. Bearing in mind the recorded state of the castle after this first siege, it is not surprising that she was to confide to her son on 9 October that she 'has taken a very great cold, which has made me very ill these 2 or 3 days'. She died the following day, but her fame as commander of the beleaguered garrison of Brampton Bryan was to spread throughout the country.

The castle was again attacked in the spring of 1644 by a new force under the command of Sir Michael Woodhouse. He had just taken Hopton Castle where eleven of the small garrison of fourteen had been massacred after surrendering. The defence of Brampton Bryan by some seventy men was as strong as before, but the attackers made use of mines and had better artillery which damaged the walls to such an extent that eventually the defenders had to surrender. The whole building was then sacked and burnt and the prisoners, including Sir Robert's three younger children, were transferred to Shrewsbury.

But within a couple of years the royalist cause was completely lost and Sir Robert's steward was able to claim recompense of some £13,000 including £200 for a study of books. This sum should perhaps be compared with the modest £1,000 which the Countess of Kent was awarded in compensation for the slighting of Goodrich Castle.

The preacher at Robert's funeral concluded his sermon with the wish that 'the Lord repair the Ruines of this Castle and build up this great Family'. By the early 1660s Sir Edward was building a new house of seven bays under a hipped roof. This was eventually incorporated into the present mansion which is still the home of the Harley family.

The engraving produced in 1731 by Samuel and Nathaniel Buck shows the ruins behind the well-tended gardens of the new mansion. The remains of the great hall and the porch with its rectangular windows, on the far side of the courtyard from the extended gatehouse, still stand two stories high. The ranges that ran on the two sides of the courtyard—the solar on the one side and the servants quarters on the other, are shown as low walls. (Robinson Cas., 8-16; VCH, 233; RCHM, **3**, 19-21 + plan; Salter, 11-12;

Treasures, 3; TWNFC, **1882**, 189-93; **1918**, 216-19; **1986**, 514-5; HAN, **57**, 25; **59**, 44 + plan; HAS, **6** & **39**; Williams, 1956; Slade, 1981, Webb, 1879; Lewis, 1854; Remfry, P.M., 1996)

**Lower Pedwardine mound** (SO 367 705)
About 2km south of Brampton Bryan Church, this much-altered mound is roughly circular and about 25m in diameter. It rises to a maximum of about 3m above the surrounding ground and has a slight ditch on the south. A bailey has been suggested. (VCH, 224 + plan; RCHM, **3**, 21; Treasures, 4; RSB, 1)

**Upper Pedwardine motte & possible bailey** (SO 365 707)
This mound is about 0.4km north-west of the one at Lower Pedwardine. There is no obvious reason for the two being so close together. The southern part of the mound, which was originally about 33m across, has been partly cut away by a farm building. It has been suggested that the mound includes traces of a tower and that there was a small bailey on the southern side. The site is confused by the later farm buildings. Circular foundations further to the south probably represent a dovecot. (RCHM, **3**, 2; Treasures, 4; RSB, 1 + plan opp. 20; HAS **57**, 23 + plan on 27)

# Bredenbury

**Sawbury Hill moated site** (SO 626 553)
Some 3km west of Bromyard and 2km south-east of Bredenbury, Sawbury Hill is on the north side of the A44. There were slight traces of a moat there around 1900. (VCH, 249)

# Bredwardine

**Castle site 1** (SO 335 444)

> A motte and bailey
> Location: Immediately to the south of the churchyard
> Access: A public right of way from the church follows
> the western side of both sites

Bredwardine, (probably 'plank settlement' from OE *bred* 'board' and *worthign* 'an enclosure'), has been the site of an important crossing of the River Wye for many years, first by ford, later by ferry and more recently by bridge. Just south of the churchyard and adjoining the Wye are earthworks and foundations described by the Royal Commission as being a motte and bailey. The mound and its associated foundations are probably those of the building illustrated in Robinson's 'Castles' and built or substantially reconstructed by Roger Vaughan in 1639-40. It is possible that this building could have replaced an earlier building described by Silas Taylor in 1650 as being the 'ancient Castle of Gronw', presumably after Hywell ap Gronwy who died 1106/7. It is suggested that this is the Lann Iunabui of the *Liber Landavensis*. However, there is a second possible site further to the south (see below). (Robinson Cas., 20-24; VCH, 233-4 + plan; RCHM, **1**, 26 + plan - xxxvi; Salter, 13; Treasures, 22; HAN, **48**, 4)

**Castle site 2** (SO 337 440)
South of the site described above are two small valleys across which banks have been built to form fishponds. South again, the wooded area widens out, still with the river on the east, and here excavation has revealed traces of two phases of timber buildings followed by at least three phases of stone buildings, the whole lasting from the twelfth to the sixteenth century. Whilst the earlier periods could well represent the remains of a castle or defended site, the fourteenth century buildings appear to be little more than a farmhouse complex. (as above and TWNFC, **1956**, 182-3; **1969**, 476; **1970**, 159; **1971**, 281; **1972**, 392; HAN **16**, 3; **17**, 6; **19**, 5, & **23**, 2-3)

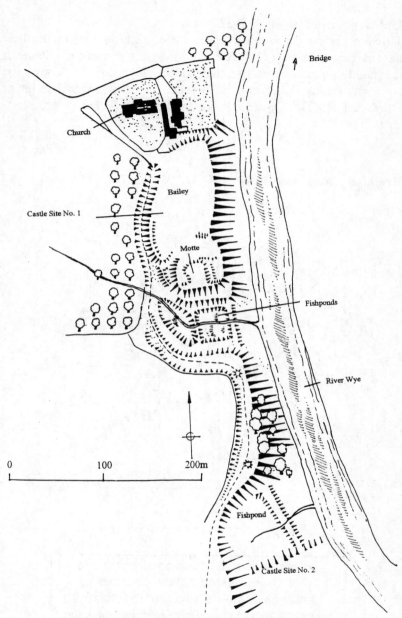

*Plan showing the two castles at Bredwardine*

**Old Court moated site** (SO 337 440)

This is a reasonably well-preserved moated site just to the north of the fourteenth century Old Court and 0.3km north of the church. It is roughly square with 30m long sides and rising 5m above the surrounding, low lying ground. It must surely be a predecessor of Old Court. (RCHM, **1**, 26; TWNFC, **1958**, 127-8; Treasures, 22)

# Breinton

**Breinton Camp moated site** (SO 473 395)

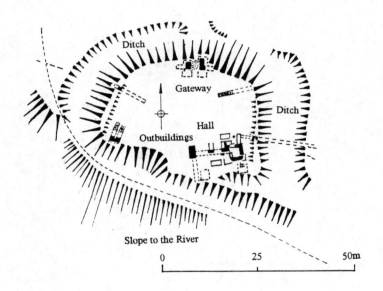

*Plan showing main excavation areas*

> The earthworks and ditch stand on the edge
> of an embankment above the river
> Location: 50m south-west of the church
> Access: A public footpath runs round the south
> and west sides of the site

Breinton is just west of Hereford and the Camp is high up on a bluff above the left bank of the Wye some 50m south-west of the church. A track that originally led to a ford across the river runs just to the west of the Camp. There is a spring of pure water at the bottom of the bluff. Excavations at the Camp between 1959 and 1962 established that it consisted of an irregularly shaped enclosure, about 36m by 25m, surrounded by a low perimeter bank and thin curtain wall, with a dry ditch up to 2m deep and 5.5m wide on all sides except the south, where the ground falls steeply away to the river bank. The entrance was on the north side where there was a stone gateway with a 2m wide cobbled track. The stone footings of the main buildings, interpreted as an upper hall but including a cellared portion, were found in the south-eastern corner of the enclosure. There were also traces of timber buildings to the south-west. The site was occupied by c.1150 and abandoned after the collapse of part of the main building in the thirteenth century. There are traces of earthworks towards the church and it has been suggested that the moated site could have been the site of the first vicarage associated with St Michael's church. A recent suggestion that this was a castle motte with a D-shaped shell keep is considered unlikely due to the insubstantial nature of the stonework as a whole. However, the outlying earthworks on the north and north-east could easily be described as a series of baileys. (VCH, 252 + plan; RCHM, **2**, 27 + plan - xxvi; Salter, 13; Treasures, 55; TWNFC, **1921**, lxix & 81; **1959**, 243; **1963**, 272-94; HAN, **50**, 43; **63**, 29 + plan)

# Bridge Sollers

### Knapp Farm possible motte and bailey (SO 414 426)
About 10km west from Hereford on the A438, the bridge at Bridge Sollers replaced the historic ford in 1896. Knapp Farm, of seventeenth century date, is on the left bank of the River Wye near where the track to the ford led down to the river. The motte, if that is what it is, is very small and would only have taken a small tower. There could be a bailey, well hidden underneath the farm, and another large one has been suggested to the north, cut in two by the A438. There is sufficient stone around the site to indicate stone building(s) on the motte and possibly in the bailey. (RSB, 1; HAN, **65**, 26 + plan)

# Bridstow

**Wilton Castle** (SO 590 245)

Many of the external masonry walls survive
Location: On the right bank of the Wye,
just upstream of Wilton Bridge
Access: A public footpath leads past the castle to its east
and from which it can be seen

Wilton means 'the estate amongst the willows' which well describes the castle which is on the left bank of the Wye just upstream of Wilton Bridge, between the river and the A40. The earliest reference to the site is about 1150, and there was certainly a castle at Wilton belonging to the Longchamps family at the end of the twelfth century. From them it descended to the De Grey family and continued in their hands until it passed by a family arrangement to the Hon Charles Brydges. During the seventeenth century Civil War it was the home of Sir John Brydges who attempted to avoid the conflict by undertaking military service in Ireland. He was the husband of Mary, the eldest daughter of Sir James Scudamore of

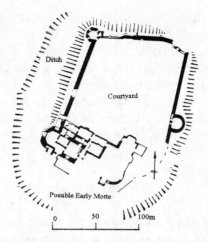

Ditch

Courtyard

Possible Early Motte

0    50    100m

Holme Lacy and sister of the Royalist Governor of Hereford, Sir Barnabas Scudamore. When Brydges returned to England to recruit for the losses in his regiment he categorically refused to allow his house to be occupied as a royal garrison. This annoyed Barnabas Scudamore and Harry Lingen who decided to take direct action. The house was described by Silas Taylor as 'a very fayre sweet dwelling house ... which in ancient times was a castle ... ye place was very unlikely to have made a garrison (it being seated not in a castle-like but house-like building).' Even so, Scudamore and Lingen arranged for a body of soldiers to burn the house to the ground one Sunday morning whilst the family was at church. It was not until the nineteenth century that parts of the ruin were incorporated into a new house.

It has been suggested that the earliest castle was of motte and bailey type, but there is no evidence to confirm this theory. A ditch still survives on the west and north, but on the south side it has been almost entirely filled in and on the east there is just a scarp slope to the river. The surviving masonry consists mainly of the local red sandstone although there is some tufa re-used in the house. The stonework follows the original earthworks in a quadrilateral design with towers at the corners. In the sixteenth century a house was apparently built in the southern part of the castle, incorporating the south-western tower, and it was this house that was destroyed by fire in the Civil War and reconstructed in the nineteenth century.

The building periods are undoubtedly complex—it would seem likely that the gateway was originally in the south wall, where the sixteenth century house was built and that the fourteenth century reconstruction changed the earlier castle into something little more than a fortified house. By the sixteenth century all pretensions to defence had been virtually abandoned in favour of a comfortable dwelling. (Robinson Cas., 143-5; VCH, 252; RCHM, **1**, 29-31 + plan; Treasures, 77; RSB, 1 + plan opp 18; Salter, 48-9 + plan; HAN, **58**, 43-5)

# Brilley

### Brilley Green possible castle site (SO 273 488)
Brilley is in the far west of the county and Brilley Green is about 1km south-east of the church. This earthwork, on a steep bluff over-looking a deep dingle, could well be entirely natural, but it has been suggested that it is the site of an eroded motte and bailey. (HAN, **57**, 43 + plan - 42)

### Cwmma Farm Tump (SO 276 514)
North of Cwmma Farm and 2.8km north-east of the church, this circular mound is 27m in diameter at the base and rises some 5m above the lowest part of the ditch. A stream that runs through the ditch on the west could have made this a wet moat. There is a possible bailey hidden in trees and undergrowth. (VCH, 224 + plan; RCHM, **3**, 23 + plan - xxix; RSB, 2; HAN, **50**, 43)

### Knapp Farm, Little Merthyr possible castle site (SO 266 487)
It has been suggested that beneath the present farm buildings there could be the remains of an early fortified site, but there is little if any surface evidence. (HAN, **57**, 43)

# Brinsop

**Brinsop Court moated house** (SO 446 458)

Brinsop Court, some 10km north-west of Hereford, is a first class example of a fourteenth century manor house surrounded by a rectangular moat. There is a stone bridge at the south-western corner. At one time it had two towers flanking a drawbridge, apparently on the northern side. It belonged to the Tirrell family in the thirteenth and fourteenth centuries, but had been acquired by the Daunceys by the fifteenth century. (Robinson Man., 43-5; VCH, 249; RCHM, **2**, 29-31; TWNFC, **1882**, 234; **1910**, 166-171; HAN, **62**, 38-40)

**Moated site** (SO 446 456)
There is a rectangular moated site some 0.2km south of Brinsop Court. It is now very overgrown. (RCHM, **2**, 31; VCH, 249; Treasures, 33; HAN, **62**, 39)

**Church earthworks and possible moated site** (SO 442 448)
Earthworks around Brinsop Church and the surrounding buildings cover an area of some 4ha and doubtless represent a deserted medieval village. To the north-east of the church is a rhomboidal-shaped enclosure surrounded by a moat. (VCH, 252-3 + plan; RCHM, **2**, 31-2 + plan; Treasures, 32; HAN, **62**, 40-1 + plan)

# Brockhampton-by-Bromyard

**Lower Brockhampton moated house** (SO 688 560)

> Medieval great hall and solar on a moated site with
> a small timber gatehouse
> Location: 4km east of Bromyard
> Access: In care of the National Trust and open to the public

Lower Brockhampton (*brook settlement*) lies in a secluded valley and in the fourteenth century belonged to a family that took their name from it—the de Brockhamptons. The ruined sandstone chapel that stood just to the west has been dated to the twelfth century. In 1283 the de Brockhamptons sold the estate to Robert de Furches, but it then passed back to a descendant of the de Brockhamptons, John Domulton, in 1403. Domulton is generally accepted as the builder of the great hall that still stands in the wet-moated site.

Alterations and additions were made to the house in subsequent years. The construction of a timber-framed gatehouse that spanned the moat, probably took place in the late fifteenth or early sixteenth centuries. The manor came into the hands of the Habington family and then, by marriage in the mid-sixteenth century, to the Barneby family. In 1726 Bartholomew Richard Lutley, a nephew of the last of the direct-line Barnebys, inherited the estates and adopted the old family surname. He married late in life and in the 1760s commissioned the Shrewsbury architect Thomas Farnolls Pritchard to design a new mansion. Brockhampton House stands on higher ground amidst extensive parkland to the south of the moated site.

The older building was used as a farmhouse for many years and a first floor was inserted into the great hall. The building became almost derelict and in 1871 the then owner, John Barneby (Lutley) arranged for its restoration. In 1946 the Brockhampton estate was bequeathed by John Talbot Lutley to the National Trust who manage the 1,680 acre estate and have carried out extensive restoration work to the house and gatehouse.

This is a fully moated site, apart from a short section of the south arm. The main complex on the island comprises a medieval great hall (now without the inserted floor), an attached solar wing and more modern extensions to the rear. The close-studded jettied gatehouse, guarding the main entrance across the moat, is a later addition, probably of around 1600. (Robinson Man., 48-9; VCH, 249; RCHM, **2**, 32-3 + plan; Treasures, 36; HAS **201**)

# Brockhampton-by-Ross

**Moated site** (position uncertain - not found on map)
Close to the eastern bank of the River Wye and some 8km north of Ross, the VCH records that 1.2km north of Brockhampton Park 'is a rectangular moat with some slight remains of masonry where the gatehouse, with a portcullis, stood. Adjoining this moat on the east side is another and much smaller moated inclosure.' (VCH, 249)

**Fawley 'Camp'** (SO 580 307)
This earthwork, some 0.5km north of the sixteenth century Fawley Court, is shown by the VCH as a heavily embanked oval enclosure (c. 60m by 30m) on high ground next to the minor road that overlooks the Wye. By 1931 it was described merely as a slight sinking. There is now little to see and its origin and purpose is uncertain. (VCH, 256; RCHM, **2**, 36)

# Buckton & Coxall

### Upper Buckton Farm mound (SO 383 733)

Buckton and Coxall parish is on low lying land to the west of Leintwardine. This oval mound, to the south-west of Buckton Farm and close to a mill leat running from the Teme, is about 39m across at the base and rises about 4m above the now dry ditch. It is possible that the leat could, at one time, have fed the ditch. There is some stone in the mound, but insufficient to be certain that stone buildings were involved. There may have been one bailey under the present farm buildings, but there is also some evidence for a second on the flat ground to the west of the motte. Parch marks, that have been seen by one writer, could suggest that this bailey had been walled, but eroded embankments often produce a similar effect. (VCH, 224-5 + plan; RCHM, **3**, 27; Treasures, 2; RSB, 2; HAN, **50**, 43; **57**, 24 + plan)

### Mounds (SO 394 741 & SO 394 738)

These two mounds lie about 1km east of Leintwardine. The northern one is 74m by 57m and 3m high above a slight ditch which could be modern. The other is more irregular, about 65m by 39m, and also about 3m high above a slight ditch. Both are in marshy ground and their purpose is uncertain. It has been suggested that they could even be natural mounds. (RCHM, **3**, 29; Treasures, 2; HAN, **61**, 7)

# Burghill

### Moated site (SO 479 446)

Burghill is 5.5km north-west of Hereford. A moat some 40m north-west of the church, was totally filled in around the turn of the century. It consisted of a small square platform surrounded by a moat and had an outside rampart on the south and east to act as a dam to form a water level. (VCH, 249 + plan; RCHM, **2**, 43; Treasures, 34)

# Byton

**Possible motte & bailey** (SO 372 642)
This site, 6.5km south-west of Wigmore and just to the south of
Byton Church, was first recognised as a castle by Roger Stirling-
Brown in 1967. He describes it as consisting of a motte, with traces
of a former shell keep, and a possible gatehouse to the south. The
bailey is to the north and includes the church. There are traces of
other enclosures nearby. Documentary sources date it back to
c.1150. (RSB, 2 + plan opp.; HAN, **58**, 29-30 + plan - 31)

# Canon Frome

**Moated site** (SO 645 436)
Some 8km north-west of Ledbury, the Court (sometimes called the
Strong House) was originally moated. This was the building that
was involved in the seventeenth century Civil War. The present
Court, just to the north of the church, was built in 1786, but incorporates parts of the early seventeenth century building. Traces of
the moat were apparent around 1900. Until recently it was used as a
secondary school. (VCH, 249; RCHM, **2**, 45)

# Canon Pyon

**Moated site** (SO 474 512)
East of the A4110 and some 3.2km north-east of the church and
200m north of The Cotts farm, this site was once described as being
a considerable and perfect rectangular moat with a causeway on the
southern side. Some masonry has been seen on the platform, but the
moat has since been filled in. It adjoins a right-of-way. (VCH, 249;
RCHM, **2**, 47; Treasures, 30)

**Lawton's Hope moated site** (SO 472 502)
In the same area as the previous site, this moated site is described as
being some 50m square with a retaining bank on the south-western
side. A stream runs along the north-east and north-west sides, but
the moat is largely dry. (Treasures, 31)

# Castle Frome

### Ringwork & bailey (SO 670 458)

This site is on the south-west side of Fromes Hill some 0.3km east of the church. It is in an extremely strong position, but is largely concealed by post-war afforestation. The ringwork is some 45m in diameter and rises about 4m above the bailey. It was described by the RCHM as a motte with a sinking in the top, but in view of its size, a ringwork is more likely. Traces of a possible shell keep have been noted. Except on the west, where there is a scarp slope, the ringwork is surrounded by a ditch with a causeway to the south-east. The bailey, with its deep ditch, surrounds the ringwork to the north, east and south. The entrance to the bailey was apparently by a causeway across the ditch on the southern side. The site is very overgrown making identification of features difficult.

Its size and situation makes it very likely that Castle Frome was the stronghold from which Walter de Lacy's estates in the Frome valley were controlled. As such it must have been built just after the Conquest. It was in the king's hands from 1155 to sometime after 1216 when it was restored to the de Lacys. Gilbert de Lacy borrowed £600 from Walter de Lacy of Weobley in 1244, probably to complete the castle at Frome or to rebuild a substantial part of it in stone. (Robinson Cas., 62-4; VCH, 225; RCHM, **2**, 49; Salter, 13; RSB, 2; Treasures, 38; TWNFC, **1894**, 184; HAN, **50**, 43; **59**, 23-6; **60**, 7-8 + plan)

### New Birchend moated site (SO 666 447)

1.2km south of the church, this is a well-preserved moated site. (VCH 249; RCHM, **2**, 49; Treasures, 38)

### Millend Farm possible castle site (SO 656 453)

This site, 1.3km south-west of the church, close to the River Frome and just to the north of Millend Farm was discovered from aerial photographs. It has been suggested that it could be of medieval origin and possibly a castle. (HAN, **59**, 24; **60**, 49 + plan)

# Clifford

**Clifford Castle** (SO 243 457)

A large motte with the remains of a polygonal keep,
together with various outer works
Location: Adjoining the B4350 on the western end of the village
Access: By permission from Betty Parkinson
at the house by the Motte

Clifford is on the right bank of the Wye, facing Radnorshire across
the river. The castle stands on a cliff above the river near a point
where it could be forded. It is one of the five castles in Herefordshire
mentioned in the Domesday Survey and built by William fitz Osbern
between 1069 and 1071. By the time of the survey it had been
granted by the king to Ralph de Tosny and was probably being used
as a base for operations into Wales. Walter Clifford, the son of
Richard fitz Pons, came to the fore following the Anarchy in the late
1130s, and probably assumed full control of the de Tosny manors
some time after he married Margaret Tosny. The castle is the reputed
birthplace of 'the fair Rosamund'—Walter's daughter and the ill-
fated favourite of Henry II. The castle must have been kept in reason-

able condition and stayed in the hands of the Clifford family until the 1260s when Matilda Clifford, the widow of William Longespey, Earl of Salisbury, became the baroness of Clifford. There was then a curious twist, for John Giffard of Brimpsfield apparently used Clifford as a base in the Barons' War, abducted Matilda, raped her and forcibly married her. For this he was fined, but Matilda appears to have accepted the *fait accompli* and stayed with John in her Marches estates. Apparently Richard II and his uncle, John of Gaunt, stayed there in 1381, but, once the Welsh were conquered, the castle was of no further importance and was allowed to deteriorate. It was last used in the early fifteenth century and took no part in the seventeenth century Civil War.

The earthworks, about 26m above the Wye, consist of a circular motte which rises about 10m above a dry ditch on the north-east and south-west sides. The other sides have natural scarps, that on the north-west having been cut more sharply when the Hereford to Hay railway was built. The motte is some 30m across and includes the remains of an irregular polygonal shell keep. Some years ago the foundations of a square keep were found in the centre of the mound. The gatehouse faces east and is flanked by two D-shaped towers and, although only standing some 1m high, it includes traces of a portcullis groove between the inner and outer arches. It leads into a courtyard with doorways into each of the gatehouse towers. The hall-block, probably of two stories with the great hall directly above service or storage rooms, is on the north side of the courtyard. To the west is a well-preserved D-shaped tower of two stages. The south-west tower is mainly buried, but the plan of the south tower is apparent. There are garderobes associated with both west and south towers. It is apparent that there are several different construction periods represented in the upstanding masonry. The main work, the D-shaped towers and possibly the hall, are probably the work of the Tosnys in the early twelfth century.

To the west is a small triangular-shaped bailey. The main bailey is to the east and was of considerable size. It is largely surrounded by scarp slopes, but there are traces of a rampart at the north and south-east angles. It is connected to the motte by a sloping causeway that crosses the motte ditch (possibly an example of Victorian 'improvements').

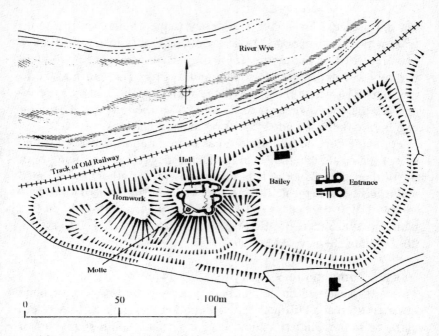

Almost central to the bailey was an irregular-shaped mound that was excavated in the early 1950s. It contained the lower parts of a substantial gatehouse and barbican with a passage some 18m long and 3m wide. At each side of the entry there are the remains of small round towers, and at the inner end a rectangular tower with a portcullis. Walls led off this gatehouse to both north and south for a short distance but were then completely robbed out. It would appear that this structure, which is probably of early thirteenth century date, was designed to split the bailey into two parts—an inner and an outer ward. (Robinson Cas., 25-30; VCH, 234 + plan; RCHM, **1**, 39-41 + plan; RSB, 2 + plan opp. 6; Salter, 14-16 + plan; Treasures, 21; TWNFC, **1889**, 366-372 + plan; **1924**,151; **1927**, lxvii - lxviii & 147-48; **1952**, 27-28 & 82-84 + plan; **1986**, 246-51; HAS, **56**, 27-29 + plan; Remfry, 1994)

### Old Castleton motte & bailey (SO 283 457)
Some 4km east of the main castle, this reasonably well-preserved motte and bailey castle stands on a slight rise overlooking a bend in the Wye. The large motte stands 9m above the ground to the north,

but only some 2.5m above the kidney-shaped bailey on the south from which it is separated by a dry ditch. Traces of masonry have been recorded on the motte. The bailey was surrounded by a ditch, partially lost underneath the road, and a bank. The hall may be to the south-east where there is a slight platform. The entry was probably on the south where there is a break in the rampart. There are two lightly-defended outer courts on the east and west.

For some considerable time it has been thought that this was the site of the castle mentioned in the Domesday Survey as being built by William fitz Osbern. This theory has recently been questioned and it has been suggested that it was built by fitz Osbern's brother-in-law, Ralph de Tosny. (VCH, 234-5 + plan; RCHM, **1**, 38-9 + plan - xxxvi; Salter, 35; RSB, 2; Treasures, 21; HAN, **50**, 45; **56**, 26-7 + plan; Remfry, P.M., 1995b)

## Newton Tump motte & bailey (SO 293 441)

This well-preserved motte and bailey castle is on low lying ground between Merbach Hill and Little Mountain and guards the western entrance to the Golden Valley. It is about 2km south-south-east of Old Castleton. The bailey forms a quarter-circle with the north and east sides straight and the south and west sides curved. It is surrounded by a slight rampart and ditch. The oval-shaped motte is totally enclosed in the north-western angle and is also surrounded by a ditch. A small stream—the Bach Brook—that runs past the site to the north may well have been used to flood the ditch. Some 90 years ago, the Victoria County History recorded possible traces of masonry on the small motte—this could represent a polygonal tower similar to that at Snodhill. A stone wall, exposed in a cutting through the bailey rampart on the northern side, was up to 1.5m thick and probably represents the bailey defences. There was an entrance on the southern side and possibly a south-eastern corner tower. The mound on the eastern rampart may represent an internally-projecting gatetower.

Indications of earthworks to the south of the entrance may represent some form of barbican. Aerial photographs have suggested further enclosures both to the east and to the west of the bailey and a possible chapel site to the south-west. To the east are traces of two fishponds. The whole complex could well be a failed borough foundation with a village enclosure in the fields to the south-west. (VCH, 235 + plan; RCHM, **1**, 39 + plan - xxxvi; Salter 35; RSB, 2 + plan opp. 2; Treasures, 22; HAN, **50**, 45; **54**, 28 + plan - 29; **55**, 36-37 + new plan - 38)

### The Bage motte and possible bailey (SO 297 434)
An oval motte in the Golden Valley, some 2.3km north-west of Dorstone and 1km south-east of Newton Tump Castle in Clifford parish, was discovered recently during tree felling operations. It is almost exactly on the boundary between Dorstone and Clifford parishes and has previously been described under both headings. The steep mound is 61m by 56m at the base and is on the edge of a spur partly cut away on the east by the now abandoned Golden Valley railway. The flat top of the mound is about 6m across and lots of large stones are clearly visible. Damage from the railway construction and more recent farm tracks is such that there is only the faintest evidence for a bailey and there is no trace of a ditch around the mound. (Treasures, 23; RSB, 3; HAN, **38**, 12-13 + plan & sketch)

### Mound (SO 249 427)
A possible ringwork and castle or siege castle has been postulated just to the north of Mouse Castle (in Cusop parish). (RSB, 3)

### Mound (SO 245 464 approx.)
A second possible castle site, to the north of the main castle, has been noted on air photographs between the old railway and the river. Investigations on the ground have failed to find anything resembling a castle—it is probably a land-fill or quarry for the railway. (HAS, **63**, 5; info. P. Remfry)

# Collington

### Martin's Castle moated site (SO 649 604)
Some 6km north of Bromyard and adjoining the B4214 is this roughly rectangular but well-formed moat that still goes by the name of Martin's Castle. (VCH, 249; RCHM, **2**, 51)

# Colwall

**Herefordshire Beacon, The Citadel** (SO 760 401)

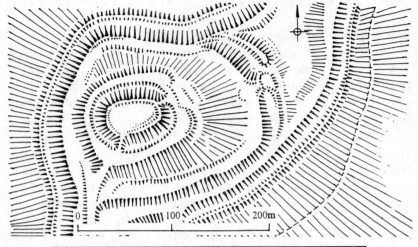

---

Mound and defended enclosure
Location: Part of the Herefordshire Beacon hillfort
towards the southern end of the Malvern Hills
Access: A public footpath leads from a car park
on the A449 along the crest of the hills

---

Herefordshire Beacon is an Iron Age hillfort towards the southern
end of the Malvern Hills. It is irregular in shape, generally
following the contours, and has a massive inner rampart and ditch.
In total it covers an area of about 13 hectares. Within the enclosure
and occupying the roughly circular hilltop is an inner stronghold
defended by a series of ditches and terraces. The summit has been
scarped to form an oval mound with a surrounding ditch. The
mound has an inner rampart with two entries, one from the south
and the other from the north-east. This inner mound—called The
Citadel—together with the defended enclosure on the north-east,
probably represents a ringwork and bailey. Excavations took place
in the late 1870s and the pottery found was re-assessed in the early
1950s and given a broad twelfth century date. (VCH, 205-6 + plan;

RCHM, **2**, 55-57 + plan; TWNFC, **1880**, 212-4; RSB, 3; Treasures, 70; HAS, **50**, 43; **66**)

**Cummins Farm moated site** (SO 738 410)
At Cummins Farm, some 1.2km south of the church is a four-sided enclosure much obliterated on the south. (VCH, 249; RCHM, **2**, 53)

**Brockbury moated site** (SO 746 419)
About 0.8km south-east of the church and 100m north-north-east of the seventeenth century Brockbury Hall, is a triangular enclosure with a further system of ditches extending to east and west. (VCH, 249; RCHM, **2**, 53-4; Treasures, 70)

# Combe

**Castle mound** (SO 348 635)
On the western border of the county, this small mound (about 36m diameter and 2.4m above the surrounding dry ditch) is on marshy ground on the south side of the Hindwell Brook close to its confluence with the Lugg. The ditches are well silted up due to regular flooding. There are traces of a possible bailey to the west, but the site has suffered some modern damage.

It was a member of the marcher lordship of Stapleton which the lords of Richard's Castle set up on several waste manors in 1086. A charter of 1244 is witnessed by a John de la Combe as was a later one of 1249, both concerning Presteigne. (VCH, 225 + plan; RCHM, **3**, 33; RSB, 3; Treasures, 7; HAN, **65**, 34; **66**)

# Cradley

**Seed Farm moated house** (SO 704 476)
In the eastern part of the county, 3km west-north-west of Cradley village and a short distance north of the A4103, is the sixteenth century or earlier Seed Farm. It is surrounded with a moat forming an island of roughly oval shape. (VCH, 249; RCHM, **2**, 62; Treasures, 37)

**Mound** (SO 756 483)
The RCHM described this mound as being about 2.4km north-east of the church, near the east side of the road. They described it as partly natural, but artificially heightened and with a causeway on the north-east side. It is not shown on maps though the description fits a mound in a field at the grid reference given. A ditch runs downhill from the possible causeway in a south-westerly direction, helping to isolate the mound from the rest of the hillside. (RCHM, **2**, 64)

# Croft

**Croft Castle** (SO 449 655)

> A mainly fifteenth and sixteenth century castle with later additions.
> Several of the living rooms are open to view
> Location: 7km north-west of Leominster
> Access: In the care of the National Trust and open to the public

The main buildings form a rectangular plan with a central courtyard. Each angle is finished with a cylindrical tower and there is a service range continuing northwards from the north-west corner. Apart from the east range, which was totally reconstructed in the latter part of the eighteenth century, the main parts of the castle are of fifteenth and sixteenth century date. This was the building described by Leland as being 'dyched and waullyd castle-like'. The castle is reputed to have been dismantled by the Royalists during the Civil War in 1645 and has had many alterations since.

Croft was held by one Bernard under William of Écouis at the time of the Domesday Survey. He is said to have been a Croft, but the earliest recognised member of the family was Hugh de Croft in 1243. Tradition has it that it was a Croft who helped in the rescue of Prince Edward, when he was a captive of de Montfort at Hereford, and his delivery to Wigmore in 1265.

During the Civil War, Sir William Croft was taken prisoner at the siege of Hereford in 1643 and two years later was slain, fighting for the king, at Stokesay Castle in Shropshire. His brother, Herbert Croft was successively dean and bishop of Hereford. It was the bishop's son and heir who was eventually granted a baronetcy as a small recognition of the sacrifices that the Croft family had made in the service of the king and sat in Parliament for many years as member for Herefordshire. The Crofts still reside in the castle although it was in other hands for parts of the eighteenth and nineteenth centuries. The building and grounds are now in the care of the National Trust. In the house it is possible to see several of the living rooms, together with furniture and paintings. (Robinson Cas., 32-38; Robinson Man., 80-83; RCHM, **3**, 35-6 + plan; Salter, 17-18 + plan; Treasures, 6)

# Cusop

## Cusop Castle (SO 239 414)

Close to the Breconshire border, this earthwork is some 1.5km
south-east of Hay-on-Wye and just to the south-west of the parish
church. In the mouth of Cusop Dingle, it consists of an irregular
oval-shaped court with the remains of a ditch and a possible entry
on the north-east. The ditch has been destroyed on the north and
north-west by the road and on the remaining sides there is a steep
scarp. Foundations of a stone curtain have been found on the bank
with evidence for buildings on the south. Traces of a stone gateway
were found in the late eighteenth century. (Robinson Cas., 40-41;
VCH, 225 + plan; RCHM, **1**, 47 + plan - xxxv; Salter, 18-19 + plan;
RSB, 3; Treasures, 42; HAN, **50**, 43; Info. P. Remfry)

## Mouse Castle (SO 247 424)

2km east of Hay-on-Wye and a similar distance north-east of Cusop
Castle, Mouse Castle is in woodland on top of a small hill with a
good outlook to the west and north. It comprises an oval enclosure
with a ditch and a small external rampart. There are steep slopes on
all sides, but a possible entry on the south-east. The motte is central
and the sides have been quarried away leaving almost vertical sides
some 2m high. The bailey is poorly defined and there are other
earthworks present, but well hidden in the woodland. It has been
suggested that there is a possible siege castle or ringwork just to the
north in Clifford parish. (VCH, 235 + plan; RCHM, **1**, 47 + plan -
xxxv; Salter, 35; RSB, 3; Treasures, 40; HAN, **50**, 44)

# Dilwyn

## Castle site no. 1 (SO 416 544)

The small village of Dilwyn, about 2km west of the Roman road
that followed the Welsh border and a similar distance north-east of
the castle at Weobley, has several defended sites. This one, originally described as a simple moat, is in the southern part of the
village. It is almost circular, about 50m in diameter, and surrounded
by a mostly wet ditch. There are traces of a ringwork rampart with

indications of buried stone within. An excavation some years ago exposed the corner of a square building with a wall thickness exceeding 2m that could have been a rectangular keep. The large bailey was to the east with two fishponds and an embankment creating its boundary on the south-east and the road to the east and north. There are traces of a platform on the east of the bailey, but the northern half has been largely destroyed by a recent housing development. There is still water in part of the moat.

Although Dilwyn belonged to William de Écouis at the time of the Domesday Survey, it was given to Godfrey de Gamages and for a long time became the centre of their estate. In the early thirteenth century it was held by William de Braose, but by the mid-thirteenth century the manor may have been split into two parts belonging to the fitz Warins and the Mallorys. This could provide a possible explanation for the several castle and/or moated sites in the parish. (VCH, 249 + plan; RCHM, **3**, 39 + plan 41 & xxix; Treasures, 17; RSB, 3; HAN, **13**, 6 + plan; **50**, 43; **60**, 50-53 & 57-8 + plan)

### Fields Place moated site (SO 418 538)
About 1km south of the church and on the southern side of Stretford Brook is an almost square moat with a mostly wet ditch. There are the remains of a bridge abutment and seventeenth century pottery has been found, but the site is probably earlier. (VCH, 249; RCHM, **3**, 39; Treasures, 18; HAN, **60**, 57; **64**, 8 + plan)

### Castle site no. 2 (SO 416 538)
On the opposite side of the Stretford Brook to the Fields Place moated site and partly cut by the road, aerial photographs have suggested a possible motte and bailey castle. The motte was just to the east of the road with a bailey cut in two by the road. A possible second bailey and fishponds lie between the motte and the stream. (HAN, **55**, 16; **60**, 56-7; **64**, 8 + plan)

### Castle site no. 3 (SO 418 524)
A possible third castle site has been suggested here, but is very suspect. Whilst there is nothing on the ground at the grid reference given to suggest a castle site, a few mounds to the east near Stocking farm could mark the sites of earlier buildings. (HAN, **62**, 4)

**Little Dilwyn moated site** (SO 438 539)

2.5km east-south-east of the church and beside the stream just to the south of Little Dilwyn Farm is a rectangular moat and a possible deserted medieval village. (Treasures, 18)

# Dinmore

**Mound** (SO 488 505)

There is a mound, about 25m in diameter and rising 1.5m above the surrounding shallow ditch, some 0.25km east-north-east of the Chapel of St John of Jerusalem. This chapel is the surviving part of the Dinmore Preceptory of the Knights of St John of Jerusalem founded about 1190. This was the Order of Knights Hospitallers whose English houses were dissolved in 1540. Although the mound may not be associated with the Order, the possibility has to be accepted. (RCHM, **2**, 68)

# Donnington

**Moated site** (SO 708 342)

3.6km south of Ledbury and 70m south of Donnington Church is a moat of rectangular shape and still partly wet. The island is about 35m square with some scarping and there is a causeway across the moat on the north. (VCH, 249-50 + plan; RCHM, **2**, 69; Treasures, 73)

# Dorstone

**Dorstone Castle** (SO 312 417)

| |
|---|
| Large motte with associated bailey |
| Location: To the west of the village centre, some 0.3km from the church |
| Access: Public footpaths pass to the immediate south of the site |

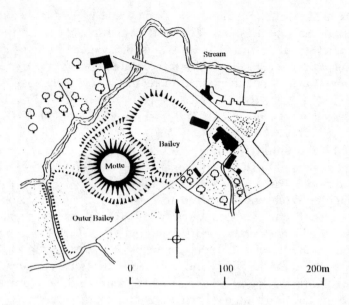

Stream

Bailey

Motte

Outer Bailey

0          100          200m

Towards the upper end of the Golden Valley, this motte and bailey castle is in a small valley immediately to the west of the village centre and some 0.3km from the church. The oval motte rises about 9m above the bottom of the surrounding dry ditch which has an outer bank towards the stream on the north. The flat top of the mound is quite large, measuring 33m by 26m and probably contained a shell keep. The partially-buried foundations include traces of a D-shaped tower flanking the entrance. The remains were examined in a 'scratch dig' some years ago when the bases of two possible buttresses, the base of a portcullis slot in the gateway, and a possible postern gate in the gate tower were revealed.

The kidney-shaped bailey, that adjoins the motte on the north-east, contains traces of buried foundations. Loose stone includes voussoirs and dressed tufa. All traces of the bailey ditch on the south are lost in gardens and the return to the north is only seen as a scarp above the stream. It is possible that the stream could have been diverted to make a wet ditch, at least around the motte. The whole site covers just about one hectare.

Dorstone was held by the de Solers family from the late twelfth to the fourteenth centuries, but the castle is probably earlier and may relate to the *Dodintune* of the Domesday Survey that belonged to Drogo, the son of Poyntz. The castle was probably refortified in 1403 after it was entrusted to Sir Walter Fitzwalter by Henry IV. It may have been one of the castles that suffered during the Glyn Dwr uprisings for it is not mentioned thereafter. (Robinson Cas., 42-3; VCH, 236 + plan; RCHM, **1**, 57 + plan - xxxv; TWNFC, **1888**, 224-5; Salter, 19 + plan; RSB, 3; Treasures, 42; HAN, **50**, 43)

### Mynydd-brith motte & bailey (SO 280 415)

3.2km west of Dorstone village and immediately south-west of Mynydd-brith Farm is an oval mound some 32m by 30m with a surrounding ditch and a scarped reasonably flat enclosure on the south-west. The top of the mound is some 6m above the ditch and has suffered considerably from later building works making its original nature uncertain. There are traces of a larger enclosure that includes the farm buildings and possible indications of a deserted medieval village. Pottery ranging in date from the Saxo-Norman to the late medieval period has been discovered on the site.

Mynydd-brith has been identified with the reasonably important settlement of *Ruuenore* of the Domesday Survey which, along with Dorstone, belonged to Drogo. *Ruuenore* is annotated *Fagemeneda* in the Herefordshire Domesday which is a hybrid English/Welsh name meaning 'variegated mountain'. In 1577, the spelling has become *Fowmynd* and by 1786, *Vowmynd*. In modern Welsh Mynydd-brith means 'speckled mountain'. In 1835 this area was shown on Bryant's map as the 'Township of Vowmine'. (VCH, 236 + plan; RCHM, **1**, 57; Treasures, 42; RSB, 4; HAN, **50**, 44; **62**, 5)

### Nant-y-Bar motte & bailey (SO 279 410)

Some 0.5km south-west of Mynydd-brith and 200m north-west of Nant-y-Bar farm on a small rise is a circular mound some 34m in diameter and rising about 33.5m above the surrounding ditch. There are traces of a causeway across the ditch on the north-east side of the mound and the summit has traces of a rampart around the top that might conceal the remains of a shell keep. There is a small bailey and some signs of a larger enclosure. (VCH, 236; RCHM,**1**, 57; Treasures, 43; RSB, 4; HAN, **50**, 44)

# Downton on the Rock

**Motte & bailey** (SO 427 735)
Some 2km east-south-east of Leintwardine and 100m west of the old church, is a mound, some 21m across at the base and 3m high. There is a slight sinking in the top of the mound and it could have possessed a tower with a forebuilding or barbican. There are traces of a bailey and other outer enclosures, but modern disturbances have made the site difficult to interpret. (VCH, 226; RCHM, **3**, 45; Salter, 19; RSB, 4; Treasures, 2; HAN, **48**, 14; **50**,43)

# Eardisland

**Motte & bailey** (SO 421 586)
Immediately to the north of the parish church is a mound surrounded by a wet moat. It is about 45m in diameter at the base and rises some 5m above the moat level. The top is some 22m across and could have taken a shell keep. The moat is fed by a cutting from the River Arrow which is less than 100m away to the north. There was a causeway across the moat on the north-west but this has been removed. The extent of the bailey is probably represented by the church road on the west and south-west and by the stream cutting on the east. In 1650, Silas Taylor mentioned 'an old moated hall wch they call the castle' at this site.

Eardisland, worth £12, was held by Earl Morcar from the king at the time of the Domesday Survey. After 1236 it was held of the de Braose family who were probably responsible for building the castle. Later it was one of the possessions of the Mortimers. (Robinson Cas., 129; VCH, 226 + plan; RCHM, **3**, 47 + plan - 49 & xxix; Salter, 19; Treasures, 15; HAN, **62**, 14 + plan - 15)

**Monk's Court mound** (SO 420 588)
On the north side of the River Arrow and some 0.3km to the north-west of the castle is a small mound. It is roughly circular, 28m across at the base and rising no more than 1.5m above the surrounding ground. There are slight traces of what is now a dry moat. The mound is made of a mixture of stone and river gravel and

there are slight traces of what may be an outer work on the east. (VCH, 226 + plan; RCHM, **3**, 50 + plan - 49; Treasures, 14; HAN, **62**, 15-16 + plan)

**Burton Court motte & bailey** (SO 423 573)
Burton Court is about 1.2km south of Eardisland Church. There are traces of what could be a motte, cut into by the Court building. The early fourteenth century Great Hall of the Court is in the assumed bailey. (RCHM, **3**, 47; RSB, 4; HAN, **62**, 21 + plan; **63**, 13 + new plan)

# Eardisley

**Eardisley Castle** (SO 311 491)

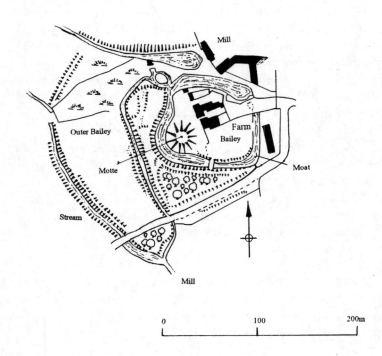

> Large moated enclosure with a motte
> Location: Just to the west of the church
> Access: A track passes to the south of the site

Eardisley is one of the suggested line of defended sites constructed in the western part of the county shortly after the Norman Conquest. It was described as being in the middle of a wood and possessing a *Domus Defensibalis* (fortified house) at the time of the Domesday Survey. At that time it was held by Robert de Baskerville of Roger de Lacy.

Eardisley motte and bailey castle consists of an oval, moated enclosure with a causeway to the north-east and a motte on the south-west side. The motte is 30m in diameter at the base and rises some 4m above the level of the bailey to a flat top some 13m in diameter. There is no ditch between the motte and the bailey, but the moat around the bailey is still wet and fed by a small stream on the north. The bailey contains Castle Farm and farm buildings of eighteenth century and earlier date. There are signs of a possible gatehouse and drawbridge pit. There are two long, narrow enclosures on the west, both of which appear to have been surrounded by ramparts and wet moats fed by a second stream. The Victoria County History records that the two streams that feed the various moats then also fed two mills, one to the north and one to the south of the castle.

The motte could well have been crowned by a tower, for many years ago, when the moat was cleaned out, a large block of masonry was found along with spear heads and armour. Daub and medieval pottery were found in the bailey in 1994.

Eardisley was probably the chief residence of the Baskervilles in 1272 when Walter de Baskerville had a licence from the bishop 'to hold divine service in an oratory built within the walls of the castle.' It probably continued as such until the Civil War when, it is recorded, that 'roysters from Hereford', as *Mercurius Civicus* calls them, 'burnt Sir Robert Welch's house, Eardisley Castle, and other houses ...' It appears that the castle was burnt to the ground, only one of the gatehouses escaping. (Robinson Cas., 44-48; VCH, 236-7 + plan; RCHM, **3**, 52-3 + plan - xxix; Salter, 19 + plan; RSB. 4 + plan opp.; Treasures, 20; TWNFC, **1904**, 256-62; HAN, **50**, 44; **57**, 42 & 45; **62**, 10)

**Lemore possible motte & bailey** (SO 310 517)
2.5km north of Eardisley and a little way to the east of the A4111 and north of Lemore Farm is this circular enclosure surrounded by a partly wet moat. Locally it is known as Martin's Castle. Although virtually level with the surrounding ground, there are traces of stonework about 2m thick that have been interpreted as the remains of a polygonal shell keep rising from the bottom of the moat. There are also traces of an encircling bailey which, although it is much ploughed-out, is said to include traces of a curtain wall. Twelfth to fourteenth century pottery has been found here. (VCH, 226 + plan; RCHM, **3**, 56; Treasures, 19; RSB, 5 + plan - opp. 4; HAN, **55**, 28-30 + plan; **57**, 43)

**The Camp possible motte & bailey** (SO 287 520)
In a rather remote situation some 4km north-west of Eardisley and about 2.4km west of Lemore is this circular enclosure some 42m in diameter, surrounded by a dry ditch with traces of an outer bank to the southern half. (VCH, 250 + plan; RCHM, **3**, 56; RSB, 5; Treasures, 18; HAN, **64**, 8)

**Bollingham Mound** (SO 301 527)
Bollingham House and the twelfth century chapel are 3.6km north of Eardisley. There is a mound here that could be related to the *Burardestune* of the Domesday Survey which became *Bollingshulla* in 1137. The Domesday name includes *burhward*, a common Welsh Marches word meaning 'fort guardian.' However, *Bollingshulla* may be 'hill of the pollarded tree.' There is a possible large outer bailey or village site to the south. (RSB, 5; HAN, **55**, 44)

**Woodsheaves Mound** (SO 288 492)
2km west of Eardisley and 2km north-east of the possible site at Millhalf, Whitney, there is a low oval mound. It is suggested that there are indications of a V-shaped ditch, but this is probably a natural feature. (HAN, **57**, 44)

# Eastnor

**Eastnor Castle** (SO 735 368)

The so-called Eastnor Castle was built to the design of Sir Robert Smirke for the first Lord Somers in 1815. It is an early example of Norman revivalist work and is rectangular in plan with four circular embattled towers at the angles, and a central keep. It is reached by a low gatehouse with round towers on the roadside between Ledbury and Tewkesbury. The castle stands above the site of the old mansion-house of Castleditch, which—it can be assumed from the name—was a defended house. (Pevsner 123-4)

**Bronsil Castle** (SO 749 372)

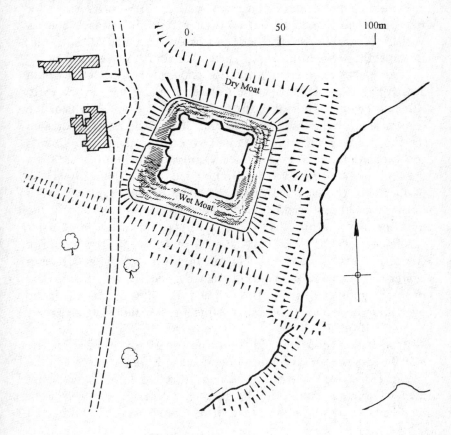

When built, this was one of the most modern buildings of its kind
in Herefordshire, for the licence to crenellate was only issued in the
mid-fifteenth century. Bronsil is well hidden under the shadow of
the Midsummer Hill Iron Age hillfort at the southern end of the
Malverns. It has always been part of the civil parish of Eastnor, but
has undergone a gradual transformation in name. In the thirteenth
and fourteenth centuries it was called *Brankswellesiche* or
*Brankewallefeld(e)*, identified as 'Branoc's Spring', Branoc being a
Welsh personal name. Later variations include Bremisfeld,
Broomshill, Bromehill, Bransill, and other similar derivatives.

Nothing is known about the early history of the site, but it would
appear that Sir John Beauchamp owned a house here in the early
fifteenth century. He was Justice of South Wales, a Knight of the
Garter, and eventually Lord Treasurer of England and was created
the first Lord Beauchamp of Powyk by Henry VI in 1447. John's
son Richard, the second Lord Beauchamp, obtained a licence from
the king in 1449, renewed in 1460, which allowed him to enclose
300 acres of parkland at Bronsil and crenellate his residence. Such
licences had been granted for several hundred years, but by the
mid-fifteenth century they were few and far between. Caister
Castle, near Great Yarmouth, and the magnificent Herstmonceux
Castle in Sussex, were both built in the first half of the fifteenth
century as rectangular enclosures surrounded by wet moats. The
former is similar in size to Bronsil, and the latter demonstrates the
overriding importance given to a symmetrical exterior, again exem-
plified at Bronsil.

Bronsil was transferred to the Talbots, earls of Shrewsbury, by
marriage, but the Beauchamps continued to have an interest in the
castle. However, Richard's son John, the third Lord Beauchamp,
died without issue and the title became extinct. The estates were
then divided amongst the grand-daughters of the first Lord, and

*The gatehouse north tower, when still standing in 1990*

Bronsil apparently went to Margaret, who married a William Reed. It was in the second quarter of the sixteenth century that John Leland travelled through the area and noted that 'Here is in the clyving of an hille a castelle having fair towrres.'

Towards the end of the sixteenth century the Reed family began to suffer from a ghost at Bronsil. The nocturnal perambulations of this restless spirit were so troublesome that the family could not gain any sleep. Gabriel Reed, the then owner, was so worried that he eventually consulted a Mr Allen of Gloucester Hall in Oxford, who was an acknowledged expert in such matters. Mr Allen advised that it was necessary to obtain 'a bone of the first Lord Beauchamp' and he assured Gabriel Reed that there would be no further problems so long as this relic of the former owner remained within the castle walls. Apparently the first Lord Beauchamp died abroad, and arrangements had to be made for some of his bones, consisting of several vertebræ, to be sent from Italy in a box. From then on, the box was kept in the castle, the spirit was pacified, and eventually the bones were regarded as a family heirloom. When the Reeds moved to New Court at Lugwardine, the wonder-working bones went with them. A box labelled 'Lord Beauchamp's bones' was still at New Court in the eighteenth century but has since disappeared.

Although the final demise of Bronsil Castle is not recorded, it may well have been abandoned by the family in the early seventeenth century. Robinson says simply that 'it was burnt in the Civil Wars', but there is no mention of this event in the standard work by Webb. However, it was certainly ruinous by 1731 and could well have been burnt.

Although in ruins, Bronsil continued to be held by the Reeds until 1774 when it was sold to Thomas Somers-Cocks. The Cocks lived at Castleditch, also in Eastnor parish, an old mansion which had originally been the home of the Clinton family. Castleditch mansion no longer survives—it was replaced by Eastnor Castle, built in 1815 by the first Lord Somers above the site of the old mansion-house. Bronsil Castle is still part of the Eastnor Castle Estates.

Most of the external walls of Bronsil Castle were standing in 1731 when Samuel and Nathaniel Buck visited the site and produced their engraving. Another drawing, described as 'being

THE SOUTH WEST VIEW OF BRANSTILL CASTLE, IN THE COUNTY OF HEREFORD.

Malvern Hills

THIS CASTLE stands in a solitary Place at the Foot of the west-side of Malvern Hills, its quadrangular Oblong is encompass'd by a Double Ditch of the same form as is here represented, and appears by several circumstances in the Remains themselves, as well as by other concurring Tokens to be a Place of very great Antiquity tho' we shall not pretend to determine that it is Roman. There is a very lately discover'd in it, a Cavern which is not yet open'd. — — This Rede Esq. is the present Proprietor thereof.

S. & N. Buck delin. et Sculp. 1731.

more correct', was made by Kennion in 1779, but this must be viewed with some caution for he noted that one tower alone was then left whilst he drew it relatively complete. Certainly, by the mid-nineteenth century most of the walls had been demolished, presumably to furnish materials when the nearby house was built. The site was then probably landscaped to produce a typical Victorian romantic ruin, complete with a 'rustic' stone bridge giving access across the moat.

Even allowing for all this work, the basic plan, consisting of an almost square island surrounded by a wet moat, now about 18m across, can still be appreciated. The island has sides about 36m in length and was originally totally enclosed by a curtain wall which continued down into the water. Fragments of this wall can still be seen when the water in the moat is at a low level. At each of the four corners was a lofty tower, probably octagonal in shape although they are shown semi-circular on the Bucks' engraving. There were also intermediate towers on each side except for the west. Here was the entrance passage flanked by a pair of octagonal towers and probably incorporating a drawbridge. A small part of the northern tower survived until a major collapse in 1991. There had been an earlier fall about the turn of the century.

The gatehouse tower which, until the collapse, survived to a height of some 10m, had three stages divided by moulded string courses. The lowest stage was featureless apart from a circular hole, some 0.2m in diameter, near its base. This hole, formed by two large ashlar blocks, was probably a drain. However, the Bucks' engraving shows a curious feature in the same area—a feature repeated in the sketch published in Robinson's *Castles of Herefordshire*. This consists of four circular holes set in a diamond pattern, giving an impression of a typical defensive cruciform-shaped opening, but without the vertical and horizontal members. It was presumably designed as a form of gun port, with the gunner sighting through one hole and firing through another. The Bucks' engraving also shows the lowest stage of the tower with a splayed base, but in reality there are no indications of such a feature, even when the moat is almost dry during the summer.

The second stage had two, almost complete, chamfered arrow-slit shaped openings at different levels, one low to the right and the other high in the left-hand face. Hardly any of the third stage survived to the middle of the nineteenth century, but Buck shows it with another arrow slit. There are no indications of the design of the upper works, but, following the permission granted in the mid-fifteenth century, some form of crenellation must be assumed.

The whole of the island is now covered in undergrowth and the internal arrangements of the castle are not obvious—the only upstanding feature apart from the gatehouse tower being part of a newel stair associated with a masonry fragment in the north-eastern corner. However, the most likely arrangement would have consisted of a series of buildings adjoining the curtain wall on all four sides, leaving a central square courtyard about 18m across. The main hall would have faced the entrance gateway, with the service wing on one side and the private accommodation on the other. The only documentary reference to internal buildings refers to an underground chamber. It is mentioned in the caption to the Bucks' engraving as a 'cavern ... not yet open'd', but was described thirty-eight years later in 1769 as 'a very remarkable cavern'. It apparently lay towards the south side of the island. Was the chest of money, which tradition says was buried on the island, deposited in this cavern? The tale records that it was guarded by a raven and could only be found by the rightful owner who, rather inevitably, must possess the Beauchamp bones!

The moat, which is now crossed by a small, nineteenth century, stone bridge, was partly cleared about 1840 when weapons, large buckles, oddly-shaped spoons, and many large, rounded stones were found, but they have since disappeared. There is a slight outer bank to the moat and, on the east and south, there are earthwork traces of the second moat shown on the Bucks' engraving and described by Robinson. On the north and west any traces of this outer moat would have been infilled when the landscaped gardens were created. The outer moat was probably of a similar width to the existing inner one—they were about twenty metres apart. To the south-east of the moat is a wooded area with clearly defined earthworks which may have been fishponds or could have been associated with the mill mentioned in a deed of 1569.

Should Bronsil be considered as a castle, or was it an elaborate castellated mansion with more pretensions to symmetry than to defence? Although these late castles could still be defended if necessary, and the provision of moats—which were often wide and deep—aided this function, the site was often chosen for the convenience of the owner and for the provision of water for the moat rather than for the defensive potential. Although it is likely that there was a dwelling-house at Bronsil before the licence to crenellate was granted in 1460, and that some parts of that building may well have been encapsulated within the fifteenth century work, the impression gained from the surviving features and from the illustrations is of a 'show-piece' castle so typical of the period. Such buildings, often erected by the lesser noblemen who had made good, included features which were characteristic of earlier castles, but were used for display rather than being functional. Regular elevations, containing imposing gatehouses with elaborate towers which included cruciform slits, gun ports and fancy machicolations were typical. The impression, as in the similar creations of the nineteenth century, was of a theatrical backdrop for chivalric fantasies.

The double moat at Bronsil was an exceptional extravagance which must have added materially to the cost. Although it has been suggested that one moat was used to preserve the level in the other, it is more likely that this was yet another attempt to create an exaggerated defensive feature and thus make the castle look even more imposing.

Castles such as Bronsil were built to satisfy the pride of the owner, to give an expression to his importance, and to allow him to live out his fantasies. To his descendants they may have been little more than a curiosity—a rather awkwardly designed house with a rather large maintenance bill. Bronsil survived for about 200 years, with a variety of owners and occupiers, until it was abandoned or went up in flames during the Civil War. Since then stone-robbing has reduced it to little more than an earthwork, but buried under the overgrown island is a wealth of archaeological information which one day may be exposed to allow the full history of this Herefordshire castle to be fully understood. (Robinson Cas., 17-18; VCH, 253 + plan, RCHM, **2**, 74 + plan - xxvi; TWNFC, **1880**, 216; 291-2, Salter, 12-13 + plan; Treasures, 72; HAN, **43**, 9; HAS, 81 & 138. Shoesmith, TWNFC forthcoming.)

# Eaton Bishop

**Eaton Camp possible castle** (SO 455 394)
This triangular promontory camp of Iron Age date, 1.3km east of the church and overlooking the River Wye, is well known and is described with a plan in RCHM. It has recently been suggested that there is a motte at the eastern apex of the triangle containing some buried stone, with indications of walls, including traces of mortar, extending out from the motte along both embankments. It is possible, therefore, that the site had both an early and a late use. (RCHM, **1**, 62 & plan - 61; HAN, **65**, 28-9 + plan)

# Edvin Loach

**Motte & bailey** (SO 662 584)
Motte and bailey which encompasses the present church and churchyard. The Victorian church is built on the outer edge of the ditch that surrounded the motte which is just outside the churchyard to the east. It has been suggested that the motte could have had a shell keep, but evidence is slight. The bailey defences more or less follow the edges of the churchyard with the ruins of the eleventh century church inside. This is a similar situation to that at Urishay in Peterchurch parish. The bailey ditch has been filled in recently. Other enclosures may exist under the farm to the west, and to the south. (Treasures, 36; RSB, 6; HAN, **50**, 44; **59**, 13 + plan - 14)

# Edwin Ralph

**Motte & bailey** (SO 644 575)
Some 2km west-south-west of Edvin Loach, this motte and bailey earthwork is about 100m west of the church. It consists of a low mound, some 37m in diameter and hardly any higher than the surrounding ground, surrounded by a partially wet moat. Traces of stone walls have been noted around the edge and foundations immediately north of the ditch could represent a gatehouse or bridge. The main bailey, which could have been walled, is on the north and there is another possible enclosure on the east. If so it would have included

the twelfth century church. (VCH, 237 + plan; RCHM, **2**, 77; Treasures, 28; RSB, 6 + plan opp; HAN, **5**, 1; **50**, 44; **59**, 14 + plan)

# Ewyas Harold

**Ewyas Harold Castle** (SO 384 287)

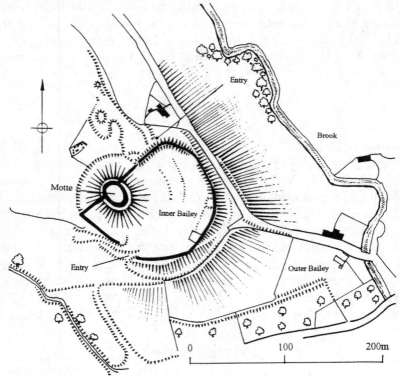

*Plan with an indication of the position of buried walls*

> A large motte with various earthworks forming the bailey
> Location: 200m west of the church
> Access: A public footpath skirts the south and west of the site

Ewyas Harold lies at the southern end of the Golden Valley. The castle occupies the end of a spur running out from the west side of the valley. The Domesday Survey records that 'Alfred of Marlborough holds the castle of Ewyas from king William. The king

104

himself granted him the lands which Earl William, who had re-fortified the castle, had given him.' This pre-Conquest castle was probably built by Osbern Pentecost, the uncle of Alfred of Marlborough. Earl William was, of course, William fitz Osbern, Earl of Hereford. It passed by marriage first to the Tregoz family and then to the de la Warres, then to the Beauchamps and from them to the Nevilles, and eventually into the hands of the Earls of Abergavenny, without playing any great part in any events of historical importance.

It was probably Robert I de Ewyas, the son of the Harold that gave the castle its permanent name, who was responsible for its reconstruction, for moving the Benedictine priory from Dulas to its site next to the castle and also, probably, for removing the Domesday borough from its site in the outer bailey of the castle to a new site east of the Dulas brook, where the modern village stands.

Leland noted a 'great parte of Mapheralde Castell [from Map-Harold—son of] yet standinge and a chapell of Seint Nicholas in it. Ther was sumetyme a parke by the castell. The castell stondythe on a mene hill, and on the right banke of Dules broke hard in the boton by it. There is a village by the castle caullyd Ewis Haralde ...' In 1645, Symonds noted that the church and castle were 'ruynous and gone.' Late in the eighteenth century Powell recorded that 'not a vestige of a wall appears above ground though I was advised that they had been dug up at times and were three yards in breadth in some parts.'

The RCHM, quite rightly, describe the castle as a remarkable example of a motte and bailey earthwork. The almost circular motte averages 70m in diameter at the base and is 32m across the summit. It rises some 13m above the ditch that separates it from the spur, and 15m above the eastern kidney-shaped bailey. There is no indication of a ditch between the motte and the bailey although this could have been filled in. The bailey is defended variously by scarp slopes, ramparts and ditches, with an original entrance probably on the north. To the south is an outer, lower bailey and excavations within it some years ago provided an indication that the original village had been in this area. To the south again is an area which, it has been suggested, could have been used for fishponds. It is thought that the priory was just within this lower bailey. It has been suggested that there is another enclosure on the spur to the north-west, above the deep ditch which separates that area from the motte.

An attempt has been made recently to show the possible design of the stone castle. Based on very limited evidence, it includes a shell keep on the motte with a possible stair adjoining the curtain wall on the north-eastern side of the motte leading from an entry into the bailey from the north. The plan also shows the inner bailey walled with two or more towers around the perimeter. There does not appear to be sufficient evidence to accept the details of this plan as anything more than one set of possibilities out of many. (Robinson Cas., 58-61; VCH, 237-8 + plan; RCHM, **1**, 64 + plan - 63; Treasures, 49; RSB, 6; Salter, 20; HAN, **35**, 15 + plan opp.16; **47**,13; **48**, 19-25 + plan; **57**, 7-11; **60**, 18-20; **63**, 9 + new plan)

# Eye, Moreton & Ashton

### Ashton Castle tump (SO 514 650)

About 0.2km west of the A49 the 'castle' consists of a roughly circular mound 30m in diameter at the base, occupying the north-western end of a small spur on the northern side of a stream. It stands 2m above the ground on the south-east, where there is a slight ditch and 5.8m above the end of the spur. There is a faint indication of a bailey. The site is naturally defensible. (VCH, 227 + plan; RCHM, **3**, 59; Salter, 10; RSB, 6; Treasures, 10;)

### Lower Ashton 'Camp' (SO 517 643)

0.8km south-south-east of the 'castle', on the other side of the A49 and south-east of Lower Ashton Farm, Ashton 'Camp' is more like a castle than the 'castle' above and consists of an irregular platform, rising some 3m above the surrounding ground, with two mounds on it. The larger, north-western mound is almost square, about 32m across and 1.3m high. The smaller mound is circular, 14m in diameter and about the same height. It has been suggested that this mound incorporates the foundations of a small round tower and that there are traces of a wall joining the tower to the rectangular mound. There are traces of a ditch around the north side of this mound, which could be a building platform. Scarping on the south and west provide some indication of what appears to be a bailey of a concentric castle. (VCH, 257 + plan; RCHM, **3**, 61 + plan - xxviii; TWNFC, **1883**, 174; **1958**, 127; Salter, 10; RSB, 6; Treasures, 11; HAN **50**, 44; **60**, 40-1 + plan)

# Felton

**Moated site** (SO 574 473)

Some 2km west of the Burley Gate roundabout (A417 & A465) and south-west of Hinton Farm is this roughly rectangular moated site. The platform is often under water and may have been almost totally removed at some time in the past. (RCHM, **2**, 79; Salter, 52)

# Foy

**Eaton Tregoz Castle, possible site 1** (SO 605 281)

Some 5km north of Ross, Foy is a parish that is mainly on the left bank and within a meander of the Wye, but also includes some land on the right bank. This area is variously known as Hill of Eaton or Eaton Tregoz; the hamlet near the river now being known as Hole-in-the-Wall. The family of Tregoz were lords of Ewyas Harold and of considerable importance in the thirteenth century. Robinson suggests that John Tregoz lived at Eaton and, in 1280, endowed a chapel in his castle there. In 1302 he was succeeded by William de Grandison who had a licence to crenellate his mansion at 'Eton' in 1309. In 1420 the building included a hall with a buttery and pantry and a great chamber above; a parlour; a chapel; several other chambers; a kitchen, bakehouse and brewery; stables and barns; a lower and outer gate, both with chambers over; and two mills. The castle at Eaton Tregoz continued to be used, mainly by the Abrahall family, until the property was divided in the latter part of the seventeenth century.

The site of this castle is now rather a puzzle. Various suggestions have been made including this site which has also been described as a possible Iron Age promontory fort. It is apparently the 'Camp Field' described by the Royal Commission and described by RSB as a low mound and bailey with some mortared stones on the site. Another possible site is that of Eaton Farm on Hill of Eaton, but again there is a total lack of evidence. (Robinson Cas., 49-51; RCHM, **1**, 67-8; Salter, 20; RSB, 7; HAN, **25**, 11-12; **64**, 31-4)

**Eaton Tregoz Castle, possible site 2** (SO 612 287)
An 1805 description notes that: 'At a place called Hole-in-the-Wall are the remains of some ancient building, consisting of the foundation of some well built walls with huge stones lying about. The site is now occupied by many cottages.' Kelly's Directory for 1891 is more definite: 'There once existed here a strongly fortified castle, dismantled and left ruinous during the feudal wars; only a portion of one of its walls now remains.' It would seem that Court Farm and the adjoining cottages are all parts of this 'castle' complex. The eastern-most cottage (once the 'Anchor and Can') has a cruck frame which should be pre-1500 and Court Farm contains a stone-vaulted cellar and an ogee-arched doorway. In 1971 dressed stones were found in the vicinity including transoms or sills and others with roll-moulding and chamfers. Much of the area was overgrown when visited in April 1995, but it would obviously repay further study as and when the undergrowth is cleared. (Robinson Cas., 49-51; RCHM, **1**, 67-8; Salter, 20; HAN, **25**, 11-12; **64**, 31-4)

# Garway

**Garway Hill Common earthwork** (SO 440 251)
Garway is a large parish adjoining the River Monnow in the south-western corner of Herefordshire. Garway Hill Common is about 3km north-west of the church and this curious earthwork is on the southern slope, not far from the summit. It is roughly rectilinear, being about 53m by 60m measured from the tops of the continuous ramparts. These ramparts are about 3m high above the external ditch. There is a causeway across the ditch on the north, which continues as a slightly sunken way, and another on the south that continues for some distance as a wide, raised grassy way. Similar small rectangular earthworks can be found throughout the Welsh Marches and further afield. They could be of any date from, during, and after the Roman period. Geoffrey of Monmouth has this as the castle where Vortigern was burnt to death. (TWNFC, **1967**, 42-3; Treasures, 75; info. P. Remfry)

# Goodrich

**Goodrich Castle** (SO 577 200)

Extensive remains of a mainly twelfth
and thirteenth century castle
Location: 1km north-north-east of Goodrich village
Access: In the care of English Heritage and open to the public

Goodrich village is almost midway between Ross and Monmouth, at the mouth of a long bend of the River Wye that includes Welsh Bicknor and Coppet Hill. The castle stands on a ridge above the river, in ruins since it was slighted and made uninhabitable after the Civil War in 1646. Fortunately it did not suffer from the depredations of stone robbers as happened to many other castles in the area. It was probably saved by the early tourists who, during the eighteenth and nineteenth centuries, made the celebrated tour up the River Wye from Chepstow, past the ruins of Tintern Abbey and thence to Monmouth, Goodrich and Ross. They appreciated the romantic splendour and mysticism of this remote castle, isolated on a spur of ground above the river. It is reputed to have been here, in 1798, that Wordsworth met the little girl whom he immortalised in his poem *We are Seven*. The castle, now under the guardianship of English Heritage, continues to attract many tourists, but the feeling of mysticism which enchanted the early tourists has sadly disappeared with the advent of concrete paving, wooden handrails, safety fencing and carefully mown grass.

The castle was founded on an estate held by Godric Mapson and called *Hulla* in the Domesday Book. The extent of this estate seems to coincide with that of the sixth century *Mainaur Garth Benni* and with the modern parish. The earliest mention of a castle is in 1101 and by 1146 it was described as *Castello Godrici*. Whoever was the original builder of the castle—was it the Godric Mapson who held the estate in 1086, or was it built by someone else and only named after Godric at a later date—his choice of this strategic site was superb. If you stand on top of the keep and gaze down towards the broad sweep of the River Wye as it flows around the meadows below the castle, and then look to the left, where a valley leads down to the river, you can understand how the castle controlled the ancient ford there which the Romans used for their road from Gloucester to Monmouth and Caerleon—the equivalent of the modern A40. This ford, and the more convenient ferry that eventually replaced it, continued in use throughout the medieval period. It was during a crossing of this ferry that Henry, Earl of Derby (later Henry IV) heard that his son, the future Henry V, had been born at Monmouth Castle. In gratitude for the information he gave the boatman the monopoly of the ferry for life.

The steep slope downwards from the spur of land, and the valley which leads up from the ford, together acted as natural defences for the castle from the west and north, and it was only the level ground leading towards Goodrich village that needed extra protection. The deep, rock-cut ditches, which are one of the most impressive features of the castle, were the medieval answer. But these may not have been the original defences. Recent aerial photographs indicate the lines of earlier ditches outside the rock-cut ones, but also curving round the castle site. Were these ditches associated with a timber palisade, which could have enclosed this easily defensible peninsula site shortly after the Norman Conquest, or are they much earlier than the castle and of Iron or Dark Age date?

The mid-twelfth century keep has been known as Macbeth's or Macmac's Tower since the seventeenth century, apparently because at one time it was the place of imprisonment of an Irish chieftain of that name. It stands on the far side of the courtyard from the entrance and is the earliest surviving part of the castle. It is an aesthetically pleasing building constructed of a well-coursed greenish conglomerate, possibly from Coppet Hill, which contrasts with the local red sandstone of the rest of the castle. Although small (the rooms are a mere 4.3m square), with only one room on each of the three floors, it has excellent proportions and was built as a defensive work to the highest standards of the time. The original entry was at first-floor level, leading into the main room—there would have been an external wooden, and probably withdrawable, ladder or staircase from the courtyard. This doorway was converted to a window in the fourteenth century and a new doorway was then inserted at ground-floor level into what had previously been the basement. Although the keep continued in use throughout the life of the castle, it soon became an unimportant building, partly hidden behind the later timber structures which were built against it.

The keep may well have been built by Richard 'Strongbow' de Clare in the 1160s. His son, Gilbert, died a teenager, and Strongbow's great inheritance devolved on his daughter, Isabella. In 1204, when she was 17, King Richard I arranged for her to marry the 43 year old William Marshall, soon to become the Earl of Pembroke. William died in 1219, and was succeeded in turn by his four sons. By 1245 they had all died and, shortly afterwards, Goodrich and Pembroke both passed to William's granddaughter, Joan, Countess of Pembroke. She married William de Valence who held Goodrich for nearly half a century until his death in 1296. It was during this period that Goodrich was almost completely rebuilt by William and his son Aymer. Records of grants of timber and financial help from the king suggest that there were two main building phases—1260-66 and 1280-90—with some additional roofing in 1296. By the time this work was finished the castle as we know it had been built.

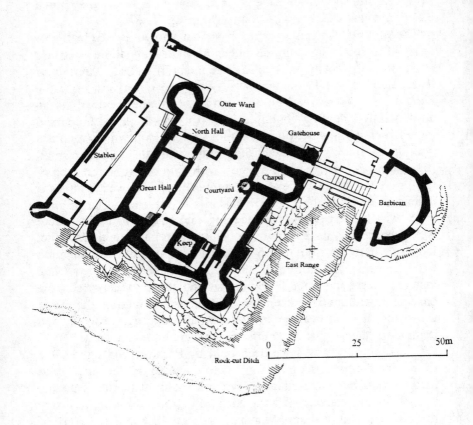

The external shape, a rectangle with three semi-circular corner towers and an elaborate gatehouse and chapel tower on the fourth corner, is apparent on the approach to the castle. But it is from the keep that the full extent of the later thirteenth century living accommodation can be appreciated. To the left are the kitchen and the doorway and windows of the great hall; ahead and beyond the well are the remains of a second large hall which included a basement. The chapel tower and gatehouse fill the far right-hand corner, and wall foundations on the immediate right indicate the position of a lost eastern range of buildings. These, together with the rooms in the corner towers, provided ample residential accommodation within the massive walls of the castle.

By the end of the thirteenth century most of the stone-built castle was as we see it now. Although it was to remain in use for a further 350 years, during which time many improvements and additions were made, these were mainly in timber and have since disappeared leaving behind the bare bones of the earlier work.

The great hall was the main part of the state accommodation of the castle. It would have been a magnificent room—Silas Taylor, visiting the castle in 1655, ten years after it had been ruined during the Civil War, saw 'a beame of oake intire without knott or knarle of 66 feet long and held 20 inches of 2 feet square the whole length. The hall itself was 60 feet long allowing 3 feet for the beame in the wall'. The three large windows in the curtain wall all had window seats, and what would have been an enormous hooded fireplace in the same wall is nearer to the 'high' end of the hall, where the lord of the castle and his distinguished guests would sit at meals.

The north range consisted of a ground-floor hall approached from the great hall through an ante-chamber, and a basement or lower servants' hall, approached from the ante-chamber by a flight of steps. A tall column supporting an arcade separated both of these halls from the north-west corner tower. This, always known as the Ladies Tower, suffered the brunt of the attack during the Civil War and little remains above the basement level. It would doubtless have had two more floors—the upper one being a private chamber. The north hall was radically altered in the fifteenth century by the insertion of a first floor just below the tops of the twin arcade arches. The roof must have been raised at the same time and the new floor would have contained a series of lodgings or bedrooms, presumably with a corridor or gallery along the courtyard side.

It was probably about this time that a two-storey timber-framed block was built between the north range and the gatehouse. The ground floor would have been an extension of the gate passage, but the first floor would have contained further chambers and a continuation of the north range corridor as a passage providing access to the gallery in the chapel through what now appears as a rather odd, high-level blocked doorway. The outlines of this lost block can be traced on the stone walls.

The gatehouse passage, which included a drawbridge, two portcullises, murder holes, and a guard passage in the thickness of the wall, is one of the most impressive defensive works of this type in the country. The stone-paved room above the passage would have contained the mechanism for the portcullises and a sleeping chamber for the guard. A room, now lost above the front of the gate passage, would have included the apparatus for raising and lowering the drawbridge.

Next to the gatehouse, and effectively part of the same building, is the chapel tower. New timber floors have been inserted in this building and the extent and dimensions of the chapel can now be fully appreciated. The sedila and aumbry next to the altar are noteworthy features, but the decoration was originally much more splendid. In 1655, Taylor saw 'a chapple with the picture of a Talbot on the South wall with the Garter of St George about it and an Earle's coronett upon it'.

The octagonal tower on the corner of the chapel contains a spiral staircase which now leads to the room above the chapel but originally went all the way up to the roof and may well have acted as a look-out point. This first-floor chamber, one of the most pleasant in the whole castle, would originally have been used by the priest but, when the castle was not in regular use, would have been part of the constable's accommodation. From here a passage, built in the thickness of the south wall leads to the wall-walk on the east side of the castle.

From this wall-walk the full complexity of the various buildings which once filled this side of the castle can best be appreciated. Looking back to the chapel tower and forwards to the wall of the north-east tower, the scars left by two distinct and different roofs can be seen. The earlier building—probably a hall—had a simple lean-to roof, but its replacement was much higher. A glance at the octagonal tower attached to the chapel givers an indication of the true extent of the building which belonged to it. Gaping holes show the positions of the first and second floor doorways which led into this range. Although the traces are relatively insignificant, they are sufficient to postulate a large, three-storey, timber-framed building running the whole length of the courtyard from the chapel to the far corner tower. Along the courtyard front would have been first and

second floor galleries providing access to the individual rooms or lodgings. The provision of such accommodation for senior retainers and visitors was a relatively common feature in castles and in roadside inns during the fifteenth and sixteenth centuries.

It would appear that the eastern hall and the chambers that replaced it had a similar relationship to the south-eastern tower as the other halls had with their towers. One doorway led down to the basement and a passage led to the ground floor. The external flight of stairs, leading to the first floor, would have been totally enclosed within a timber structure. This tower has fireplaces on both ground and first floors, indicating two chambers or lodgings. The basement would doubtless have been used for storage.

In the fourteenth century an outer wall was built on the north and west sides of the castle. It was not of any great height and, although it included corner towers, had little defensive potential. It enclosed an outer ward which included a timber-framed barn-like building that contained stabling, tack-rooms and hay storage for over 100 horses.

Although Goodrich Castle had a strong gatehouse with an impressive arrangement of defensive works, this was not considered sufficient and an additional building—in effect another small castle—was built on the outside of the defensive ditch. This building—the barbican—was probably single-storied and was surrounded by its own ditch. The entrance, which included doors, a portcullis and a drawbridge, was as strong as that at many a castle. This was an important part of the overall defences and it was from within this building that the horses were led down a flight of steps to the stables in the outer ward.

The picture of Goodrich Castle which has emerged from a close study of the fabric is that, after the great rebuilding of the thirteenth century, it underwent a process of gradual change from being a 'castle' to a 'home'. The thirteenth century fortress with its large halls designed for communal living and with only a few private chambers for the lord and his distinguished guests, slowly became a large fifteenth century house, still enclosed within the defensive walls, but containing a rabbit warren of small rooms mainly built of timber.

Joan, the Countess of Pembroke, died in 1307. The castle then passed to her son, Aymer, and the outer ward and barbican may have been his reaction to the lawless state of England during the reign of Edward II. After Aymer's death the young Despenser managed, both by threats and by the imprisonment of the rightful heir, Elizabeth Talbot, to take over Goodrich, but his success was short lived for he was executed in Hereford on 24 November, 1326. Eventually the Talbots established their rightful claim and Goodrich became their principal seat. They were doubtless responsible for many of the internal alterations during their long residence.

In the mid-fifteenth century John Talbot, the ablest soldier of his day, was created first Earl of Shrewsbury. He had much power in the area and Leland, touring the border between England and Wales between 1536 and 1539 noted 'Herchenfeld [Archenfield] is a great lordship longging to the Erle of Shrewisbury, and lieth betwixt Monemuth and Hereford ... They cary their prisoners to Castle Goderyce sumwhat out of Erchynfeld but longging to the Erle of Shreuisbyri.' Between the keep and the south-east tower is the entry to that dungeon, a low, dank, vaulted room without any window.

*Reconstruction showing the courtyard of Goodrich Castle in the fifteenth/sixteenth centuries*

In the early seventeenth century Goodrich, by then belonging to another Elizabeth Talbot who had married Henry Grey, Earl of Kent, was in the care of a bailiff, although it was apparently still habitable. By this time, the kitchen, if not other parts of the castle, was supplied with running water which came through a long lead pipe across the valley from springs on the opposite hillside to the west. The deep well in the courtyard must have been disused by that time for, during the Civil War, the defenders suffered a severe blow when the Parliamentarian troops cut off their piped water supply.

In 1642, at the beginning of the Civil War, Goodrich was garrisoned by parliamentarian troops under Colonel Robert Kyrle of Walford Court. He was responsible for much local plundering which included regular raids on the New House, the home of Thomas Swift, the royalist vicar of Goodrich and grandfather of Dean Swift. But, in December 1642, a large royalist army came up from South Wales and the castle was evacuated. For some 18 months there was a stalemate, until, in the spring of 1644, with parliamentary forces in control of Gloucester, Henry Lingen, royalist sheriff of Herefordshire, placed a garrison at Goodrich. By August 1644 the garrison numbered over 100 men and horse, and Lingen had fortified the ferryman's house and strewn the ford with caltrops (four-spiked iron balls) to make it impassable by horsemen.

By 1645 the situation had started to deteriorate for the royalists. Hereford was under siege by a large Scottish army who spent much of their time plundering the surrounding villages. The king managed to raise the siege and knighted Henry Lingen whilst he was in Hereford, but in December another parliamentary force had surprised and taken the city. Sir Henry and fifty of his men only escaped by crossing the frozen River Wye and retreating to Goodrich.

By early 1646 all the royalist armies had been dispersed and the king was in flight to Scotland. In the whole of the west only the two castles at Goodrich and Raglan continued to be garrisoned for the crown and parliament moved against them. By then Lingen's force had grown to some 200 men and, in preparation for a long siege, he began to requisition food and arms throughout the neighbourhood. The scene for the final battle was set when Colonel John Birch with 500 horse and foot, advanced on Goodrich.

They first took out the guard at the ferry crossing and then, under cover of an attack on the main gate, broke into the stables, removed the horses and fired the building.

Birch had to leave the siege for a few days, but he returned at the end of March and established a fortified camp on the opposite hillside. He had insufficient armament to subdue the castle and obtained 'the great iron culverin' from Gloucester and two other guns from Ludlow. His pioneers then started to make defended positions near the castle from which they could mine beneath the walls. Birch also had a special mortar piece cast which would carry a shell of above two hundredweight—this was Roaring Meg which still stands in the grounds of the Churchill Gardens Museum in Hereford. 80 extra barrels of powder were requested from Parliament.

The beginning of the end was now in sight—although the defenders were still in high spirits and had carried out several successful sallies, killing some 24 parliamentarian troops, they could not long survive against the weight of armament now arraigned against them. Breaches were appearing in the walls and 'not a roof was entire' within the castle. By then the mine had been dug some ten yards through solid rock beneath the outer wall towards the Ladies Tower. An attempt was made by the defenders to dig a countermine, but this was totally defeated when the tower was sent crashing down on their entry. By this time the castle was open to assault and the defenders had little choice but to surrender, hauling down their colours on 31 July. According to tradition Lingen and 50 'gentlemen and others of quality' and 120 soldiers marched out to a lively tune (now lost) called *Sir Henry Lingen's Fancy.*

In 1647 parliament ordered that Goodrich should be slighted and that all works associated with the 'troubles' should be dismantled. The Countess of Kent was offered £1,000 in compensation. It would appear that the castle had been so badly damaged by Birch's battery that the only slighting considered necessary was the stripping of lead from the surviving roofs, but all traces of the Civil War leaguer, the mines, and the gun emplacements were backfilled and buried. The castle was left to gently moulder in dignified retirement, visited only by the occasional antiquary, until its tourist potential began to be appreciated. (Robinson Cas., 65-70; VCH, 254; RCHM, **1**, 74-78 + plan; Salter, 21-23 + plan; Treasures, 81; HAN, **60**, 49; HAS, 30, 54, 68, 73, 94, 100; Radford, C.A.R., 1958)

## Goodrich Court gatehouse (SO 567 206)

This large gatehouse, built on the approach to the enormous early nineteenth century castellated mansion erected by Blore for Sir Samuel Rush Merrick, is on the south side of the main road from Ross to Monmouth. Built of red sandstone with round towers and machicolations (an extended gallery around the top of a tower with holes in the floor to drop missiles on attackers), the mansion—more like a castle that the genuine item—was used as a school during the Second World War but was then abandoned and was demolished in the early 1950s. (Pevsner, 139; TWNFC, **1977**, 175-84; Anon nd.)

# Grafton

### Possible castle (SO 494 369)

3.5km south-west of Hereford, an aerial photograph has shown a possible motte in an irregular enclosure with one, or in places, two ditches. There are no traces on the ground, although crop marks have been seen. (HAN, **56**, 31; **58**, 42)

# Harewood

### Elvastone moated site (SO 524 283)

Harewood is 12km south of Hereford on the A49. RSB suggests that there was a low level moated site at Elvastone, 0.7km south-east of the disused church of St Denis, that has since been ploughed out. Certainly, there are no clear signs left on the surface. (RSB, 7)

# Hentland

### Chapel Tump (SO 539 243)

0.5km south of St. Owen's Cross on the A4137, Chapel Tump has been much altered by the addition of cottages and gardens. There was an oval enclosure of about 0.3 hectares with traces of a bank on the north-east and south-east sides. The ditch on the south-west side described by the Royal Commission as being cut into the rock has since been infilled. The interior of the enclosure was about 1.6m above the bottom of the ditch. The only portion remaining is a mound in the garden of Meek's Cottage. (RCHM, **1**, 86; Treasures, 76; HAN, **62**, 45; **64**, 14)

### Gillow Manor moat (SO 532 254)

1.3km south-west of Hentland Church, Gillow Manor dates from the latter part of the fourteenth century and consists of four ranges built around a small courtyard. It has a projecting gatehouse with embattled parapet on the south-western side. The moat formerly surrounded the house and formed a square outer enclosure on the south-western side. (VCH, 250; RCHM, **1**, 86-7; HAN, **62**, 43-45)

# Hereford

### Hereford Castle (SO 512 396)

Earthworks remain on Castle Green, together with part
of the moat to the north and what may have been
the watergate and later Governor's House
Location: to the east of the cathedral
Access: Now forms a public park

When Leland visited Hereford in the early sixteenth century he
noted that the castle 'hath bene one of the fairest, largest and
strongest castles of England'. He went on to say that 'I take the
castle to be of as great circuit as Windesore'. After reading that, the
modern day visitor may feel rather disappointed to find only Castle
Green—a large, pleasantly landscaped area on a cliff above the
River Wye where people play bowls or laze in the sun. However,
the surrounding earthworks and part of the moat that survives gives
a slight impression of the defended area. There are no upstanding

walls and no large castle mound is left to give a true indication of what was once one of the most important castles in the country.

But, underneath the well-cut grass of the Green and under the adjoining Redcliffe Gardens, some 1300 years of the history of Hereford lies hidden. Here, after a dry summer, the buried foundation walls of the castle begin to show as brown parched lines in the otherwise green grass. Even deeper, and only seen briefly when a sewer was laid across the Green in the nineteenth century, are the drains belonging to the castle—massive stone-walled passages in which Walter Pilley, a noted antiquarian saw 'two or three skeletons, also a pitcher jug in perfect condition. Unfortunately while the workman was lifting it up, a mass of earth fell, breaking it all to pieces. Close to this was a deep well, walls lined with stone'.

Hereford has a long and distinguished history—it was the earliest Saxon town built west of the River Severn and is one of the earliest examples of a post-Roman town to be laid out with a formal plan. The diocese, and possibly the cathedral, was founded in AD 676, but the city was pre-eminently a royal foundation, with a strategic importance based on its command of a major route into central Wales and its position astride a recognised ford across the River Wye.

The earliest town defences so far established date from the mid-ninth century. They encircled the immediate area of the cathedral and the small town that had grown around it. By about AD 900 they had been extended and rebuilt to include Castle Green. The new work was well constructed and designed to look impressive from the outside. A series of closely-spaced vertical posts were set into the ground a short distance behind the inside lip of a broad ditch. Split logs were placed horizontally on top of each other behind them, against which layers of turves were laid to form a rampart. The resultant face, which would have included an upstanding breastwork, would have been about 4m high.

Timber defences such as these would have had a limited life span, and it was not long before the whole circuit was improved with the addition of a stone wall in front of the timber face. It was probably about 2.5m high and 2m wide, and would have had a timber breast-work continuing above it to protect the defenders. The top of the rampart would then have acted as a fighting platform and, for ease of access, a road was constructed on the inside of the embankment. Although this early defensive work lies well-buried underneath the eastern earthwork which now encloses the remains of Hereford Castle, a re-built section can be seen to the north of Castle Green at the rear of St Owen's Court. This, then, was the first defence built around the area which, much later, was to become Hereford Castle.

Although within the defensive enclosure, Castle Green was never a residential part of the city. Well before the Norman Conquest it was the home to a religious community which could well have been established before there was a cathedral at Hereford. The original foundation may have been associated with the spring which was later said to have had miraculous powers as St Ethelbert's Well. The religious settlement was eventually dedicated to St Guthlac, who had apparently fought on the Welsh border, but had retired to become a hermit in the Fens. He died in AD 715 and was buried at Crowland in Lincolnshire. Eventually, some of his remains were moved to Hereford for, during the reign of Edward I, a fire occurred in the royal castle which apparently destroyed the wooden shrine which covered the saint's remains. Clearly, at some time well before the Norman Conquest, Hereford had a special place in the development of the cult of St Guthlac.

Surrounding the monastery of St Guthlac was a large burial ground which was in use before before the beginning of the eighth century. It was not just for the use of the monks—it was a cemetery for the whole of the local community and continued to be used as such for a period of some 500 years. Many burials have since been exposed and from these observations it can be suggested that up to 15,000 individuals are buried under the Green. Although this seems a very large number, it only involves some 30 burials a year, suggesting a population of less than 1,000.

Archaeological excavations in 1960 and 1973 examined some 85 burials and radio-carbon dating established that most were of an earlier date than the foundation of the castle. The excavations also uncovered the stone foundations of two buildings, both oriented in an east-west direction. The latest of these was a small stone church about the same size as the one at Kilpeck. It was probably built in the second half of the eleventh century and eventually became the castle chapel, surviving until the end of the seventeenth century. It almost certainly replaced a timber church built on a slight artificial mound perhaps as early as the seventh century. The other, which was re-built at least once, may have been a mortuary chapel. It was probably demolished before 1100. These remains, together with an unexcavated building that stood between them and which can be seen as parched marks in the grass, are considered to be part of the monastic settlement of St Guthlac.

Ralph, the son of the Count of Vexin, was made Earl of Hereford about 1046 and is accredited with constructing a castle at Hereford and installing a Norman garrison at some date before 1052. This was one of the earliest Norman castles in England as distinct from the defended towns of the late Saxon period. Ralph's castle would have had to be positioned within the defended Saxon town, which was bounded on the north by Eign Gate Street, High Town and St Owen's Street. The castle would have been much smaller than the great royal fortress of the thirteenth century and probably consisted of little more than a simple motte with a tower on the summit. The most promising suggestion is that Hogg's Mount, at the north-eastern corner of Castle Green, is this castle. The site, which at that time was next to the east gate of the city, would have been one of the few available sites within the otherwise closely packed settlement.

Ralph's castle was overrun and destroyed by the Welsh in 1055 when the town and cathedral were burnt and Gruffydd ap Llewellyn took 'vast spoil and booty'. There is no indication that this early castle was repaired by Harold Godwinson who, after pursuing the Welsh, returned to Hereford 'which he forthwith fortified with gates and bars and with a broad deep ditch'. It is likely that the castle site was neglected from this date until the Norman Conquest eleven years later.

In 1066 William fitz Osbern, Lord of Breteuil in Normandy, was created Earl of Hereford. He was specifically charged with building castles on the Welsh border and it would seem inevitable that he was responsible for at least re-building the castle at Hereford—the centre of his palatinate—if indeed he did not reconstruct it entirely. A castle was certainly in existence in 1067 when it was harassed by the Saxon, Edric the Wild.

*Hereford Castle as it would have been in the seventeenth century, taken from Speede's map and Leland's description*

It is most likely that William erected the large motte, which stood to the west of Castle Green in the area that is now Redcliffe Gardens, and built a tower upon it. He then joined it with an embankment to Hogg's Mount. This embankment, combined with the existing Saxon town defences on the east, would have isolated St Guthlac's monastery and the cemetery within the new castle bailey without any infringment of their land ownership.

The pre-Conquest castle of Earl Ralph and the replacement of fitz Osbern were both probably built of timber. The main castle mound would have been surrounded with a palisade and ditch and crowned with a wooden tower. Most of these early castles were built of readily available timber rather than stone, which would have taken considerable time and effort to quarry.

The early post-Conquest history of the southern Welsh March may have been totally different had William fitz Osbern not been killed in Flanders in 1071. In only five short years he had made the border area safe and had effectively re-designed Hereford by reconstructing the castle and by building a new market place outside the Saxon defences—the area we now know as High Town. His son and heir, Roger, took part in an unsuccessful attempt to depose the king and as a result his estates, including the castle of Hereford, became crown property.

Henry I ascended the throne in 1100, succeeding his brother William Rufus. He reigned ably for 35 years and, before his death, nominated his daughter, Matilda, as his successor. However, the Council of Barons did not consider that a woman was fit to rule and offered the throne to Stephen de Blois, nephew of Henry and grandson of the Conqueror. This uncertainty about the succession and the 'Anarchy' that followed resulted in many castles being built in the Welsh marches and had a considerable effect on Hereford and its castle.

Early in 1138, Geoffrey Talbot garrisoned the castle on behalf of Matilda. Stephen marched on the city and whilst he was besieging and taking the castle 'the insurgents set fire to the city and all below the bridge over Wye was burned own'. At a later date, according to Henry of Huntingdon, 'Talbot returned ... and burned down all the other side of the Wye'. Matilda landed in England in 1139, when the greater part of western England seceded from Stephen. Miles of Gloucester joined Matilda's party and, after routing Stephen's men at Wallingford, seized the city of Hereford. However, the castle continued to hold out and towards the end of 1139 was besieged by both Miles and Geoffrey Talbot who, by then, had joined forces. The description of the siege by Robert de Bec, one of Stephen's adherents, may be an eye witness account.

'Geoffrey Talbot ... endeavoured to besiege the soldiers whom the king had left in the town of Hereford as defenders of the country and ministers and guardians of his right. And entering into the church of the episcopal seat, dedicated to the Mother of God, and irreligiously driving away the ministers of God's table, he rashly introduced a company of armed men, and turned the house of prayer, the place for the propitiation of souls, into a den of war and blood. It was really horrible, and not to be borne by persons of pious dispositions, to see the abode of life and salvation changed into a retreat for plunderers and fighting men; the citizens in tears uttering loud cries, either because the burial-place of their friends was thrown up against the ramparts of the castle, and they saw the bodies of their relations, some half putrefied, others very lately buried (a cruel spectacle), drawn without remorse from their graves;

or because on the tower, whence they used to hear the sweet and peaceful summons of the bells, they now saw engines erected and missile weapons thrown against the king's men. Geoffrey, therefore, from the church vehemently assaulted the king's soldiers, who were shut up in their castle; and Milo of Gloucester, on the other side, very much streightened them, so that at last they were forced to surrender the castle of Hereford.' The cathedral tower had become a siege castle.

The burial place referred to is likely to have been the one which surrounded St Guthlac's monastery rather than that close to the cathedral—the latter would have been of no help in attacking the castle. The description suggests that the king's forces had retreated to the tower on the motte—the final defensible position—and that the attackers were approaching across Castle Green, digging protective ditches as needed and totally ignoring the monastic community. The attacking position on top of the cathedral tower, the ditches within the cemetery, and the attackers 'on another side' all indicate that the motte was the one which, it has been suggested, was built by William fitz Osbern on Redcliffe Gardens rather than the earlier mound built by Ralph before the conquest.

Shortly afterwards 'the church of St Peter situated in the market place and the church of St Guthlac, unsuitably situated within the circuit of the castle' were united to endow a new monastery, built by Bishop Robert de Bethune in the Bye Street suburb of the city. The new monastery has long since disappeared—it fell a victim to the dissolution and was eventually replaced by the Nash-designed County gaol. This was demolished in 1930 and the site is now occupied by the bus station and part of the County Hospital.

Meanwhile, 'the motte of Hereford with the whole castle' was granted by Matilda's son, Henry II, to Roger of Gloucester in 1154, but following a rebellion in the following year he resumed possession and for the rest of its history Hereford was a royal castle maintained by the sheriff.

From the middle of the twelfth century documentary references to the castle become more common and it is evident that, throughout the latter half of that century and the first half of the thirteenth, the castle received almost continual attention. Accounts of the money spent give an indication of the work carried out, and the occasional survey provides a graphic picture of the nature and condition of the buildings throughout the whole castle.

The timber tower on the motte was not the first part of the castle to be replaced in stone—in 1181-2 a lime-kiln was built to provide the necessary material to rebuild a defective section of the wall. The great keep, on top of the western mound, was probably built at the beginning of the thirteenth century, about the same time as a 'small tower' was built at a cost of £100. The walls and bridges needed regular repair in the first half of the thirteenth century and a new tower had to be built in 1239-40 to replace one which had collapsed.

Although more than £100 was spent on various parts of the castle between 1250 and 1252 this does not appear to have been sufficient to maintain the many buildings, for a survey in 1254 disclosed several major problems. The roof of the great tower needed repairing and the steps leading up the motte were in such poor condition that they needed to be completely rebuilt. In addition, the 'Jews' prison'—presumably used partly for the protection of Jews as moneylenders—which was below the ring wall of the keep, was unroofed and both the gates leading into the castle needed repairs. A regular problem was the south wall which was often in danger of being undermined by the River Wye. The sheriff was allowed £60 to spend on the necessary repairs to the wall, to make a quay to protect the castle wall from slipping into the river, and to complete the buttresses between the castle gate and the 'new tower'— presumably the one built in 1239-40.

King John and his successor Henry III were regular visitors to Hereford and doubtless occupied the state quarters which were in the bailey of the castle rather than in the great tower. A thirteenth century description gives an excellent indication of the number and variety of the buildings then present in the area now known as Castle Green. There were the king's great hall, the king's small hall, chambers for the king and queen and their knights, the county hall, an almonry, a counting house, a stable, two gaols, an exchequer chamber, a building in which siege engines were kept, and the usual offices (kitchen, bakery, etc.).

The stored siege engines presumably included the mangonels and petards which John fitzTerrick and Roger Carter had been appointed to survey in 1232. Such machines could throw stones of nearly a hundredweight (51kg) and had a range of 400 to 500 metres. In 1242, John and Roger le Werrur, who were surveyors of the king's works and engines of war at Hereford, testified that they spent £7 8s. 6½d. in the workmanship of the said engines and a total of £12 1s. 4d. in the construction of a trebucket, a large rock-throwing catapult.

The royal apartments had to be maintained to a high standard and in 1233, Henry arranged for a 'fair and becoming chapel' 25 feet long to be built at the end of the oriel in his chamber. Improvements in 1245 cost a total of £176 7s. 10d.—the king's chamber was just whitewashed and wainscotted but the queen's chamber was lengthened by 20 feet, wainscotted and painted, and provided with a wardrobe, a fireplace, and a privy chamber. In 1256, a new kitchen was needed, and a chamber for the king's clerks was built in the 1260s.

During this same decade Hereford featured prominently in the Barons' Wars. For a time the castle was the headquarters of the Baronial Party and had Peter de Montfort as its governor. It was here that Prince Edward, the eldest son of the king, having been taken prisoner with his father at the battle of Lewes, was brought by his captor, Simon de Montfort, Earl of Leicester. Edward was kept only under light guard, even though dissatisfaction was growing at de Montfort's increasing power, and was permitted to exercise himself on horseback on Widemarsh Common. From here, having exhausted his guards' horses in races, he climbed a fresher mount and escaped to Wigmore Castle, home of the Mortimers.

Some work was authorised at Hereford during this period including repairs to the keep and the towers belonging to the inner bailey; the curtain walls, including those sections which 'descended from the keep', and the 'two towers of the castle' which are presumed to have been at the corners of the eastern arm of the bailey.

In addition to the chapel attached to the king's oriel, there was a second chapel within the bailey, dedicated to St Martin. This may have been the one which was repaired in 1283-4 at a cost of £10 6s. 8d.—possibly the 'faire chapell of St Cuthebert' (a changed or mistaken dedication) seen by Leland in the sixteenth century.

Leland's chapel, described as having its east end built '*opere circulari*' was doubtless the one that was partially excavated in 1960.

The Edwardian conquest of Wales between 1277 and 1282 meant that the castle at Hereford lost much of its strategic importance almost overnight. Indeed, according to an inquisition in 1281, Hugh de Turbeville, when sheriff of the county, had burnt and destroyed the king's houses, engines of war, and military stores in the castle to a value of £100. Infuriatingly no reason is given.

Surveys in 1291 and 1300 indicate that the roof timbers of the great hall were beginning to decay due to the loss of lead and shingles, the roof of the county hall needed repair, and some 65 feet of the curtain wall had fallen. The almonry, which had been built in 1233, had apparently been demolished. Some repairs were undertaken in 1307 when twelve oaks, fit for timber, and stone from the quarries, were taken from Haywood Forest to repair the king's houses in the castle and also for repairing the walls and towers. This must have been purely a holding operation for when Queen Isabella, the wife of Edward II, came to Hereford in 1326 she was lodged in the Bishop's Palace, the castle apparently being once again in disrepair. By 1377 the buildings were becoming ruinous and in 1387 Richard II granted rights of pasture and herbage in the castle to Roger Ploughfield.

At the beginning of the fifteenth century there was renewed disaffection in Wales which led to the Owain Glyn Dwr uprising. As a result repairs at the castle were undertaken including the re-roofing of the great tower, repairs to the corner towers and the chapel roof, and the replacement of the riverside wall with an oak paling fence, 140 feet long. Altogether just under £100 was spent and 351 oak trees were taken from Haywood Forest. This was to be the last major attempt to keep the castle in good repair and thereafter it was allowed to fall gradually into decay.

When Leland visited the city a hundred years later he noted that 'the hole castle tendithe toward ruine' and that the main drawbridge was 'clene downe.' Even so, he provided one of the best descriptions of the main parts of the castle although it is obvious that many of the buildings in the bailey area had already disappeared. He describes both the motte and the bailey as being surrounded by water fed by the stream which also encircled the city wall. He then went on to describe the motte which, rather confusingly, he calls the dungeon: 'The dungeon of the castle is highe and very stronge, havynge in the utter waull or ward 10 towres *forma semicirculari*, and one great towre in the inner ward.'

The main entrance to the castle was about half-way along the north side of the bailey. Leland records that: 'There was a great bridge of stone archis, and a draw bridge in the midle of it, to entre into the castle'. He also mentions 'a faire and plentifull springe of watar within the castell, and that and the pece of the broke comminge out of the diche dyd drive a mille within the castle'. Speede, in his map of 1610, shows the castle very much as it had been described by Leland some 60 years earlier. Apart from the main gate and the water gate, he only shows two buildings in the bailey—a square tower and a small building assumed to be St Martin's Chapel. According to the map, the curtain walls still stood around the whole circuit, and the great keep with its encircling, multi-towered high wall continued to overlook the city from the top of the large mound. It was not many years afterwards that it saw its next action.

Herefordshire was essentially a royalist stronghold during the Civil War although several of the principal families supported parliament. In September, 1642, the Earl of Stamford's army took the city by surprise and occupied it for a short while before being forced to retreat to Gloucester. In 1643, the city defences needed some work—the ditch was only knee-deep in water and the gates needed repairs—but there appeared to be a lack of enthusiasm and co-operation amongst the citizens to safeguard the city. Sir Richard Cave, who was a senior officer in Hereford at the time, made several recommendations including 'that the way under the castle, being upon the same bank, very plain and open as a highway, should be strengthened with a good work and turnepike, to hinder any entrance by land under the castle, or by water in boats, secondly that a breast-work should be cast up to defend the entrance into the castle by the mill, as plain and open a place as the other, only there is a small ascent'. He estimated that the work on the bank of the river would take a hundred men two days. Nothing was done, and when Sir William Waller appeared the city immediately surrendered. Waller and his troops soon left Hereford and it was re-occupied by royalist troops under the redoubtable Barnabas Scudamore who rapidly put the city into a position to resist a siege.

The Battle of Naseby in 1645 was the turning point in the war and Prince Rupert retreated first to Hereford then to South Wales. He was followed by the Scottish Army under the command of the Earl of Leven who, by 30 July, had invested the town on all sides. Scudamore's efforts had been successful and the response of the citizens was totally different to that two years earlier. The city had been put into a proper state of defence and a strong garrison installed. Well over a thousand of the citizens took up arms or mended the defences as they were broken down—even the women and children took part. The heroic defence continued for some five weeks, repulsing attacks on the Wye Bridge by demolishing an arch, countermining at Friars Gate and St Owen's Gate, and firing cannon from the castle. Eventually, hearing of the impending approach of King Charles with a relieving force, the 'Scotch mist began to disperse' and by 4 September the king was in Hereford. During his short visit he knighted Barnabas Scudamore for his valiant efforts and graced the city by adding to its arms a bordure of St Andrew's crosses and the motto *Invictae fidelitatis praemium*. It is evident that although the castle played little part during the siege it must have suffered from the Scottish batteries on the south side of the Wye and in the Bartonsham meadows.

Some three months later Hereford was taken by Colonel Birch who was then made governor of the city and took up residence in the Bishop's Palace. He appreciated that there would be considerable difficulties in keeping the city with its predominately royalist citizenry so took immediate steps to protect his garrison. His secretary Roe recorded that 'by your speedy ffortifieing the castle you secured that cittie for the parliament with a few men, soe that though you tooke the place but the 24th day of December, 1645, yet in the beginning of March followeing you had soe strengthened the castle that with the helpe thereof 460 men kept that citty.'

The extent of Birch's work is unknown, but it can be estimated from a survey and valuation of the castle by the Surveyor General's office in 1652, a bare six years later. 'All that scite of the ruinous castle of Hereford, with the appurtenances scituate and being in the parish of St John's and near unto the college and city of Hereford, and adjoining to the river Wye; being surrounded on the west, on the north, and on the east, by a wet moat, and on the south by the river Wye; part of which ruinous castle hath for enclosure thereof the ruins of an old wall, with divers fortifications built upon the said wall, and without the same; together with a certain dwelling house now standing in the said castle, called the Governor's Lodge, consisting of three rooms below stairs and three above, besides garretts and necessary rooms, with two little rooms adjoining to the said house towards the entering into the said castle; all which said scyte within and without the walls, together with the said dwelling house and moat, containing by estimation five acres and a half, more or less, we value to be worth per annum £6 10s.'

In addition there was 'All that tower scituate in the west part of the castle, and upon the mount called, the Castle Hill, commonly called the Keep, built with stone, having a rampier or wall of stone, about the same, upon the said Castle Hill, which said tower is now covered with lead, taken from the chapter-house belonging to the cathedral. All the materials of lead and stone, with the timber of the said keep, we value to be worth, upon the place, in gross £40.

'The old ruinous gatehouse standing and being in the old ruinous walls on the north side of the said castle, covered over with part of the said lead taken from the chapter-house aforesaid: the lead and other materials of the said ruinous gatehouse we value to be worth upon the place, in gross, £25.

'There are two ruinous houses standing and being within the said castle, one of which said houses hath been used for the main guard in the said castle; the other for quartering of soldiers in the said castle, the materials of which said houses we value upon the place, in gross, £20.

'Memorandum—The said castle standing upon the river Wye, the possessors thereof, as we are informed, have claimed a privilge of fishing in the said river, and probably have enjoyed the same, but by reason of the discontinuance of inhabitation in the said castle, the said fishing hath of a long time been discontinued, yet we conceive that there is a right of fishing belonging to the said castle, at least so far as the bounds thereof do extend along the said river Wye.'

It would seem that Birch had carried out some repair to the outer walls and re-roofed the main towers. Some buildings must have been in usable condition, for he kept his garrison there for some time after the war.

The castle was eventually sold to Sir Richard Harley and several of his friends for 'publique use and benefitt, and the advantage of the countie of Hereford and the inhabitants thereof'. Shortly afterwards, Harley granted the castle to the Justices of the Peace for the county. The garrison moved out and the demolition contractors moved in. In 1653, a 'grate part of the stone of the castle was disposed to the College of Hereford (the College of the Vicars' Choral) to build their new dining hall, and somme to the city of Hereford to build the Tolsey'.

In 1677, John Sylvester prepared a plan of the castle showing his proposed alterations. This indicates that most of the buildings had been demolished although the castle mound still survived. Some buildings also remained, and the gatehouse on the northern side of the bailey was eventually repaired and used for the storage of the records of the county. The house which still stands at the south-western corner of the bailey is in part of thirteenth century date and may have been the castle governor's house at some time. Part of it is presumably the water gate shown on Speede's map of 1610. Sylvester shows it as a dwelling house, part of which had been burnt. A little while afterwards it was noted that 'the gravell of the Castle Mount hath been disposed of by order of sessions'. The initial landscaping may well have taken place shortly after Sylvester drew his plan.

In 1752, the city magistrates leased the Green to an odd organisation called 'The Society of Tempers' whose aims were 'The promotion of amiability and good temper'. The Society was probably responsible for much of the landscaping as we know it now. Taylor's plan of 1757 shows paths and walks similar to those which exist at the present day although at that time the moat still encircled the bailey on the east and the water within it still supplied the Castle Mill. By that date most of the mound had been removed and the area in front of it, adjoining the Wye, had become a coal wharf. The Society of Tempers was eventually dissolved in 1831. Two years later the county magistrates leased the Green to the City Council for a period of 200 years at a rent of £1 per annum. The Council is still responsible for its maintenance and upkeep.

A memorial to Lord Nelson was built in the middle of the Green in 1809 and the eastern part is now fenced off as a bowling green. A stone buttress, built at the southern corner of the bailey in 1975, conceals the pumping mechanism which keeps Castle Pool, the last surviving fragment of the castle moat, full of water. After the motte had been removed the area which it had occupied was partly used for housing and partly as gardens. This continued until 1969 when the triangular area was landscaped and a bandstand, seldom used but often vandalised, was built. The bandstand was demolished in 1996. The Victoria Suspension bridge built in 1897 replaced the historic ford which crossed the Wye below the castle.

In 1796, Price described the public walk around Castle Green as being 'esteemed superior to any other walk of the kind in the kingdom' because of 'the variety of beautiful objects seen from it, which must strike the admiration of every curious traveller who chooses to visit it'. The views are still as excellent as they were 200 years ago and the Green with its buried archaeological treasures is now preserved as a scheduled ancient monument. (Robinson Cas., 72-75; TWNFC, **1884**, 161-164; **1960**, 343-57; **1971**, 211-224; VCH, 238-9 + plan; RCHM 126; Salter, 26-27 + plan, RSB, 7; Treasures, 56; Shoesmith, 1980a and b)

# Hope Mansell

**Moat House moat** (SO 624 197)
On the southern border of the county, 5.5km south-south-east of Ross and 100m north-west of the church, there are a few traces of a moat at the appropriately named Moat House. (VCH, 250; RCHM, **2**, 90; Salter, 52)

# Hope under Dinmore

**Hampton Court** (SO 520 524)

A fifteenth century castle much altered over the centuries,
but still retaining considerable elements of the original work
Location: 6km south of Leominster, to the south of the A417
Access: Presently undergoing alterations
to become a conference centre

In 1865, the Rev Charles Robinson wrote 'There is no mansion in
Herefordshire which can vie with Hampton Court in interest or in
beauty'. He compared it with Holme Lacy, a very large mansion a
few miles south of Hereford, but said that that building had undergone 'so many alterations that it was almost impossible to detect
any traces of antiquity.' With Hampton Court, standing close to the
River Lugg some 6km south of Leominster, the converse is true.

The building dates back to the time of Henry V when Rowland
Lenthall (a gentleman of an old Herefordshire family) took a
retinue of 8 lancers and 33 archers into the field of Agincourt in
1415. For his efforts he was knighted, enriched with some of the

spoils of victory, and 'began the new buildings of Hampton Court.' The building was probably completed by 1435 when a licence to crenellate was issued and an agreement was reached to enclose 1,000 acres as a park.

In about 1510, the mansion was sold to Sir Humphrey Coningsby who was a Justice of the King's Bench. It was to stay in the hands of the Coningsby family until 1808. John Leland visited Hampton Court on his travels through England and Wales in the late 1530s describing it as 'a goodly mansion house', and was interested in the early plumbing for he indicated that the original owner had 'brought from a hill a spring of water and made a little pool with it in the top of his house.' This was apparently in the entrance tower where traces of the cistern were still visible in the mid-nineteenth century.

Notable amongst the members of the Coningsby family was Sir Thomas Coningsby who held high command under the Earl of Essex and was in the army sent to the aid of Henry IV of France. A contemporary writer records that he was 'a great master of economy hating luxury and avarice with equal violence—his house, or let us call it a college, was full of the sons of gentlemen who at his expense were instructed in the arts of riding, fencing and other manly activities.'

He was the founder of Coningsby's Hospital in Hereford. He established it 'in thankfulness to God for his defence and protection as well in travels by sea and land, as also against malice and practice at home'. This was in 1614 and it was built in the form of a quadrangle containing 12 houses. One house was for the chaplain; the others for 'Old servitors' at least half of whom should be old soldiers. Coningsby provided them with 'a suit of ginger colour, of soldier-like fashion, a cloak of red cloth to wear as he goeth abroad, and a gown of red cloth to be worn in the hospital.' This clothing is said to have inspired the red and black of the Chelsea Pensioners. The hospital still survives in Widemarsh Street in Hereford.

Sir Thomas's son, Fitzwilliam, was sheriff of Herefordshire and took part in the English Civil War in the 1640s, aiding in the defence of Hereford against the parliamentarian troops. The eventual financial losses to the estate due to sequestration were immense, but the family fortunes were restored by his grandson,

Thomas, who opportunely managed to save the life of William III the day before the Battle of the Boyne in Ireland in 1689. William won the battle and Thomas received an Irish peerage, becoming Lord Coningsby of Clanbrassil. On his return to England he was responsible for many of the alterations to Hampton Court carried out around 1700.

The full extent of this restoration work is somewhat complex and not fully understood, but it probably included a transformation of the north front into an ordered, castellated composition. This consisted of four balancing towers surrounding the great entrance tower, which remained as the dominant feature. Such a composition would have been unexceptional in the second half of the eighteenth century, but was remarkable for the very early 1700s. The date is confirmed by the lead work on the towers which bears the date 1710. A formal garden was laid out at the same time time, but all traces had been lost before 1800 when a picturesque landscape, possibly the work of Repton, took over. Similarly, all traces of Coningsby's internal works have also disappeared, apart from an exceptional chimney piece that was in the great hall until the 1840s.

Stukeley visited Hampton Court in 1714 and described how, in the hall, 'at dinner time, one of the ancient bards in an adjacent room played to us upon the harp, and at proper intervals threw in many notes of his voice, with a swelling trill, after a surprising manner, much in the tone of a flute.'

Although Lord Coningsby had considerable influence throughout the country and became Lord Lieutenant of Herefordshire in 1715, he was well known as a tyrant and, to say the least, became totally unbalanced in his later life. Hampton Court must have become a strange and unhappy place as he suffered a series of lawsuits that were essentially self-inflicted and, in 1721, he ended up in the Tower of London for having libelled Lord Macclesfield, the then Lord Chancellor. It must have been a relief to the many local people whom he continually harassed when he died in 1729.

Hampton Court passed to his daughter, Frances, and in 1754 his granddaughter married the 4th Earl of Essex. Their son, George, Viscount Malden and later 5th Earl of Essex, inherited the estate in 1781 and a few years later remodelled the building. This was very much in the Gothic Revival style and included many of the crenellations. It could well have been the work of James Wyatt, who at that time was working on Hereford Cathedral following the collapse of the west tower on Easter Monday, 1786.

The estate was sold in 1810 to the Arkwright family and extensive alterations were carried out for the rather unfortunate John Arkwright who, in 1834, wrote 'comfort is the only consideration which has induced me to make any alteration.' John was the grandson of Sir Richard Arkwright the inventor and industrialist. The father and son architectural partnership, William and John Atkinson of St John's Wood, produced a set of drawings, but unfortunately Charles Hanbury Tracy became involved. The latter, who can only be seen as an enthusiastic amateur architect, apparently created many problems to be resolved by the poor John Arkwright. It seems that the Atkinsons were responsible for the cloistral idea and for preserving the north front. However, Hanbury Tracy rebuilt the south-east and south-west blocks—a composition that lacks both conviction and balance. It is not surprising to find Arkwright writing 'I am convinced that there never was a man with less architectural taste or feeling than myself.' But the work continued and Arkwright suffered further qualms both of conscience and of finance, for the original estimate of £10,000 was to become a final figure of over £27,000.

What has remained after all this work? The basic courtyard plan of the building seems to be original with the semi-fortified gatehouse or entrance tower in the centre of the north range. Indeed, the reveals of the archway are grooved to take a portcullis. The chapel, at the north-eastern corner of the courtyard, is also of fifteenth century date. The two-storey porch on the courtyard side of the south range is of the same date and probably led into the screens passage of the Great Hall which would probably have taken up much of the south range. This has been lost, but Hanbury Tracy's entrance hall at least contains the Coningsby chimney-piece that came from the Great Hall.

The Arkwrights sold the Court to a Mrs Barrell in 1912. Twelve years later it was acquired by Viscountess Hereford in whose family it remained until the 1970s. The building now has new American owners who are carrying out extensive repair work. (RCHM, **3**, 68-70 + plan; Salter, 25; Treasures, 30; Cornforth, J., 1973)

# How Capel

**Mound** (SO 613 306)
Some 6.5km north of Ross, and on the eastern side of the Wye, the mound, which stands some 3.5m high, is just to the south-east of the church. Some masonry has been found in the area. (Salter, 50; HAN, **64**, 7)

# Huntington

**Huntington Castle** (SO 249 539)

Some overgrown stonework remains on the bailey circuit
Location: 0.5km north of the thirteenth century church
Access: A public path passes through the south of the site

The castle is in Huntington village, on the western border of the county some 6km south-west of Kington and 0.5km north of the thirteenth century church. The motte, about 38m across at the base, is to the south-west of the oval-shaped inner bailey. Apart from the west, where there is a steep scarp, the mound and bailey are

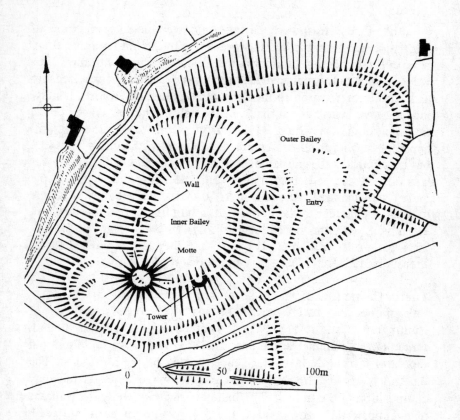

Wall

Outer Bailey

Inner Bailey

Entry

Motte

Tower

0    50    100m

surrounded by a ditch with traces of an outer bank on the south and east. There is a crescent-shaped outer bailey to the north-east with a ditch on the east and north. A causeway across the inner bailey ditch on the eastern side marks the position of the former gatehouse. The bailey was enclosed by a curtain wall that continued up the motte on both sides. One fragment, some 6m high, stands on the west side and the foundations can be traced around the circuit. There are the remains of a thirteenth century semi-circular mural tower with descending stairs on the north side and a chamber to the east. The foundations of a second semi-circular tower have been excavated on the south-south-east. Until recently there were traces of what was probably a circular tower on the motte. The whole site is very overgrown. There are vestiges of the failed borough in the field to the south.

Although the earthwork castle could well date to the time of King Stephen when the Welsh were active in the border areas, there is no definite mention of Huntington Castle by name until the 1220s when it apparently replaced Kington Castle as head of the lordship and barony of Kington in the time of Reginald de Braose. It may, indeed, have been built at that time, initially of stone. Traces of the failed borough, for which a July fair was granted in 1256, are still apparent on the ground. Repairs were made to the castle in 1403, but by 1460 it was returned as worth nothing. However, one tower was still in use as a prison in 1521. The keep and much of the bailey wall was still standing in 1670. Within the bailey was 'the hall and a chamber to the north of it, a building styled the octagon, and a well.' (Robinson Cas., 76-79; VCH 239-40 + plan; RCHM, **3**, 75 + plan - 76; TWNFC, **1914**, 31-2; Salter, 29 + plan; RSB, 8; Treasures, 17; HAN, **37**, 8-10 + plan opp. 10; **64**, 8; **66**)

### Turret Castle (SO 259 534)

This motte and bailey castle is just over 1km south-east of Huntington Castle in Hell Wood. It consists of a circular mound, some 48m in diameter at the base and 8m high above the ditch that separates it from the irregular-shaped bailey on the north-east. The flat top is about 23m across and badgers have exposed the clay composition of the mound. The bailey is surrounded by the remains of a rampart that may conceal the foundations of a curtain wall. There is a ditch between it and the spur to the east that appears to be an outer enclosure. The entrance is on this side, but no traces of a gatehouse can be seen.

This may well be the original castle in this area, superseded by the site north of the church by 1228. If so, it was one of the possessions of William fitz Osbern, Earl of Hereford, and his son Roger, and could have been an intermediate link between Clifford and Wigmore. (RCHM, **3**, 75 + plan - 76; Salter, 44; RSB, 8; Treasures, 17; HAN, **37**, 8-10; **50**, 45)

### Hell Wood (SO 258 532)

The late Richard Kay discovered another motte just a short distance south of Turret Castle. It is a ridge-end site formed by cutting a ditch across the promontory and scarping a motte. (HAN, **66**)

**Turret Tump mound** (SO 246 521)
This site is 2km south of Huntington Castle and 2km south-west of
Turret Castle at Little Hengoed. It consists of a circular mound,
26m in diameter at the base and rising 5m high, that occupies the
top of a knoll. It has been suggested that there could have been a
round or polygonal tower on the motte. There are slight traces of a
ditch on the south side. The farm to the west may be on top of the
bailey area. (VCH, 227 + plan; RCHM, **3**, 77; Treasures, 18; RSB,
8; HAN, **66**)

**Mound** (SO 248 516)
0.5m south-south-east of Turret Tump is another mound, again on a
slight natural knoll. It is about 40m across and rises 2.7m above the
surrounding ground. (RCHM, **3**, 77; Treasures, 18; RSB, 8)

# Kenderchurch

**Mound** (SO 415 294)
Some 3.2km east-north-east of the castle at Ewyas Harold and
1.6km north-east of Kenderchurch Church, this mound is north-east
of Howton Farm between the A465 and the railway, and is well
visible from the latter. It is about 41m in diameter and about 2m
above the surrounding ground. The top is flat and there are slight
traces of a ditch around it. (VCH, 227 + plan; RCHM, **1**, 152;
Treasures, 49; RSB, 8)

# Kentchurch

**Kentchurch Court** (SO 423 259)
Kentchurch parish adjoins the River Monnow—the boundary
between England and Wales—some 2.5km south-east of Pontrilas.
Kentchurch Court was a fourteenth century castle or fortified manor
house, largely rebuilt by Nash in 1795. The medieval features
include the gateway to the south-west of the house and the tower at
the north-western angle of the building, heightened and given
battlements by Nash.

Kentchurch is reputed to be the eldest house of the Scudamore family in Herefordshire and the place where Owain Glyn Dwr ended his life. (RCHM, **1**, 153-4 + plan; Salter, 30; Treasures, 75; Whitehead & Shoesmith, 1994; Hodges, 1995, 165-6)

## Tump (SO 421 270)
About 1.3km north of the church and to the east of Bowlston Court Wood is a mound, roughly oval in shape, the top being about 16m by 13m and some 3.6m high above the surrounding ditch. The ditch is dry apart from on the west where a small stream runs through it. The top of the mound, though small, has traces of three separate platforms. In 1949, the southernmost platform included stone debris considered to represent a rectangular building with the floor some 0.6m above the general level of the top of the mound. There were other traces of stone around the perimeter which could represent a shell keep. The entry was on the eastern side where there were traces of a wide causeway. There may be slight earthworks on the south, but the site is now very overgrown. (RCHM, **1**, 153 + plan - xxxiv; Treasures, 50; RSB, 9; HAN, **42**, 14-15 + plan opp 15; **50**, 43; **51**, 11-12 + plan - 15)

## Moated site (SO 421 257)
0.4m from the River Monnow and 100m south-east of Kentchurch Church, this fine rectangular moat is supplied by water from a nearby stream. The entrance is on the north-eastern side. (VCH, 250 + plan; RCHM, **1**, 153)

## Twyn-y-Corras motte & bailey (SO 418 249)
Corras is 1km south of Kentchurch Church. The motte was damaged by a World War II pill box that has since been removed; the bailey is partly under a modern house. To the south of the motte is a second bailey that contains, amongst other buildings, a chapel excavated in 1988. The original chapel had an apsidal east end typical of an early Norman manor chapel, later replaced with a squared east end. The chapel was enlarged at some time after 1200 and given a square stone tower. It was probably demolished around 1400, perhaps as a consequence of the Black Death. (Treasures, 76; RSB, 9; TWNFC, **1989**, 194-208; HAN, **8**; **58**, 18 + plan; **59**, 5-7 + plan)

# Kilpeck

**Kilpeck Castle** (SO 444 305)

> A motte with stone fragments of a shell keep, together with
> the ditches and ramparts of its baileys, and the mounds
> and banks representing the medieval village
> Location: The castle is to the west and the village site
> to the north-east of the church
> Access: A footpath leads onto the castle site,
> whilst a public road crosses the village site

The origins of Kilpeck go back to a period well before the Norman
Conquest when the independent kingdom of Ergyng or Archenfield
encompassed a large area on both sides of the River Wye. Formed in
the post-Roman period, it probably continued as a semi-autonomous
state into the tenth century. The kingdom was converted to
Christianity at an early date, the chief saint being Dubricius or
Dyfrig and many places are associated with his name. However, a
small group of churches in Ergyng have a dedication to Saint David
or Dewi including Much Dewchurch, Little Dewchurch, Dewsall
and Kilpeck. The Dewi commemorated was probably a local man of

Ergyng rather than his more celebrated namesake from Wales. The earliest and most important was probably Much Dewchurch—*Llandewi Ros Cerion*—which had an abbot in the first quarter of the seventh century. The first mention of Kilpeck is in the mid-ninth century when Ffanu, son of Benjamin, freed *Ecclesia Cilpedic* with its 'ager' (either the circular churchyard, or earthworks since buried underneath the later castle). *Peddig* was probably a personal name whilst *cil* means a nook or retreat.

Kilpeck Church is deservedly world-famous as the best surviving example of the remarkable Herefordshire School of Sculpture. It was built in the second half of the twelfth century, but one fragment, at the north-west corner of the nave, is puzzling. This piece includes typical late-Saxon long-and-short work and could be a fragment of a much earlier building.

The Domesday Survey notes that Kilpeck (entered as *Chipeete*) belonged to Cadiand before the Conquest, and that in 1086 it was in possession of William, son of Norman de Plies. The lordship included sufficient arable land for three ploughs, but there were an additional 57 men with 19 ploughs. These were probably free Welshmen for they paid no formal taxes nor did any service (except in the king's army) for their lands, and only provided William with 15 sesters of honey (one sester equates to about 32 ounces) and ten shillings annually. There is no mention of the church or the castle but the estate was valued at £4.

William fitz Norman had other manors in Herefordshire and Gloucestershire with a total value of £18 2s. and more lands in Sussex centred on Bramber. However, it is likely that his main income came from the lucrative position of king's forester for the forests of Dean, Treville and the Hay of Hereford for which he paid £15 annually. It was presumably William or his father who built the simple motte and bailey castle at Kilpeck which still forms the central part of the castle earthworks. The principal buildings would almost certainly have been of timber and would have included a keep on the motte and possibly a great hall and a chapel in the bailey.

Indeed, the chapel provides the first documentary reference to the castle in 1134. This was when Hugh Forester, later known as Hugh de Kilpeck, the son of William, endowed the new priory he had built at Kilpeck with the revenues from several churches

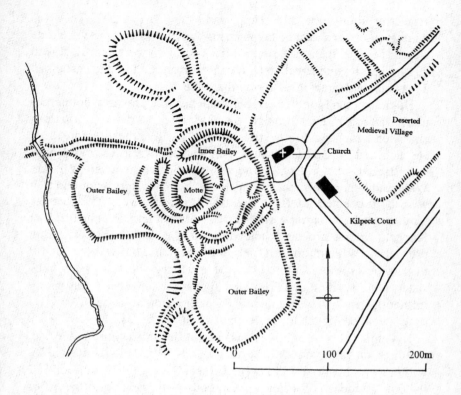

including St David's at Kilpeck and St Mary's *de castello*. Hugh was very much part of the local gentry in Herefordshire and was probably responsible for building the church at Kilpeck and for reconstructing the castle in stone at some time before his death in 1169.

His son Henry and his grandson John, who successively inherited the estate certainly had less influence and power, possibly due to the decrease in income from the forests due to gradual clearance. In 1195 John was described as holding 'a poor fief owing only the service of one knight'. John died relatively young in 1204 leaving a young son, Hugh, as his heir. As was normal at that time, the king appointed a responsible person to manage the estate until Hugh came of age. This was William de Cantilupe, sheriff of Herefordshire and steward of the royal household. William moved into Kilpeck Castle and apparently continued to administer the estate for some time after Hugh came of age in 1209. This was doubtless due to an act of favouritism by King John, who visited de Cantilupe at Kilpeck on some three occasions between 1211 and 1214. With regular royal visits it can be assumed that the castle had a reasonable degree of luxury by that time.

Hugh eventually took over the estate but was probably not particularly effective even though he was one of the eight barons entrusted with negotiating a truce with Llewellyn the Great in 1231. He died in 1244 and his estates were split between his two daughters; Isobel, the eldest, taking Kilpeck. She married William Walerand—an unfortunate alliance for their two surviving children were both deemed idiots. It was on Christmas Eve, 1259, that the king granted William a weekly Friday market and an annual fair at Kilpeck, which probably helped boost the settlement's faltering prosperity. William himself had no direct heirs, but was successful in passing on the estate to Alan de Plugenet, the son of his half-sister, when he died in 1273. Alan appears to have been reasonably influential and was summoned to parliament as a baron several times between 1295 and his death in 1298.

His son, also Alan, was successful in inheriting the estate, although on rather doubtful legal grounds. When he died in 1325, without producing any children, Kilpeck had a total value of £62 0s. 6d.—evidence of a fairly prosperous settlement—but thereafter it went into a rapid decline. This was probably because Alan's heir was his sister Joan, and she handed over the estate to a distant cousin, Eleanor de Bohun, who was married to James Butler, Earl of Ormond. By the time James died in 1338, Kilpeck had decreased in value by almost two-thirds. What had happened in just 13 years to cause such a drastic change in fortune? The most likely reason was that the Butlers became absentee landlords and the castle was deserted. The famines in the early part of the fourteenth century and the Black Death in 1349 probably sealed the fate of the whole settlement which had grown in the shadow of the castle. Even the priory, a cell of Gloucester, suffered from the general decline and although it survived with a prior and one monk, it was regularly unable to pay its dues and was dissolved in 1428.

Kilpeck continued to be held by the earls of Ormond for many years, but when Leland visited in the 1530s he merely noted the 'castel of Kilpeck by Herchenfeld belongging to the Erle of Ormond' of which 'sum ruines of the waulles yet stonde'.

The estate eventually fell into the hands of the Pye family of the nearby house, the Mynde, and by 1635 the castle was described as 'decayed, a park around it now'. Having been abandoned for some 300 years, it is rather surprising to find that sufficient was left of the buildings for them to be garrisoned for the king during the Civil War. It was never put under siege, but at the end of the war the parliamentarians slighted what remained to ensure that it could never be used as a stronghold again.

Kilpeck was not just a castle in isolation—it was and is a classic example of a planned mediaeval settlement laid out next to the Norman castle. The present road system respects this lay-out and can be used as a guide. Approaching from the main A465, through St Devereux, across the railway and up the hill, the visitor arrives at a crossroads. To the right is the turning to Kilpeck Church and to the left the road to Much Dewchurch. The road ahead continues for some 80 metres and then turns abruptly right to the modern village. The crossroads is at the site of the gateway into the defended mediaeval settlement on the right, and hidden in the hedge-line are traces of the embankment which would originally have been surmounted with a strong defensive work—either a palisade or a fence of brushwood and thorn palings. The road ahead, as it curves to the right, follows the line of these defences.

The road to the church passes through the long-abandoned settlement, following the original road towards the church. In the field on the right, the irregular, slight mounds and banks represent the positions of long-lost houses and plot boundaries. Just before the church on the right recent excavations have shown that a track led around the churchyard to a metal-working area, well away from the main part of the village and the castle because of the danger from fire. The present road curves to the left, around the attractive seventeenth century Kilpeck Court, to a small car park adjoining the churchyard. From the mid-thirteenth century onwards this was probably the area used for the Friday market. There was probably an entry from the market area to the castle, but few traces remain.

In the centre of the castle is an impressive motte some 8 metres high and completely surrounded by a ditch. The flat, almost circular top includes the slight remains of what was a polygonal shell keep, most likely built in the twelfth century as a replacement for the original wooden tower. The remains comprise two large fragments of a structure which had an external diameter of about 30 metres. The north fragment includes a fireplace with a circular flue and two round drain-holes piercing the wall. The other piece has the remains of an oven, with the springing of an arch across its front, built into the angle with an internal cross-wall.

There is hardly sufficient left to appreciate what the castle was like when King John visited it in the early thirteenth century. There would probably have been a causeway crossing the outer part of the ditch on the east which would have led to a timber gatehouse with a drawbridge. Wooden steps would have led up the mound to a defended gateway in the perimeter wall of the shell keep. This would have led through to a central unroofed area or courtyard with a series of buildings, probably of stone but possibly of wood, which would have backed onto the defensive wall. The wall was probably of sufficient height to have included a wall walk all the way round it.

The main problem with such shell keeps was that the heavy masonry had to be placed right on the lip of the artificial mound so as to gain sufficient room for a central courtyard. Although the mound would have had a hundred or so years of consolidation since it had been built, the ground was bound to be unstable. The stone keep at Kilpeck probably suffered as much from unstable foundations as it did from the slighting after the Civil War.

Between the motte and the settlement was a kidney-shaped bailey which still has an impressive ditch and rampart around it. Part of this area is now taken up with an extension to the graveyard of St David's Church. A trial excavation, in 1982, to the north of the graveyard exposed traces of roads and buildings which had fallen into disuse by the fourteenth century. The bailey would have contained the many auxiliary buildings which were part of the medieval castle. The main entry was on the south where there is a gap in the rampart and a small mound which could well conceal the foundations of part of a gatehouse. South of this is another, lightly defended outer bailey, and there were two other enclosures on the west and north, but the latter has almost disappeared due to ploughing. West of the castle is a small dingle containing a stream.

The remains of a dam crossing the dingle represents the site of a fishpond or a mill pool.

Originally the settlement earthworks would have joined up with the castle defences at the north-east and south-east corners. The north-eastern junction is still apparent but the other is now obscured by modern housing and gardens.

Although little masonry survives at Kilpeck, the extensive earthworks of the castle and the laid-out plan of the adjoining settlement complement the magnificent Norman Church and make the whole site worthy of a visit. (Robinson Cas., 80-84; VCH, 240 + plan; RCHM, **1**, 158 + plan - 159; TWNFC, **1887**, 143-4 + plan opp 144, **1912**, 115-7, 131-5, **1992**, 162-209; Salter, 30 + plan - 31; RSB, 9; Treasures, 66; HAN, **53**, 14)

### Digget's Wood mound (SO 441 295)

In the 1930s this was described as a mound on the south bank of a stream in Digget's Wood, some 1.2km south-south-west of the church. It was round, 24m in diameter at the base and 2m high. The wood was cleared in 1951 and during 1973-4 the mound was levelled prior to ploughing and the conversion of the site to pasture. There is now no trace of it whatsoever. (RCHM, **1**, 160; RSB, 9; HAS, **36**, 6 + site map)

# King's Capel

### Capel Tump (SO 559 288)

King's Capel is a parish some 6.5km north-west of Ross, on the left bank and within one of the long meanders of the River Wye. Capel Tump, a mound just to the south-east of the church, is some 40m in diameter and rises some 4m. There are some traces of buried masonry within the 1m high embankment that runs around the flat top which is about 23m across. Although all traces of a bailey have been lost and there are no signs of ditches, the name 'castleditch field' to the south of the mound and finds from underneath the adjacent Colley's Forge suggest that this was indeed a castle. An alternative hypothesis is that the church enclosure could incorporate a large bailey. (RCHM, **2**, 98; Treasures, 68; RSB, 10; HAN, **45**, 1 & 9; **58**, 42)

# Kingsland

**Kingsland Castle** (SO 445 613)

A motte with its bailey clearly visible
Location: West of the church
Access: A public footpath runs past the site to its north

The castle, to the south of the village road and west of the parish church is some 5.5km north-west of Leominster. Around 1540, Leland noted that 'there was a castle at Kyngsland ... the diches whereof and a parte of the kepe be yet sene by the west parte of Kyngsland churche.' The motte is about 56m across at the base and rises some 5m above the marshy ground to the west. The top is an irregular oval about 26m across. The bailey is to the north and east of the motte and is separated from it by a ditch. There is also a transverse ditch across the bailey. There was a further ditched enclosure on the north that probably extended to the line of the modern road but the northern side is now lost. Traces of a ditch to the south-east may be part of a village enclosure in which there are indications of possible house platforms. To the south of the motte and on the other side of a small stream are the remains of fishponds.

The stream may well have been utilised to feed the moat around the keep and some of the wide ditches around the baileys.

The keep seen by Leland has completely disappeared, but the little evidence available suggests that there was an octagonal shell keep on the motte. Slight mounding on the north-east side of the motte ditch may represent a barbican or a bridge abutment.

Kingsland is reputed to be the site of a palace of the Dark Age King Merewald and in the nineteenth century the meadow adjoining the castle was called 'Merwold Croft'. After the Conquest this area belonged to the king but by 1135 it had been given in bail to Philip de Braose of Radnor. King John stayed there in 1216 when he was wasting the Braose lands. It was presumably the de Braoses who built this extensive castle, but it must have been abandoned by the mid 1400s as it was not even mentioned during the battle between the houses of York and Lancaster at nearby Mortimer's Cross. (Robinson Cas., 85; VCH, 240-1 + plan; RCHM, **3**, 82 + plan; Salter, 30-31 + plan; RSB, 10; Treasures, 9; TWNFC, **1930**, photo xxx; HAN, **50**, 44; **62**, 16-17 + plan)

# Kings Pyon

**Butthouse** (SO 442 489)
Butthouse is 1.6km south of King's Pyon Church and 2km west of Canon Pyon. The house is of early seventeenth century date, and the two-storey timber-framed gatehouse, a short distance north-west of the house, is dated 1632. Although not a castle and hardly defensive, this still reflects a time when an Englishman's home was his castle.

The earlier defended site is 180m north-east of Butthouse where there is a roughly circular mound, 27m in diameter at the base and 16m at the top, standing about 3m high. It has been suggested that this is a round barrow, but traces of stonework could indicate a shell keep. There are traces of a possible bailey. (RCHM, **3**, 87-88; Treasures 32; RSB, 10; HAN, **2**, 2)

# Kington

### Castle Hill (SO 292 569)

A field, about 130m north of the church and close to Bach Brook, is popularly known as Castle Hill. It contains an irregularly-shaped knoll that may have been shaped to include a small mound. The barony of Kington was probably created at the end of the eleventh century when the castle and the outlying dependent knights' mottes and baileys would have been built. The barony was never of any great importance. Repairs of a palisade at Kington Castle are mentioned in the Pipe Rolls for 1187. It is likely that the castle was destroyed in August, 1216, by King John and never rebuilt. Huntington then became the centre of the barony. (Robinson Cas., 86-7; VCH, 227; RCHM, **3**, 91; Salter, 31; RSB, 10; Treasures, 9; HAN, **17**, 5 + plan; **60**, 6-7, **66**)

# Kington Rural

### Woodville motte and bailey (SO 304 544)

This site is 2.6km south-east of Kington and south of Woodville. Although now in a rough and imperfect state, the mound is circular, 20m in diameter and rises about 1.5m above the surrounding ground. The foundation of a wall, 1.5m thick on top of the motte, has been recorded. The motte is encircled with a ditch with traces of an external rampart that may have been used to make a wet ditch utilising the nearby stream. There are traces of an outer enclosure on the north-west. (VCH, 227-8 + plan; RCHM, **3**, 96; Treasures, 17; RSB, 10; HAS, **50**, 46)

### Chickward 1, possible motte & bailey (SO 287 535)

Some 3km south-south-west of Kington, and just to the west of the road that leads to Chickward hamlet is a possible motte and bailey. The top of the mound, which adjoins the road, is irregular. There is a wet moat on the south-west and west, with a possible bailey in the paddock to the west. (HAN, **57**, 44 + plan - 47)

### Chickward 2, mound (SO 284 533)

This site is in the hamlet, 0.5m south-west of Chickward 1. South of the road and between it and the stream there is an irregular series of earthworks that could include a roughly circular mound about 1m high. There are no indications of defences and this could be no more than a house or barn platform. (HAN, **57**, 44 + plan - 47)

### Hergest, Castle Twts motte and bailey (SO 277 555)

Some 2km south-west of Kington, this earthwork is on top of a small knoll which may have been artificially steepened. There is a small motte towards the west which is 17m across at the base and rises about 1.7m above the small eastern bailey. The bailey is little more than a flattened area protected by the scarp slopes, but there are possible traces of an approach causeway. There are no traces of any stonework, although a recent writer mentions indications of a round tower and a possible barbican. It has been suggested that the work was never fully completed. (VCH, 241 + plan; RCHM, **3**, 94; RSB, 10; Treasures, 16; info. P. Remfry)

### Hergest Court moated house (SO 275 553)

A little way from Castle Twts is Hergest Court, the seat of the Vaughan family. It is said to have been built about 1430 on the site of an earlier house. The surviving parts, partly of stone and partly timber-framed, are of fifteenth century and later date. A stone outbuilding to the south is probably of fourteenth century date. The house and outbuildings are on the end of a long, narrow spur of land. There is a pool on the north-west side and the River Arrow passes to the south-east. A man-made channel and a tributary of the river help to form a partial moat. (VCH, 250; RCHM, **3**, 94-5)

# Kinnersley

**Kinnersley Castle** (SO 346 497)

Sixteenth century house built on site of earlier castle
Location: Immediately east of the church
Access: Private, but occasionally open to the public

Kinnersley is on the A4112 some 3km east of Eardisley. The present house was erected towards the end of the sixteenth century. It is L-shaped and three stories high, built of sandstone and brick, and was apparently constructed on the site of an earlier building, for from time to time foundations have been discovered below the ground. These seem to indicate a quadrangular building, encircled by a moat which was spanned on the eastern side by a drawbridge. The moat is now mostly filled in, but traces to the north and east of the house were noted by the RCHM in 1930. (Robinson Cas., 88-92; RCHM, **3**, 98-99 + plan; Salter, 31)

# Kinsham

**Lower Court moat** (SO 361 644)
Kinsham is in the north-west of the county some 11km north-east of Kington. Lower Court is 0.6km south-west of the church and the north-east wing incorporates some fourteenth or fifteenth century work. The remainder is seventeenth century or later. At one time the moat probably surrounded the house, but it is now mostly filled in. (RCHM, **3**, 101; HAN, **61**, 7)

# Ledbury Rural

**Quatsford House moat** (SO 680 404)
About 4.5km north-west of Ledbury, the late sixteenth or early seventeenth century Quatsford House and surrounding area is enclosed by a large moat. (VCH, 250; RCHM, **2**, 114, Treasures, 70)

# Leintwardine

**Mound** (SO 408 745)
Drawn to the attention of the Woolhope Archaeological Research Group in 1993 by Dr S.C. Stanford, this mound is at Kinton township, 0.4km north-east of Leintwardine Church. It is about 18m in diameter and 2.5m high. A piece had been cut out of the south-west side for a previous house and a new house had been built on the site. There are vestiges of a ditch to the north-east and to the south is a stream. A slight bank could represent a bailey.

The manor of Kinton was probably held as part of Leintwardine by a knight called Richard of Barre (the progenitor of the Birley family), from Ralph de Mortimer at the time of the Domesday Survey. (HAN, **59**, 4-5; **60**, 3)

# Leominster

**Leominster Castle (Comfort Castle?)** (SO 499 585)
In 1930 the RCHM recorded the Castle Moat, 730m south of the
church. It was a four-sided enclosure surrounded by a dry moat. A
note in 1966 said it had been excavated and built over and that it
had been a moated medieval farmhouse. The *Hereford Times* for 20
April, 1962, mentions that twelfth to thirteenth century pottery and
an arrowhead had been found there.

The site of the 'hill caulled Comforte castle', described by
Leland as being either a mile north from Leominster or half-a-mile
east, 'whereof sum ruines yet appere' and where there are 'tokens
of dyches where buildings hathe bene', can no longer be identified.
(Robinson Cas., 31; RCHM, **3**, 115; RSB, 11; HAN, **1**, 1)

# Leominster Out

**Lower Hyde possible motte & bailey** (SO 456 552)
Lower Hyde is about 6km south-west of Leominster. The area,
previously described as a moated site, consists of a low motte some
1.5m above the surrounding area. It is in the north corner of a
roughly rectangular bailey that is encircled by a moat and split into
two parts by a shallow ditch. In effect there is a small bailey to the
south of the motte and an outer enclosure to the west of both. One
recent writer suggests that it held a shell keep. The moat is wet and
was fed from a stream that runs by on the northern side. The outer
bailey until recently had a building upon it and the southern ditch of
the inner bailey is covered by a barn. A footpath runs past the site.
(RCHM, **3**, 127; RSB, 11; HAN, **54**, 32; **60**, 53-4 + plan - 57)

**Upper Hyde moat** (SO 453 552)
Upper Hyde is 0.3km west of Lower Hyde. Until recently there
were traces of a fragmentary moat surrounding the house, which is
of seventeenth century date. About 45m to the north-west of the
farm is an oval island that in 1930 was surrounded by a wet moat.
This moated island is now no more than 1m above the silted moat.
The two parts are probably connected, but no full survey has been
undertaken. (VCH, 250; RCHM, **3**, 129; HAN, **60**, 53 + plan - 57)

### Upper Wintercott moated site (SO 472 547)

Only 1.6km east-south-east of Lower Hyde is yet another moat, some 90m north of Upper Wintercott. The moat had been formed by a massive stone-faced dam and there is a possibility of a 'castle' having been built on the mound behind the moat. The island is almost circular. (VCH, 250; RCHM, **3**, 127; Treasures, 29; HAN, **60**, 55)

### Wharton Court moated site (SO 511 559)

Some 4km south-south-east of Leominster and just to the east of the Leominster by-pass, Wharton Court is a noteworthy building of early seventeenth century date that is easily identified for it has chimney stacks on all four corners. The moat is 60m east of the house and consists of a small rectangular island surrounded by a wet moat. One suggestion is that it was a duck decoy site! (VCH, 250; RCHM, **3**, 127-8; Treasures, 29)

# Leysters

### Mound (SO 568 632)

Leysters is about 9km north-east of Leominster. The circular mound is just to the south of the twelfth century church and has a surrounding ditch. The top of the mound is about 23m in diameter and 3m above the ditch. The trench in the top is a nineteenth century exploration that produced ashes, charcoal and an accumulation of rough stones, but nothing in the shape of pottery or coin. At that time it was thought to be a tumulus. There are slight traces that could be a bailey to the south and burnt patches and possible platforms could indicate the presence of a deserted village in the two fields to the east of the motte and the church. Local lore has it that a circus elephant is buried somewhere on the site! (VCH, 228; RCHM, **3**, 104; TWNFC, **1892**, 281; Treasures, 11; HAN, **60**, 40 & 42 + plan)

# Lingen

**Motte & bailey** (SO 366 673)

A good example of a motte and bailey
Location: Immediately north of the church
Access: A public footpath leads from the churchyard
over a stile and across the site

Lingen is in the north-west of the county about 5km west of
Wigmore. The castle consists of a circular motte with a rectangular
bailey to the west. The mound is some 6.5m above the surrounding
dry ditch and has a roughly level platform some 19m across
although it has been damaged on the southern side. There are traces
that may represent a shell keep with a gatehouse on the western side
of the motte. The bailey was defended by a ditch and a curtain wall,
exposed in a modern cutting, on and behind the rampart. The main
entrance was probably at the south-east corner. There are traces of
an enclosure on the east that would have connected with a stream
about 60m east of the motte that may have fed the ditches. There
are further earthworks in the field to the north, including a large,
low mound with traces of a ditch.

Turstin held the manor under the Mortimers at the time of the Domesday Survey and is reputed to be an ancestor of the Herefordshire Lingens, including the Sir Henry Lingen of Civil War fame. (Robinson Cas., 93-95; VCH, 241-2 + plan; RCHM, **3**, 136 + plan - xxviii; Salter, 32; RSB, 11 + plan opp. 20; Treasures, 5; HAN, **50**, 44; **57**, 6 & 22 + plan - 27)

### The 'Churchyard' Mound (SO 372 681)
Otherwise referred to as a tump or tumulus, this mound is about 1.1km north-east of Lingen Castle. The mound is circular, some 38m across at the top and 3.4m high. It is surrounded by a dry ditch except on the north where there is a stream. The summit of the mound is approached from the south by a slanting causeway. There are traces of an outer enclosure on the east. (VCH, 228 + plan; RCHM, **3**, 137 + plan - xxviii; Salter, 32; RSB, 12; Treasures, 5; HAN, **57**, 28; **58**, 35)

### Oldcastle Wood (SO 370 668)
About 0.4km south-east of Lingen Church, this site has been suggested as that of a castle on field-name evidence, but such names can equally apply to Iron Age hillforts. (HAN, **57**, 22; **60**, 59 + plan - 60)

# Linton-by-Ross

### Eccleswall Castle (SO 652 232)
The earthworks at Eccleswall Court, some 5.5km east-south-east of Ross on the B4224, have been described as the site of Eccleswall Castle. The flat-topped mound, which is east of the modern build-ings, is partly natural and has the remains of a ditch on the south. To the east is a terrace and to the north a large pond. There are traces of a retaining wall around the mound on the pond side. The farm buildings contain re-used stones and include a square tower, once used as a pigeon-house. There is insufficient remaining to be sure of the general disposition of the buildings and, indeed, it has been suggested that the mound could actually be the bailey! (Robinson Cas., 52-3; VCH, 254; RCHM, **2**, 121 + plan - xxvi; Treasures, 84; HAN, **60**, 22 + plan - 24)

# Little Hereford

**Motte & bailey** (SO 555 679)

Little Hereford is in the north of the county, some 13km north-east of Leominster. The church is just to the north of the River Teme and there are a complex series of earthworks surrounding it. The main part is triangular in shape, the southern side running along the river bank. To the east is a ditch with inner and outer banks that continues to the north-east of the church. There is little trace to the north-west. There is a small mound in the middle of the south side, south of the church with traces of an enclosure to the east. It is about 1.4m high. The main enclosure probably represents the defences of a deserted medieval village, but the earthworks near the river could well be the remains of a small motte and bailey. It could have been the place used for King Stephen's camp in 1140. (RCHM, **3**, 66; RSB, 12; Treasures, 10; info. B. Coplestone-Crow)

# Llancillo

**Llancillo Court motte and bailey** (SO 367 256)

> A large motte and ditch with traces of walling on its summit
> Location: Between Llancillo Court and the church of St Peter
> Access: It lies at the junction of three public footpaths

Llancillo is on the border with Monmouthshire some 4km south-west of Ewyas Harold Castle and just to the north of the River Monnow. The mound lies between the late eleventh or early twelfth century church of St Peter and Llancillo Court and south of a small stream. It is circular, about 8m high and 39m in circumference at the base, and surrounded by a dry ditch and an outer rampart. Around the top of the motte, which is about 15m across, are traces of rubble walling of what has been suggested as a round tower. However, the size could indicate a shell keep with two semi-circular buttress towers on the west forming the entrance. The internal diameter would then be about 11.5m.

There are traces of banks and ditches on both sides of the mound, some of which could be associated with providing water to the now dry ditch. There is a second, smaller mound 35m to the north-west of the large mound. It is rectangular and some 0.5m high and could represent the remains of a hall block.

There seems little doubt that this was a motte and bailey castle, probably built by a military sub-tenant of the de Lacys before the end of the eleventh century. It eventually became part of the lordship of Ewyas Lacy. The Esketot family apparently settled at Llancillo and it was probably one of them that replaced the original castle with one in stone in the late twelfth or early thirteenth century. (VCH, 228 + plan; RCHM, 1, 165 + plan xxxv; TWNFC, 1923, 287; Treasures, 50; RSB, 12 + plan opp.; HAN, 40, 6-10 + plan opp. p.9; 53, 16-18 + new plan - 20)

# Llangarron

**Wallingstones moated site** (SO 503 222)

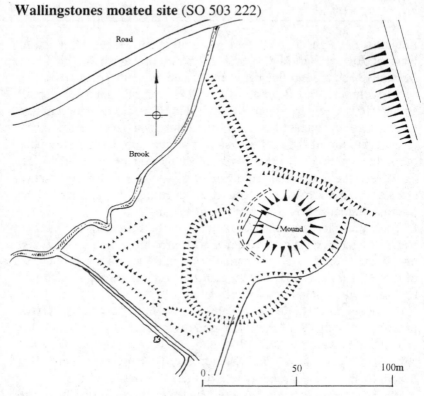

*Plan of the moated site, showing the buildings and walls which have been excavated*

A low mound surrounded by ditches and marsh
Location: 3km north-west of the church, and a
short distance south of Trippenkennett Bridge
Access: Can be seen from the road

Wallingstones is in the north-west of Llangarron parish, about 8km west-south-west of Ross. The moated site was not noted by early writers, but is of considerable importance because of the excavations carried out there between 1959 and 1963 by Norman Bridgewater and the Archenfield Archaeological Group.

*Waldygston* or *Waldyng(e)ston* was probably named after the father of Roger fitzWalding who was alive in the middle of the twelfth century. In the late fifteenth and early sixteenth centuries it was in the hands of the Maynston family.

The site consists of a low circular mound about 38m across surrounded by ditches and marshy areas. Crop marks indicate a possible enclosure to the south-west. The Nant-y-Waun Brook, which runs about 75m to the north-west, could well have been used to feed the ditches, now silted up, and the possible fishponds to the east, with water. The parish boundary follows the earthworks and indicates an earlier course of the stream.

Settlement was established on the site before 1250 and included ditch systems possibly associated with timber buildings. Within the same phase was a stone-built first-floor hall with an undercroft and a garderobe tower at one corner. It is suggested that they were built before the mound was constructed, as the mound apparently abutted the eastern wall of the hall which had foundations on the original ground surface. The mound was probably built about 1250 on which were found the remains of a building constructed at right-angles to the earlier hall. The purpose of the mound was not clear; was it just to ensure that the new building had a floor at the same level as the first-floor hall and was raised above the marshy area?

This new building could have been half-timbered. It had a stone flag floor and was probably roofed with slates and clay ridge-tiles. Early in the fourteenth century the buildings were abandoned and partially demolished. Was this, as with so many other sites, due to the Black Death?

However, newcomers arrived on the site in the fifteenth century and probably built a house on the northern edge of the mound where a wall and crude floor were found. The undercroft of the old hall was then used as a rubbish-tip. A curtain wall was apparently built around the base of the mound about the same time. The quantity and diversity of finds from this period indicates that the occupants were people of some means. Occupation probably continued into the sixteenth century after which there was extensive stone robbing. The site has since been levelled and drained.

The numerous and varied finds from the excavation, now in Hereford City Museum, are of considerable interest. Apart from the extensive collection of pottery and ironwork dating from the thirteenth century and later there was a shield boss some 18cm in diameter with a central dome and spike. It is made of thin iron and is of thirteenth century design. There was also the remains of a small balance beam of bronze, possibly used for checking coin weights. (TWNFC, **1938**, 153-4; **1959**, 243-4; **1970**, 75-116; HAN, **42**, 14)

**Langstone Court moated site** (SO 536 219)
There is a rectangular moat 1km north-west of Llangarron Church. It is a short distance south-east of Langstone Court, but on the opposite side of the Garren Brook. (RCHM, **1**, 168; Treasures, 79)

# Llanrothal

**Tregate Castle** (SO 480 171)
Llanrothal is a small parish in the extreme south of the county, approached by a minor road from Welsh Newton. 1.6km south-south-east of the restored church is the fifteenth century Tregate Castle farm. The adjacent remains are those of a motte and bailey castle, with the farm on the eastern side of the mound. The mound is about 55m in diameter rising about 4m above the bailey, which is almost entirely obscured by the farm and its associated buildings. To the south-east are a series of terraces that may have formed outer courts; alternatively, they could be later landscaping. Masonry on the top of the mound probably represents a shell keep and there are worked stones in the walls of the farmyard. (VCH, 223; RCHM, **1**, 172 + plan - xxxvi; Salter, 44; RSB, 12; Treasures, 82; HAN, **14**, 4 + plan; **47**, 12-13 )

# Longtown with Clodock

**Pont Hendre motte and bailey** (SO 326 281)

> A large, steep-sided motte with associated bailey
> Location: South of the Olchon Brook, halfway between Longtown
> and Clodock, to the west of the road
> Access: On private land, but can be seen from the road. A public
> footpath runs through the fields to the north of the Olchon

The parish church is at Clodock, on the left bank of the Monnow, in the south of this large parish, which is shadowed by the Black Mountains. Pont Hendre motte and bailey castle is half way between Longtown and Clodock on the western side of the road. It stands above the Olchon Brook, close to and west of its junction with the River Monnow. The steep-sided, circular motte, which is about 47m in diameter at the base, is 10m high above the surrounding dry ditch. The crescent-shaped bailey is on the north-east and has two lengths of rampart adjoining the motte, but otherwise depends on the scarp on the side facing the Olchon Brook. There is no trace of any masonry works.

This castle has always been regarded as the predecessor of Longtown. This is due to the reference in 1187 when £37 was spent on *Castelli de Ewias et Novi Castelli*. The new castle is presumed to be the one at Longtown and the castle of Ewias would then have to be the one at Pont Hendre. (VCH, 242 + plan - 243; RCHM, **1**, 184; Salter, 38; RSB, 13; Treasures, 49; HAN, **46**, 43 & 46-48 + plan)

**Ewyas Lacy Castle** (SO 321 292)

> Stone keep, other masonry remnants and earthworks
> Location: In the north of Longtown village
> Access: In care of English Heritage with open access

To the visitor approaching Longtown from the north, the grey tower of the circular keep perched on its high mound still dominates the village and stands out in bold relief against the dark background of the Black Mountains.

Its remote position in south-west Herefordshire must have been a problem for the commissioners sent out by William of Normandy in 1085 to compile the Domesday Survey. Even so, they found their way there and recorded it as belonging to Roger de Lacy and consisting of 'one land called Ewias within the boundary of Ewias. This land does not belong to the castlery nor to the Hundred. From this land Roger has 15 sesters of honey, 15 pigs when men are there and [administers] justice over them.' The castlery was at Ewyas Harold and Roger's right to replace the Hundred Court with one of his own emphasises its singular position. Longtown was then known as Ewias Lacy, being in the Welsh Commote of Ewias, then about to be taken over by the Norman invaders. Roger was the son of Walter de Lacy who died in 1085 from injuries after falling from St Peter's Church in Hereford.

Longtown, as its name suggests, is a long straggling village built on the ridge of ground between the River Monnow and the Olchon Brook, just above the confluence with the Escley Brook. The early Ordnance Survey plans show the castle as being on the site of a Roman fort. The compilers must have come across the same reference as the Editor of Kelly's 1891 *Directory of Herefordshire*, for hidden under the entry for Clodock, but describing Longtown, he writes the following: 'Here once stood a castle, the keep and walls of which, surrounded by a circular moat, still remain; the castle was built on the site of a Roman settlement, identified by some authorities with the station called *Blestium*, which, by others, has been fixed at Monmouth. Roman remains were found when the new school was built on the Castle Green in 1869.' The 'Roman remains' can no longer be found and apart from this information and the rectangular shape of the earthworks, there is nothing to confirm the theory of a Roman origin. *Blestium* has now been firmly fixed at Monmouth.

Considering the medieval period, it is most likely that the site was chosen for its strategic importance on the route from Hay-on-Wye to Abergavenny. However, this was neither the first nor the only castle in the area—in 1187 there is a record of expenditure of £37 on two castles, *Castelli de Ewias* and *Novi Castelli*. The original Ewias Castle, which was probably built by Roger de Lacy in the latter part of the eleventh century, may be the simple motte and bailey at Pont Hendre, close to the junction of the Monnow and the Olchon. The decision to replace it with the New Castle on a more defensible site in Longtown may have followed the seizure of the original castle by the Welsh in 1146. If this suggestion is correct, then the New Castle was probably built by Roger's great-nephew, Hugh, at some time before he was killed in 1185. Improvements and alterations could have been carried out by his son, Walter, shortly after 1189, when he finally inherited the estate, or when he returned to favour between 1213 and 1223. It was probably Walter who created the adjoining defended township, first mentioned as *Nova Villa* in 1232.

The new borough of Ewias Lacy was laid out on a regular plan to the south of the castle. The land was divided into long, narrow, 'burgage plots', occupied by burgesses paying annual rents. The settlement terminated in a small triangular market-place built under the shadow of the castle earthworks. By the thirteenth century the settlement was successful enough to warrant the construction of St Peter's Church as a chapel-of-ease, thus relieving the inhabitants of the long walk to the parish church of St Clodock, some distance down the valley. The upper part of the town, including the market-place and the church, was within a defensive embankment which would have served as an additional defence for the castle. By 1310 there were apparently some 100 burgesses in Longtown, suggesting a total population of about 500.

The present main road through the village runs to the east of the market-place and the original High Street, and continues northwards through part of the castle earthworks. To the north of the castle are traces of a further defended area. This could have been part of the castle, acting as an additional defence to the north, but perhaps more likely was an extension to the reasonably successful late thirteenth and early fourteenth century settlement. Recent excavations have shown the presence of at least one building with stone foundations of this date in this northern enclosure.

Assuming that the theories of a Roman origin for Longtown are incorrect, the earliest part of the castle is almost certainly the steep, circular mound. This may originally have been surrounded by a

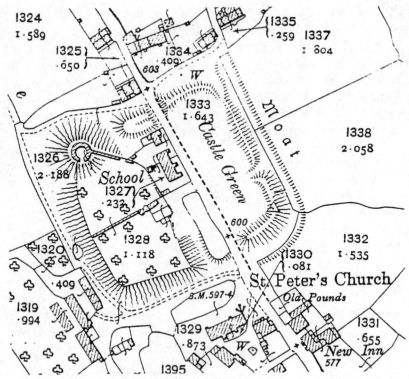

*Longtown Castle as marked on the 1904 OS map, scale 1:2500*

defensive ditch crossed by a bridge or drawbridge, but if so it has been infilled on the castle side. Steps would have led up the side of this motte to the narrow walkway surrounding the circular keep. If this keep was indeed the *Novi Castelli* of 1187, it is the earliest of the nineteen known round keeps in the Brecon region.

The great gash in the keep, which continues for the whole height of the building, originally included a semi-cylindrical buttress which contained the spiral staircase. Adjoining it at first-floor level would have been the main entrance into the keep, approached on the outside by a timber staircase which could be withdrawn in times of trouble. There are two other semi-circular projections—one is associated with a garderobe and the other which a chimney flue.

The lowest part of the keep—the undercroft—had no windows and would have been used for storage. The only means of reaching

*A cut-away reconstruction of the keep*

it would have been through a trap-door in the ground floor. This, the principal floor, had large windows in each of the three bays between the buttresses. They were widened at some time when defence was not of first importance. On the outside of one window, the semi-circular arch is carved with beaded rosettes of twelfth century date which are clearly inserted and must have been re-used from an earlier building. This room was heated by a large fireplace which would have had a projecting stone hood supported on decorated corbels. The floor was supported on one main cross-beam reinforced with diagonal braces rising from lower corbels. Joists would have run from this beam to the set-back in the masonry around the circumference, and wooden planks then completed the floor. A doorway led from this room to the bottom of the spiral stair leading to the first-floor chamber and the wall-walk.

The first-floor room would have been the lord's bed-chamber. It did not have a fireplace, presumably receiving enough heat from the floor below, but it had a private garderobe or latrine corbelled out next to one of the buttresses and approached by a passage in the thickness of the wall. The splayed windows which light this chamber are narrow but include window-seats. They are probably part of the original design. The floor was built on the same principles as the one below.

The battlements have been lost, but the wall-walk survives and would have been approached by the spiral staircase. Below the wall-walk level there are three carefully made square-sectioned holes passing through the masonry in each bay. These beam slots were designed to take the main cantilevered beams for a platform which ran around the outside of the whole keep at this level. It would have had sides and a roof and was designed to protect the castle defenders during an attack. When not needed it could be dismantled and stored in the roof space.

Externally there are two set-backs, each with a chamfered plinth, allowing the wall to decrease in thickness at higher levels. Until recently there was a large water tank sunk into the basement. This was removed during the early 1970s consolidation works undertaken by the Department of the Environment, the predecessor of English Heritage. It is assumed that they did not find the iron coffer containing a thousand golden guineas, which is reputed to have been buried beneath the keep of Longtown Castle. This was mentioned to Mrs Leather by a local informant, but he assured her that 'no-one will ever be able to get it out'.

The bailey, to the south of the motte, is an irregular rectangle about 55m wide and 90m long. There is an embankment surrounding it which includes slight traces of a curtain wall. Across the middle runs a stone wall and gateway built directly on the bailey floor and separating the area into an inner and outer bailey. The two solid semi-circular towers which flank the gateway are probably of early thirteenth century date. The towers were originally higher than now and there would have been a guard-chamber above the gate position associated with the portcullis works. The grooves for the portcullis can be seen on each side of the passage. Originally the wall, gatehouse and towers would have included a wall-walk and battlements.

The inner bailey is now a relatively smooth grassy area but would have been full of buildings and a hive of activity when the castle was in continuous use. It is likely that all the buildings would have been of timber and would have included a great hall with its service-wing, a chapel, kitchens, and perhaps a bakery and a brew-house. There would have been further buildings in the outer bailey such as stables, granaries, a blacksmith's shop and the many store sheds needed for such an isolated site during the winter months.

The entrance to the outer part of the bailey was presumably on the east side, next to the wall separating the two parts of the bailey, in the same place as the present entry. There would have been a proper gatehouse and possibly a drawbridge across the ditch.

The castle earthworks continue to the east of the present village road, forming an additional rectangle enclosed with massive ramparts. This additional area, with no trace of any stone walls on the ramparts and no apparent purpose within the general design of a castle, has led to the suggestion that the medieval builders re-used a Roman fort. Although this possibility remains, however remote, the earthworks are more likely to have been an additional enclosure, built between the two defended parts of the village and adding to the defences of the castle as a whole. It could well have had proper timber fortifications such as a palisade and fighting platform, or just a fence of brushwood and thorn palings. An early nineteenth century description refers to stone footings in this area which were removed, 'in order to apply the stone to more modern purposes'. The present road leading through the enclosure is likely to be on the line of the medieval road joining the two parts of the village together. Timber gateways at each end, and at the extremities of the village defences, are likely.

As with practically every major castle, Longtown is said to possess a mysterious underground passage. Mrs Leather records the local story that it passes underneath the Black Mountains to emerge in the Honddu valley at Llanthony Abbey!

The prosperity of Longtown and its castle seems to have been at its peak during the late thirteenth and early fourteenth centuries when it was in the hands of the de Verdon family. From then on it appears to have suffered a gradual decline. This was partly due to the lack of male issue for several generations, and probably partly as a result of the mid to late fourteenth century outbreaks of the Black Death which affected every village and town in the county. By the fifteenth century the castle had become the property of the Nevilles, Lords Abergavenny, and by this time was probably in ruins.

Apart from local tradition, there are no references to the castle taking part in the Civil War. However, cannon balls are reputed to have been found near the keep, so some military activity may have taken place.

The castle earthworks apparently had one late, rather macabre use. Alfred Watkins noted that the part of the embankment nearest to the keep was the site of the gallows—the last gibbeting being of a wife-poisoner. This was one William Jones, a native of Clodock who conspired with Susannah Rugg to poison Jones's wife at Longtown by the use of arsenic. They were executed outside St Peter's Church in Hereford in 1790 and Jones's body was brought back to Longtown to 'hang near to where the deed was committed.' (Robinson, Cas., 97-100; VCH, 242 + plan; RCHM, **1**, 181-184 + plan; Salter, 32-33; RSB, 12; Treasures, 49; HAN, **26**, 7-9 + plan; **35**, 3, 8-10 + plan opp. 10; **64**, 43 & 44-46 + plan; HAS, **104**; **234**; Remfry, 1996; Leather, E.M., 1912, 2 & 8; Shoesmith, 1994, 135)

### Great Hunthouse mound (SO 345 263)

This mound is described in the Royal Commission survey as being oval, partly artificial, with a flat top, and surrounded by a dry ditch except on the north-east and east where there is a small stream. They describe it as being 230 yards south-south-west of Great Hunthouse Farm; the grid reference given above. However, all efforts by the Woolhope Archaeological Research Group to find it again have so far been unsuccessful. (RCHM, **1**, 191; HAS, **64**, 48-9 + plan)

### Castle Bach possible castle site (SO 359 299)

The site is a platform at the end of a ridge with all the surrounding fields having a 'castle' prefix. There is a barn on a low mound but no other earthworks. (RSB, 13)

# Lugwardine

### Hemhill moated site (SO 550 413)

Some 4km east of Hereford, Hemhill moated site is a short distance north of the A438 along the turning opposite the church. The enclosure, to the south-west of Old Court, is some 20m across and is surrounded by a ditch that may well have been filled by an adjoining strong spring. There are some traces of foundation trenches. (VCH, 250; RCHM, **2**, 126 + plan - 125; Treasures, 53)

### Old Longworth moat (SO 564 393)

Old Longworth, 2km south-south-east of Lugwardine Church and close to the River Frome, may include part of a seventeenth century building but is largely rebuilt. The moat, originally surrounding this house, is now fragmentary. The chapel, formerly near the house, was dismantled and re-erected at Bartestree Convent. (VCH, 250; RCHM, **2**, 126)

# Lyonshall

**Lyonshall Castle** (SO 331 563)

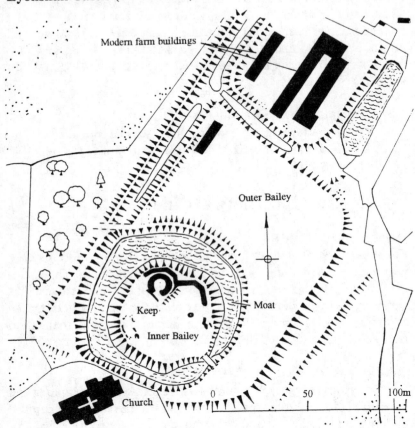

Modern farm buildings

Outer Bailey

Keep

Moat

Inner Bailey

Church

0      50      100m

A motte with remains of stonework of the keep and bailey
Location: Immediately north-east of the churchyard
Access: On private land, but glimpses can be had from the
churchyard and a footpath to the south of the site

Lyonshall parish is to the east of that of Kington. The castle is
immediately north-east of the churchyard and is very overgrown.
The inner, almost circular bailey is the closest part of the castle to

*Lyonshall Castle in 1869*

the church. It is surrounded by a wet moat and approached by a modern bridge on the south-east. About 50m in diameter, it was defended by a curtain wall of which fragments remain on the north and east. In the northern part of this inner bailey, standing on a slight rise, are the remains of a circular keep. The keep, 11m in external diameter, has its wall standing to a height of about 1.6m. The wall has a splayed string-course and a battered plinth. The walling includes the remains of three windows to the north and a possible opening to the south. Robinson suggests a flight of steps up to the opening on this side. The curtain wall encircles the keep in a polygonal way with a re-entrant on the east. This part stands some 2.5m high and at the surviving western end there are the remains of a blocked doorway. To the north-east are two projections; they probably supported a garderobe. The curtain on the east rises to a height of some 5.8m. Mounds on the western side of this bailey indicate buried sections of the curtain wall and there are traces of a rectangular building to the west that was doubtless built against the curtain wall. There is a well in the eastern part of the bailey.

The outer enclosures are to the north-east of the inner bailey. The first has a moat on the north-west and north-east sides and a scarp slope to the south-east. To the north-east again is a second, smaller enclosure with a continuation of the moat on the north-west side and a separate section of moat on the south-east. This area contains modern farm buildings that have obscured the north-eastern part of this enclosure.

This castle was probably established shortly after the Conquest and belonged in succession to the families of Lacy, Devereux and Vere. It was mentioned in 1209 as a castle and was ordered to be defended in April, 1264. A contract of 1391 between Sir John Devereux and John Brown, a mason of Hereford, describes a new stone hall to be built with walls 3 feet thick and buttresses where needed. The hall was to be 44 feet long and 26 feet wide with four doors and three large windows, one a bay of ten lights. Brown was also to enlarge and repair the gatehouse to include a portcullis and lodgings for the guard. In 1404, Walter, 5th Baron Fitzwalter, was ordered to fortify it against the Welsh insurgents under Owain Glyn Dwr. It may have been then that the relatively deep moats were constructed. The castle probably fell into disuse shortly afterwards. (Robinson Cas., 101-105; VCH, 242-4 + plan; RCHM, **3**, 142 + plan - 143; TWNFC, **1904**, 230-1; Salter, 34 + plan; RSB, 13; Treasures, 15; HAN, **22**, 4)

# Madley

### Motte & bailey (SO 418 389)

Madley is on the south side of the River Wye, some 10km west of Hereford. The earthwork, described as a motte and bailey on large scale maps, is 230m north-west of the church. It has suffered considerable change since the Woolhope Club visited in 1924 and the RCHM in the 1930s. They described the site as having a 3m high oval mound, 39m by 31m, surrounded by a dry ditch, with a bailey on the south. Modern development has obliterated much of the bailey, whilst the mound was apparently removed in 1963 without any record. Within the remaining part of the bailey there is a platform that could mark the site of the former hall and slight traces of buried foundations in the bailey bank. The motte was of a size that could have accommodated a shell keep. (RCHM, **1**, 198; TWNFC, **1924**, xxi & photo opp.; Treasures, 43; RSB, 13; HAN, **50**, 44; **51**, 27 + plan - 30)

## Castle Farm possible motte & bailey (SO 406 384)

About 1.3km west-south-west of the church, the mound at Castle Farm is a slight artificial earthwork on top of a natural mound. It is about 36m in diameter at the base, but the top is largely obscured by a seventeenth century farmhouse. There is a possible bailey to the east with scarped edges except on the west and south where there are traces of a ditch fed by a small stream. Blount described this reputed castle as a moated manor house, a description that is continued in the VCH. This is probably the site of Cublington Castle, home of the Delafields. (Robinson Cas., 39; VCH, 250; RCHM, 1, 198-9; TWNFC, **1924**, xxi-xxii; RSB, 13; Salter, 18; HAN, **50**, 44; **51**, 28-29 + plan)

## Moated site (SO 416 386)

A small, wet moated site lies some 360m west-south-west of the church, beyond a small housing estate. It is overgrown and the mound barely rises above the surrounding level of the field. (RCHM, 1, 197; HAN, **51**, plan - 30)

# Mansell Lacy

## Moated site (SO 426 456)

Mansell Lacy is some 11km west-north-west of Hereford, just to the north of the A480. The moat is 100m south-east of the church and to the east of Court Farm. It is partly wet and encloses an oval island some 27m by 33m rising about 1m above the surrounding ground. Around the base of the mound are traces of a wall foundation with a battered face. It is at least 2m thick and could be a revetment for the mound. There is a low rectangular platform on the mound that could represent a building. The crossing of the moat towards the church leads to a stony platform that could be associated with a bridge or barbican. There are other slight earthworks to the east and south and the whole may well be a low lying castle rather than a simple moated site. The two VCH references appear to be to the same site. (VCH, 228-30 + plan - 229; 250; RCHM, **3**, 147; Treasures, 22; RSB, 13; HAN, **17**, 6 + plan; **62**, 41-2 + plan)

# Mathon

**Church Farm moated site** (SO 734 457)
Some 10km north-north-east of Ledbury, the seventeenth century Church Farm is just to the south of Mathon Church. The moat, which is to the west of the house, encloses a roughly oval-shaped island. (RCHM, **2**, 142)

**Moat Farm moated site** (SO 747 447)
About 1.5km south-east of the church, this extensive moat is north-west of the seventeenth century house and encloses a roughly rectangular island. It lies, obscured by a fringe of wood, to the west of a public path. (RCHM, **2**, 142)

# Michaelchurch Escley

**Whitehouse 'Camp'** (SO 295 357)
Michaelchurch is a small village on the Escley Brook which runs parallel to and south-west of the Golden Valley. The earthwork is 2.5km north-west of the church on the summit of the ridge that separates the Escley Valley from the Monnow Valley. It consists of a small rectangular mound, 10.5m by 6m, standing 2m high, with an equally small enclosure on the north-western side, some 20m by 10m, surrounded by a rampart aome 1.5m high. There is no sign of an external ditch. There is a possible entry through the rampart at the northern corner. An oval outer enclosure, defined by scarp slopes, completely surrounds the inner earthwork except for the entrance area. A cottage, built on the eastern side of the outer enclosure, has now almost disappeared. Although the earthwork appears to be a miniature motte and bailey, it is perhaps more likely to be a defended farm or homestead. (VCH, 230; RCHM, **1**, 203 + plan - xxxiv; Salter, 50; HAN, **44**, 8-9 + plan)

# Middleton-on-the-Hill

**Moor Abbey Moat** (SO 545 634)
Some 8km north-east of Leominster on the border with Worcestershire, Moor Abbey, once a possession of Leominster Priory, is in the south of Middleton parish. The sixteenth century building, encased in stone in the eighteenth century, was formerly moated, but traces survive only on the north-western side. (VCH, 250-1; RCHM, **3**, 148-9; Treasures, 11)

# Moccas

**Moccas Castle** (SO 348 425)
Moccas Castle is only 2.5km south-east of the castle at Bredwardine. The castle earthworks were on the south side of the B4352 and just to the east of Moccas Deer Park, but due to continual ploughing little survives above the ground. It consisted of an ovoid bailey formed by scarping the slopes of a natural mound and enclosing it with a ditch which could well have been wet as the area tends to be marshy. At the eastern end was a very small motte with the top only 4m by 3m and some 4m high but with a ditch on the bailey side.

When viewed in 1953 it was considered unlikely that any portion of the castle was of masonry construction, but a licence to crenellate was granted to Sir Hugh de Freyne in 1293. The licence stipulated that he could 'strengthen it with a stone wall without tower or turret and not exceeding ten feet in height below the battlements.' It was certainly built and was probably occupied until the end of the fourteenth century. The almost total loss of any surface features of this stone-built castle or fortified manor house in what is a relatively remote part of the county is an example of the extent of loss that can so easily occur without any record. Robinson, in the mid-nineteenth century observed that 'the foundations have long since formed a quarry for road metal ...' (Robinson Cas., 106-8; VCH, 254 + plan; RCHM, **1**, 204-5 + plan - xxxvi; Salter, 35; RSB, 14; Treasures, 41; HAN, **55**, 5 +plan - 6)

# Mordiford

**Checkley, Clouds moated site** (SO 592 381)
A moated site, with a shallow moat and a low mound, in a planta-
tion near a stream. (Salter, 52)

# Moreton on Lugg

**Church House Farm moat** (SO 504 456)
Some 6.5km north of Hereford and immediately south of the
church, two arms of this large wet moat survive. The northern side
and most of the east have been destroyed by farm buildings, but
traces of an outer enclosure have been noted to the east. (VCH, 251;
RCHM, **2**,147; Treasures, 33)

# Much Cowarne

**Pauncefort Court moated site** (SO 620 472)
2km east of the Burley Gate crossroads, the moated site is at
Pauncefort Court, east of the church. All that survived in 1930 was
the dry eastern arm, since when further buildings have been erected
and roadways made. (RCHM, **2**, 59)

# Much Dewchurch

**The Camp motte & bailey** (SO 486 312)
The Camp at Much Dewchurch is about 300m to the north-east of
the church, across the road and behind the pub. Although it has
suffered some damage in recent times, this is evidently a motte and
bailey castle. It stands on the summit of a low ridge sloping away to
streams on three sides. The main earthwork consists of a roughly
oval mound, some 42m by 38m and 3m high above the surrounding
ditch. The low bank around the mound could include some stonework, possibly that of a ringwork. There were, until recently, traces
of a crescent-shaped bailey on the west and there remain traces of
two additional enclosures on the east of the mound.

Pottery from the twelfth to the fourteenth century has been found and it has been suggested that the castle was burnt in 1402-3. (VCH, 244 + plan - 243; RCHM, **1**, 52 + plan - xxxiv; Treasures, 65; RSB, 14 + plan opp. 12; HAN, **50**, 24-25 + plan - 26 & 44)

### Bryngwyn moated site (SO 484 306)

A rectangular wet moat with an entrance on the south side is in Bryngwyn Park, a little way to the north of Home Farm. (VCH, 251; RCHM, **1**, 50)

# Much Marcle

### Mortimer's Castle (SO 657 329)

A portion of Much Marcle parish, some 8km south-west of Ledbury, was given by Edward I to Edmund Mortimer, the father of the Roger Mortimer who was involved in the murder of Edward II. The church contains a monument to Blanche, the daughter of Roger and wife of Sir Peter de Grandison. The last Earl of March bequeathed his share of Marcle to Thomas Walwyn for life, and out of the ruins of the castle he built the tower of the church. The share of the manor reverted to the crown with the accession of Edward IV and was eventually sold to Thomas Kyrle of Walford.

The motte and bailey castle is just to the north of the church. The top of the motte is some 30m across and it stands about 6.5m above the encircling ditch. The semi-circular bailey on the eastern side is now occupied by cottages and gardens. Beyond this bailey on the north and east is a rectangular enclosure bounded by a rampart or scarp with a ditch on the north. There is another rectangular enclosure to the north-east. (Robinson Cas., 109-110; VCH, 244 + plan - 243; RCHM, **2**, 130 + plan - xxvi; TWNFC, **1899**, 101-2; Salter, 35; RSB, 14; Treasures, 65)

**Hall Court Farm moated site** (SO 645 353)

The VCH recorded the considerable remains of a nearly circular moat at this site north-east of Rushall and on the opposite side of the road from Hall Court Farm. The RCHM mentioned that the north-west part had been obliterated by the 1930s. By 1974, the site was recorded as being threatened by ploughing and an excavation was undertaken. The resultant report mentions that the moat had been deepened during its life to reach 2.5m deep and 9m wide. An area of the platform was examined revealing a complex of later medieval features most of which had been demolished by 1600. There were stone foundations, probably for timber-framed buildings. One building in the centre of the moated area, although badly robbed-out, was obviously of superior construction with a floor of decorated tiles. There was roofing tile and window glass amongst the demolition debris. By 1992, it was reported that the site had been almost completely ploughed out. (VCH, 251; RCHM, **2**, 130; Treasures, 63; Salter, 52 (but with the wrong grid ref); HAN, **30**, 20; **57**, 5)

**Enclosure** (SO 651 334)

The Royal Commission around 1930 described this rectangular enclosure on the west side of the road to Rushall and 0.8km north-west of Much Marcle Church. It was about 42m by 9m with a scarp at each end and a bank along each side. There was a third and parallel bank to the north, and to the west and north-west a further system of ditches. To the south-east of the enclosure was a small rectangular terrace. At that time the condition was described as good. (RCHM, **2**, 134)

**Ellingham Castle** (SO 662 333)

Robinson makes much of the fact that Much Marcle had two baronial residences, Mortimer's Castle and Ellingham Castle. He relates the latter to the manor of Hellens or Hellings 0.6km north-east of the church, formerly the seat of the Walwyn family. The present building is a good example of a late sixteenth century brick-built house although it has been reduced in size. However, again according to Robinson, Blount described Ellingham Castle as being 'in a place not far from the town, now overgrown with wood and called the Quarry Wood.' (Robinson Cas., 54-57; RCHM, **2**, 130-31)

# Munsley

### Lower Court possible motte & bailey (SO 662 408)

Munsley is close to the Roman road, 6.5km north-west of Ledbury. The mound, about 100m south-west of the c.1100 parish church, rises about 2m above the north-eastern approach. The surrounding ditch would originally have been flooded by a small stream which runs through the eastern side. The bailey was to the south-west of the mound where there is an L-shaped length of wet moat. It contains foundations of a possible barbican. Lower Court, the house on the mound, is of two stories with cellars and has some seventeenth century work. (VCH, 251; RCHM, **2**, 148-9 + plan - xxvi; RSB 14)

### Paunceford Court moat (SO 674 407)

1.3km east of the Lower Court site, the seventeenth century Paunceford Court and outbuildings are surrounded by traces of a moat to the north and south-east of the farm. (VCH, 251; RCHM, **2**, 149)

# Ocle Pychard

### Castleton Farm possible motte & bailey (SO 593 456)

A low mound with a possible bailey underneath the farm and other associated earthworks have tentatively been identified as a possible castle site. (RSB, 14)

# Orcop

### Moat Farm motte & bailey (SO 473 265)

Orcop is some 2km west of the A466 road to Monmouth and about 14km south of Hereford. The motte and bailey castle, 0.3km north-west of the church, is on low lying ground at the confluence of the Garren Brook and a smaller tributary. The motte, 7m high above the encircling moat, has an almost circular level summit about 18m across. The small kidney-shaped bailey is on the north. The stream now forms the moat on the east, with a ditch on the west and north.

The entry was on the northern side where Moat Farm now stands. When built, all the ditches would have been wet, forming the basic defence. It has been suggested that there was a polygonal shell keep on the motte. (VCH, 244; RCHM, **1**, 208 + plan - xxxiv; Salter, 35; RSB, 14; Treasures, 21; HAN, **50**, 44)

# Pembridge

### Court House moated site (SO 391 580)
Pembridge, with its famous detached belfry and many half-timbered buildings, is a large parish almost midway between Leominster and Kington. The seventeenth and eighteenth century Court House Farm is immediately south-west of the churchyard. The moat is to the east of the farm and south of the church such that the northern arm of the ditch adjoins the churchyard boundary. The western arm has been mainly filled in. The mound is about 39m by 29m with steep sides, the average height above the water level being 5m. The entrance, now concealed by farm buildings, would have been on the west. Stone around the site and used in surrounding buildings probably indicates that there was originally a fortified house on this platform. A footnote in Robinson's 'Castles' refers to Silas Taylor's visit in the mid-seventeenth century when he saw, to the south of the church, 'the mansion house where there are yet the remains of a fortified keep or small castle.' A castle was mentioned here in 1219. (Robinson, Cas., 129; VCH, 251 + plan, RCHM, **3**, 163; Treasures, 14; HAN, **62**, 18-23 + plan)

### Court of Noke possible moated site (SO 371 595)
About 2km north-west of the church and close to the River Arrow, the Court of Noke is an eighteenth century house. To the north and east of the house there is a length of mill stream with a right-angled bend. This, together with a small return scarp on the west was recognised by the RCHM as a possible former moat. (RCHM, **3**, 162-3, Salter, 52)

## Upper Wetton moated site (SO 373 537)

The Royal Commission mention the fragmentary remains of a homestead moat some 5km south-south-west of the church. There is a pool to the west of the farmhouse, but the grid reference refers to a pool in a field to the east. There is a very low lying island off centre in this body of water, but no signs of where any soil excavated to form the 'moat' may have been tumped. (RCHM, **3**, 162, Salter, 52)

## Cabal or Hunton Tump (SO 345 585)

The Tump (or Tumulus as it is shown on the Ordnance Survey Map) is almost midway between Pembridge and Kington, on low lying ground near the junction of the disused railway line from Leominster to Kington and Dolyhir and the branch that led to Presteigne. Both railways were closed in 1951.

The moated mound is steep and square in plan with a partly wet ditch on the east and south. The summit of the mound is about 22m by 18m and it stands about 4m high above the surrounding ditch. The moat was probably originally fed from a small stream on the eastern side. The original approach to the mound was by a causeway at the north-west corner; there is a modern narrow causeway to the north. There are some traces of stonework in the possible bailey on the south side. There are also traces of an enclosure to the north.

A deep trench was dug into the mound in 1874 and its upcast remains on the west and east. In addition a drainage channel was cut across the southern bailey to drain the moat and the marshy land to the west and in this cutting scraps of pottery were found. They were described as 'rims and bases of black, grey and red very rough vessels, some with a greenish glaze and some with a black manganese glaze, and also pieces of some stone bats with greenish glaze upon them where it had run off the vessels in the kiln.' Partially glazed roof tiles and early bricks were also found. It would appear that this motte and bailey castle had a later use as a pottery kiln, probably in the sixteenth or seventeenth century. Nearby is 'The Forge' which made use of ore brought from Wales by mules in the mid-nineteenth century. (VCH, 251; RCHM, **3**, 162; RSB, 16; Treasures, 14; TWNFC, **1931**, 77-79; HAN, **21**, 2-3 + plan)

**Church belfry** (SO 391 581)

It has been suggested by several writers that the detached belfry at Pembridge Church is built on a lowered motte and that the corner posts of the bell tower are the remains of a timber motte tower. However, there is no evidence to substantiate this theory. (RCHM, **3**, 161 + plan -160; HAN, **62**, 20-21 + plan and sketch)

**The Yeld moated site** (SO 351 563)

Some 4km west-south-west of Pembridge Church, the Yeld farm-house is a short distance south of the A44. The moated site, some 250m north of the farm, was completely levelled and the moat infilled in 1970. The site was examined by the Woolhope Club Archaeological Research Group and limited excavations were carried out. Three areas were examined in some detail; in the first there were traces of a small hut on the edge of the mound, in the second a cesspit, and in the third a stone-lined pit. No excavations took place in the centre of the mound which was some 40m across. The ditch, before it was infilled, was some 2m deep. Thirteenth to fourteenth century pottery was found, agreeing with the entry in the Lay Subsidy Rolls for 1334. This was a tax on wealth in the form of moveable goods rather than land, and the inclusion of the Yeld indicates that a sufficient number of people lived here to contribute to the tax. (Treasures, 16; TWNFC, **1973**, 34-38; HAN, **22**)

# Peterchurch

**The Gobbets moated site** (SO 330 404)

In the west of the county, Peterchurch is the largest village in the Golden Valley. This moated site, on the western bank of the River Dore, 3km north-west of the church, is some 300m east of the Gobbets Farm. It is in the middle of a marshy area that extends to the river and was at one time considered to be a cattle enclosure. The mound is raised above the surrounding ground and the ditch is evident on the north-east and north-west, merging into the marsh on the south-west. The eastern counterscarp bank continues to the south, apparently forming a dam across the southern end of the marsh. It appears that the mound was on the eastern side of and encircled by an artificially-formed lake. The mound is some 50m by 25m and has a depression on the top. It has been suggested that this depression could be the robbed-out remnants of a hall block. Early Norman pottery has been found on the site. (RCHM, **1**, 213; TWNFC, **1938**, xcvi - xcvii; RSB, 16; HAN, **56**, 44; **57**, 13 - plan; **58**, 53-54 + plan)

### Wellbrook moated site (SO 351 384)

Wellbrook Manor, about 0.5km east of Peterchurch Church, consists of a two-and-a-half bay fourteenth century hall and a solar. In 1922, in the orchard to the west of the house, Alfred Watkins noted two earthwork banks at right-angles to each other with a small mound or tumulus some 25m from the north-west angle. In 1924, it was reported that the mound had been demolished to extend the grounds of the house.

This was apparently not completely true, for a more recent observation has suggested that the site was partly destroyed by a modern housing estate and only one side of the mound has been cut away, showing a buried foundation. (TWNFC, **1922**, 156; **1924**, 80; RSB, 14)

### Snodhill Castle (SO 322 404)

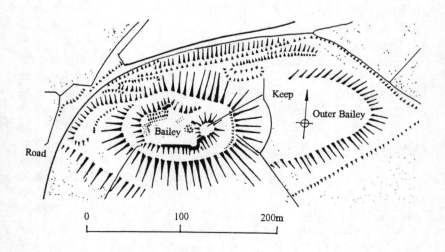

Substantial earthwork and masonry remains
Location: 3km north-west of Peterchurch Church
Access: A path leads up the motte from the west, whilst a public
footpath passes below the site to its south

Henry I gave lands in Peterchurch to Great Malvern Priory. When, in 1127, the priory exchanged them with Robert de Chandos for the Manor of Hatfield, they were called *Terra de Strada*. The Chandos family built a castle on their newly-acquired land which was called the *Castellum de Stradel* a few years later. The Pipe Rolls refer to *Snauthill* in 1196. It was described as being ruinous in the mid-fourteenth century and was one of the many castles that Henry IV ordered to be refortified in 1403 against the threat of Owain Glyn Dwr. The chapel at Snodhill is described as one of those that were damaged or destroyed during the Welsh raids up to 1406.

It was about 1540 when Leland noted: 'There is a castell a mile and more benethe Dorston apon the right ripe of Dour. It is called Snothil, and ther is a parke wallyd, and a castle in it on an hill caulled Southill, and therby is undar the castle a quarrey of marble. The castle is somewhat in ruine. Ther is a Fre Chappell. This castle longyd to Chandos.' The castle suffered a bombardment during the Civil War and, some 20 years later, much of the stonework was removed and used to construct Snodhill Court for William Prosser of London.

The chapel must have been repaired after the early fifteenth century destruction for it was still in use in the early seventeenth century. Blount, in 1675, described it as being *Infra castrum*, but in 1686 the ruins of the chapel were described as being near the 'castle of Snowdle'. The site of the chapel was uncertain in 1888 and has still not been established. It may be where there is a cottage at the foot of the hill to the west of the castle. The 'quarry of marble' remains a puzzle!

The earthworks are extensive and cover an area of some 4 hectares. On the summit is an oval-shaped high motte with an oblong bailey on the western side. The sides of the bailey and motte have been artificially steepened to form a berm. The berm has an outer revetment below the motte, effectively forming a ditch, and widens out to the west where there are traces of a causeway at the

south-west angle. The slope continues down below the berm and on the eastern side is a large triangular area, ditched on the north, that must have been used as an outer enclosure. At the foot of the slope on the west, below the bailey, there is a platform with scarped sides.

The stone keep, on top of the motte, is an irregular elongated polygon with internal measurements 7m by 11.5m. It consisted of a basement that was apparently octagonal with 2m thick walls. The surviving walls narrow above an offset to become about 1m thick and at this level the building appears to have ten sides. The entrance was on the west where the lower part of the south side remains. The surviving circular flanking tower, that contains the remains of the outer doorway and grooves for a portcullis, has a straight joint between it and the keep wall and is obviously an addition. There are traces of doorways and windows in the fragments remaining.

The bailey was surrounded with a stone curtain wall and the whole circuit can be traced. It ran down the sides of the steep motte and followed the scarp edge. On the south side, where the remains are most obvious, the eastern section including the semi-circular tower was rebuilt, probably in the fourteenth or early fifteenth century. The round tower on the north side (some 9m in diameter) contained octagonal rooms and could have been associated with a hall block; there were probably at least two other towers around the circuit as well as the entrance gateway to the south-west. There are grassy mounds along the whole of the northern part of the bailey that probably represent the walls of significant buildings. Below the scarped side of the motte, opposite the entry to the keep, is a sunken area with an external embankment. This is presumably associated with the means of access to the motte summit, effectively acting as a barbican, there being no ditch between the motte and bailey. (Robinson Cas., 121-123; VCH, 244-5 + plan - 243; RCHM, **1**, 213 + plan - 212; TWNFC, **1888**, 227-229 + plan; Salter, 41-42; RSB, 15; Treasures, 43; Coplestone-Crow, 1989, 164; HAN, **43**, between pages 14 & 15 + plan; **56**, 43 + plan)

**Urishay Castle and Chapel** (SO 323 376)

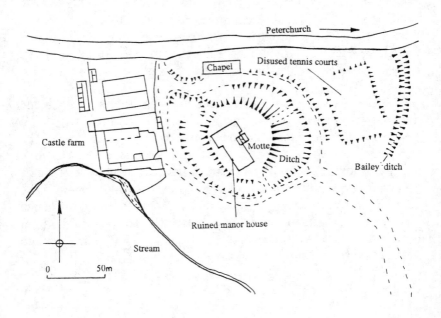

Urishay is some 2.5km west of Peterchurch, close to the summit of the ridge that separates the Dore valley from that of the Escley. It is the one hide *Alcamestune* of the Domesday Survey worth three shillings and belonging to Hugh Donkey. Originally 'the Hay', it acquired the affix 'Urry' probably from *Urrio* or *Ulric de la Hay* who was living in the mid-twelfth century.

The remains consist of a prominent motte and bailey castle in private grounds belonging to the adjoining farmhouse. The motte is some 50m in diameter at the base and rises some 6.5m above the ditch. It is occupied by the ruins of a seventeenth and eighteenth century house. Some of the window openings have been narrowed from openings which are deeply chamfered with tufa quoins that may argue for an earlier date for some of the masonry. The sides of the mound have been revetted and terraced as part of the gardens of the house. The mound was originally surrounded by a ditch of which substantial traces survive. There is a stone causeway with a culvert crossing the ditch on the south-east and the remains of a bridge on the north-east. A small stream, which now runs directly behind the farmhouse to the west of the mound, may once have been diverted to flow into the ditch around the motte.

The bailey is on the north and west and is cut by the present road. The chapel, of late eleventh or early twelfth century date, is in the northern part of the bailey, almost on the lip of the motte ditch. The eastern part of the bailey contains a flat area which is a disused tennis court. Aerial photographs provide some evidence for at least two outer enclosures. (Robinson Cas., 130; VCH, 254-5; RCHM, **1**, 211-4; TWNFC, **1987**, 686-720; Salter, 44; RSB, 14; Treasures, 44, HAN, **43**, between pages 14 & 15 + plan)

# Pipe Aston

**Tump no. 1** (SO 462 719)
In the far north of the county, this simple mound is about 0.1km north of the church and just to the east of the minor road leading towards Ludlow. It is roughly circular, rising about 7m above the wet ditch. The top is about 24m across and is said to contain some stone foundations. (RCHM, **3**, 9 + plan - xxviii; Salter, 10; RSB, 16; Treasures, 4; HAN, **50**, 43)

**Tump no. 2** (SO 462 721)
About 0.2km north of Pipe Aston no. 1 and just south of the road, this roughly circular mound is some 45m in diameter but barely 3m high. There are traces of an encircling ditch and a small enclosure on the west whilst a stream forms the northern boundary. (VCH, 224 + plan; RCHM, **3**, 9 + plan - xxviii; Salter, 10; Treasures, 3; HAN, **58**, 5; **63**, 10 + plan)

# Pipe & Lyde

**Motte & bailey** (SO 497 438)
Some 4km north-north-west of Hereford and 0.5km west-south-west of Pipe & Lyde Church, this site was discovered in 1976. It contains a large amount of loose stone, partially-buried dressed stone and buried foundations, but has only slight earthworks consisting of a raised platform surrounded by a ditch on three sides. There are also traces of a larger rectangular enclosure defined by ditches, a possible fishpond and a mill. This could well be a low-level motte and bailey castle site with wet defences, but it is equally possible that it was a lightly-defended manor house. A thirteenth century reference mentions land in the field called Middelfeld lying *sub Castello*. Middelfeld at Lyde Godfrey is assumed to be this site and was a military holding of the bishop of Hereford. It had probably disappeared by about 1320. (RSB, 16; Treasures, 35; TWNFC, **1979**, 40-43 + plan; HAN, **50**, 45)

### Lower Lyde Court moat (SO 519 440)

1.8km east of the church, the seventeenth century Lower Lyde Court was formerly surrounded by a moat, but only the northern angle remains. A holloway to the north is considered to indicate the site of a deserted medieval village. (VCH, 251; RCHM, **2**, 153; Treasures, 34)

# Pixley

### Pixley Court moat (SO 662 389)

Pixley is 1km south of the Trumpet junction, on the A438. Pixley Court, just to the south-west of the church, has a sixteenth century cross-wing. The moat, which is fragmentary, probably surrounded the church as well as the house. (RCHM, **2**, 154; Treasures, 71)

### Mainstone Court moat (SO 658 398)

Just over 1km north of the church and on the north side of the A438, east of the Trumpet junction, is the mainly eighteenth century Mainstone Court. The moat, which is to the south-east of the house, is complete being oblong in shape with a rounded south end, but without any building on the island. (VCH, 251; RCHM, **2**, 154; Treasures, 60)

### Court-y-Park moat (SO 647 397)

To the north-west of the Trumpet junction, Court-y-Park is probably of late sixteenth century date, but mainly refaced in brick. The house stands on a mound which appears to be partly artificial and several ponds probably indicate the former presence of a moat, some 90m square, surrounding the house. (VCH, 251; RCHM, **2**, 154-5; Treasures, 60)

# Pudleston

**Ford Abbey Farm moat** (SO 564 585)
Ford Abbey Farm is about 1.4km south of Pudleston Church and 6.5km east of Leominster. The core was built about 1500, but it has had several extensions since that time. There is a 30m square dry moat at the site. There is no apparent reason for the use of 'Abbey' in the name. (RCHM, **3**, 170; Treasures, 27; TWNFC, **1969**, 471-2)

# Richard's Castle

**The Castle** (SO 483 703)

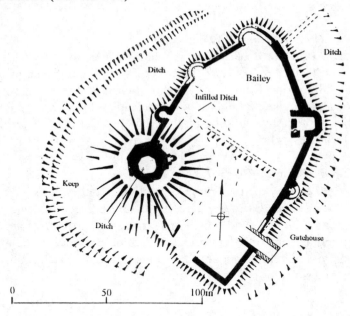

Some masonry remains on a strong motte and bailey
Location: The castle is immediately to the west of the
twelfth century parish church
Access: A path leads from the churchyard onto the site

Richard's Castle is a parish on the Shropshire border partly in Herefordshire, but mainly in Shropshire. The old church of St Bartholomew is associated with the Herefordshire portion and is 1.5km to the west of the village road. It may be significant that the bells are in an early fourteenth century tower standing well detached from the church to the east of the chancel and as far away from the castle as was possible.

The castle is mentioned in the 1086 Domesday Survey and may have been built before the Conquest for Richard Scrope, who came to England under the Confessor and whose son, Osborne fitz Richard, held it at the time of the Survey. Was it originally built as part of the response to the widespread devastation that had been caused in this area by the Welsh attack in 1052? It overlooks, and could well have controlled, the valley of the River Teme. Was its military function overtaken by the new castle at Wigmore, built shortly after the Conquest? It belonged to the 'de Say' family for a while and then passed to a separate branch of the Mortimer family. The settlement was important enough to be granted a fair and market in 1216. From the Mortimers it passed by marriage to the Talbot family in the mid-fourteenth century. By this time it was apparently in poor condition, although it was garrisoned against a possible raid by Owain Glyn Dwr at the beginning of the fifteenth century.

Around 1540, Leland noted that 'Richard's Castell stondith on the tope of a very rokky hill, well woodyd, and at the west end of the paroche churche there. The kepe, the waulls, and towres of yt yet stond but goynge to ruyn. There is a poore house of tymbar in the castle garth for a farmer. It longeth now to the king, it longed of late to the Lord Vaulx, then to Pope. There is a park empaled and well woodyd, but no dere in it.'

The defences may well have been deliberately ruined at some time during the Civil War. In 1645 a sharp engagement took place near the castle when a body of Royalists, some 2,000 strong, under Sir Thomas Lunsford, was surprised by Colonel Birch's parliamentarian troops, resulting in much slaughter.

The earthwork remains consist of a typical, but very strong, motte and bailey, both surrounded by a continuous deep ditch. The motte is some 60m in diameter at the base and although the top is now a mere 14m across, it was probably larger before the masonry keep was built. The top is some 27m above the ditch on the west, the ditch between the mound and the bailey having been back-filled. The kidney-shaped bailey had a perimeter wall and fragments up to 5m high survive above the ground in some places, and are covered in debris to form a rampart in others. There were several D-shaped towers around the perimeter and one rectangular one that was probably residential and attached to a hall similar to those at Wigmore. The entry to the bailey was on the south-east where a fragment of the south side of the elongated gatehouse remains, and there is a causeway across the ditch. There are traces of an outer embankment, curtain wall and ditch leaving the north-east corner of the bailey in a north-eastern direction. This is considered to be part of the defences that once surrounded the village.

Traces of the excavations that took place in the 1960s are still apparent. They concentrated mainly on the motte and exposed the lower part of an octagonal tower which was dated to the end of the twelfth century. On the east was a slightly later apsidal projection that may have contained the entry to the keep. When the castle became a farm, the small round tower at the bottom of the mound was converted to become a dovecot. (Robinson Cas., 118-120; VCH, 245 + plan; RCHM, **3**, 172 + plan - 173; Treasures, 4; RSB, 16-17; Salter, 39-40 + plan; HAS, **25**; Curnow & Thompson, 1969,105-27)

**Moated site** (SO 492 724)

This moated site is about 2km north-north-east of Richard's Castle Church, in the middle of Haye Park Wood. It is roughly rectangular with an inner rampart, and is surrounded by a narrow ditch with a counterscarp bank on the east. (RCHM, **3**, 172-3; Treasures, 10)

# Ross Rural

**Penyard Castle** (SO 618 226)

> Masonry remains from the fourteenth to seventeenth
> centuries, together with probably earlier earthworks
> Location: Near the top of Penyard Hill,
> 2.5km south-east of Ross Church
> Access: A footpath to the west of Lawns Farm passes to
> the north of the ruins, which lie on the edge of woodland

The castle belonged to the Talbots of Eccleswall in the thirteenth century and possibly earlier. It is built on the edge of a plateau with a steep wooded slope dropping down to the valley below. However, the slope continues upwards to the north-west, from which the site can be overlooked. There is a trace of a ditch on the south-west side and various other banks and mounds that probably cover buried walls. The upstanding remains probably date to the fourteenth century and indicate a building of some size. It was ruined by the seventeenth century and, in 1691-4, stone from the castle was used to build the Parsonage House and a barn at Weston-under-Penyard. A house was built into the ruins, possibly in the seventeenth century. The house has since become ruinous and the site overgrown.

The remains consist of a block of buildings stretching north-south. The earliest masonry consists of the north-east and south-east corners of a building at the southern end. The northern part includes the ruined farmhouse—a building of at least four separate periods that may incorporate earlier work.

The surviving remains are complex and there is now some difficulty in associating them with the RCHM description of 1930 when 'immediately adjoining the house on the south and extending to the west are remains of a vaulted fourteenth century undercroft of at least four bays. It was about 17ft wide and bases of some of the chamfered responds and of a fireplace remain.' The remains of the undercroft are again mostly buried. The RCHM also mention a fourteenth century doorway in the west wall of the house. In 1980, Richard Kay suggested that this doorway could be buried underneath the debris and that the south gable of the house contained a blocked chamfered doorway with a four-centered head. The north gable wall contained a fourteenth century two-light ogee-headed window and a narrow rectangular slit. What is inserted from the original and what is in situ is difficult to establish without detailed survey. Some similarities with Goodrich Castle have been noted and these need to be properly analysed bearing in mind the joint ownership. (Robinson Cas., 116-7; RCHM, **2**, 166; TWNFC, **1928**, 129-136; **1951**, 272; Treasures, 80; Salter, 38; HAN, **13**, 7 + plan; **37**, 3-6; **60**, 21-24 + plan; **62**, 5)

# Rowlestone

**Castle mound** (SO 375 272)
Rowlestone is in the south-west of the county, some 2km south-west of Ewyas Harold Castle. The castle mound is 100m north-east of the church. The motte is 35m in diameter at the base and rises some 4.5m above the bottom of the dry ditch. There are no indications of any stone buildings on it. Court Farm, which is of fourteenth century origin, is probably in the area that was once the bailey although there are no surviving remains of any embankment. (VCH, 230; RCHM, **1**, 223; Treasures, 49; RSB, 17; HAN, **40**, 6 & 9-10; **53**, 15)

# St Devereux

**Moated site** (SO 439 312)
Only 0.5km north of the castle at Kilpeck, this rectangular moated site is situated on the west side of the road, opposite the church of St Dubricius. The ditch is mainly filled in but the Royal Commission noted a quadrangular platform to the north. (RCHM, **1**, 225)

**Didley Court Farm motte and bailey** (SO 451 320)
1.2km north-east of the church is the early sixteenth century Didley Court Farm. The motte and bailey castle has been much cut into by the farm buildings, but the motte, about 24m in diameter at the base and 5m high, that may have included a shell keep, survives to the south-east. It has a ditch on the south-west that becomes a berm on the south-east and east where there is a scarp slope. There are traces of a crescent-shaped bailey to the north and a second enclosure to the west. (RCHM, **1**, 224 + plan - xxxv; Treasures, 64; RSB, 17)

**Trelough moated site** (SO 432 312)
Trelough is about 1km west of St Devereux Church. The present house is of early eighteenth century date and the moat that surrounded it, but was originally associated with an earlier building, is now mostly filled in. (RCHM, **1**, 224; Treasures, 47)

# St Margaret's

**Possible motte** (SO 358 339)
St Margaret's lies on the southern rim of the Golden Valley about
3km south-south-west of Vowchurch. The motte, which has also
been described as a quarry dump, is about 0.5km east-north-east of
the church. It is only some 15m in diameter and stands between 1.5
and 3m high. (RCHM, 1, 227; Treasures, 47)

# St Weonard's

**Tump** (SO 497 243)
St Weonard's stands on a hilltop two-thirds of the way from
Hereford to Monmouth on the A466. The mound, which is immediately south of the church, is some 40m in diameter at the base and
5m high. The flat top is 23m in diameter and is covered in trees and
undergrowth. It was excavated in 1855 and the cutting made then is
still apparent. The description and section published at that time
suggests that a circular bank was made around an area in which ash,
charcoal and pieces of burnt human bone were found, apparently
within a rude vault. The central part was then filled in. There was
no sign of the 'gold coffin' reputed to contain the remains of the
saint. At a later date the mound was made considerably larger and
heightened.

It would appear that although the primary use was undoubtedly a
burial mound, it was re-used as a motte, possibly with a shell keep
on top. Earlier observers noted traces of a ditch around the motte
and also a bailey to the south, but these have all been obliterated by
new roads and buildings. (VCH, 230 + plan; RCHM, 1, 227;
Treasures, 76; RSB, 17; HAN, 12, 5; Leather, E.M., 1912, 9)

## Treago Castle (SO 490 239)

> Fortified house dating from the early sixteenth century
> Location: 0.6km south-west from St Weonards village
> Access: Private, but the north front can be seen from the road

The church at St Weonard's is on top of a hill. Treago Castle lies below it and about 0.6km to the south-west. It is the ancient seat of the Mynors family. John de Mynors, who was appointed by Edward II as keeper of the Forest of Dean, was described as being of Treago.

There are no features of early fourteenth century date apparent in the building, although parts of the walls and the ground plan could be of that date. The present building was erected about 1500 and is square in plan with round towers at each corner. Two of the towers originally contained spiral stairs; the other two are larger and contained rooms. The inner courtyard, originally 8m square, was probably approached by a passage through the eastern range. The hall would then have been in the northern or western range with the kitchens to the south. The projecting three-storey porch on the north elevation is of mid-sixteenth century date. The building became a farm in the early nineteenth century and had many alterations during the 1840s including the infilling of the courtyard and the refacing of many of the walls. It is still occupied by the Mynors family. (VCH, 255; RCHM, **1**, 230-2 + plan; Salter, 43 + plan; Treasures, 78)

# Sarnesfield

### Hell Moat (SO 366 520)
Hell Moat is about 3.5km due west of Weobley in the south-west corner of Sarnesfield Coppice. The moat encloses an irregularly-shaped island, up to 50m across, with an inner bank on the north, west and south sides and an outer bank on the south and west. A small stream runs to the east, on which side the moat has suffered greatest damage. (VCH, 249, RCHM, **3**, 178 + plan - xxix; Treasures, 18)

# Shobdon

### Castle mound (SO 399 628)
The mound is 120m west of the delightful Strawberry Hill Gothic church. It is round, with a flat top some 45m in diameter rising about 3m above the surrounding land. There is some buried stone on top of the mound which is surrounded by a dry ditch. There was a causeway to the north-east, but this area has now been filled and levelled. There is a possible hornwork to the south-west. The bailey, which was on the east, has mainly been levelled and covered with a chicken processing factory. It could originally have had a wet moat.

It was probably built in the early twelfth century when Shobdon was given to Oliver Merlymond by Hugh Mortimer on condition that Oliver served him loyally. Oliver built himself a castle and was also responsible for the abbey and for the church at Shobdon. This is the church that was demolished in the mid-eighteenth century. The doorways and chancel arch, which are highly decorated in the twelfth century style of the Herefordshire School, were re-erected in the park as an eye-catcher. (RCHM, **3**, 182; RSB, 17; Pevsner, 288; HAN, **24**, 4 + plan; **58**, 30-1 + plan)

### Possible castle site (SO 408 628)

This has been described as a possible motte, ditch and counter-scarp with a bailey. The mound is quite prominent with a shallow ditch containing a pond at one point, and other embankments indicate what could be the line of a bailey. To the east runs one of the early valley defensive ditches, similar to the Rowe Ditch some 3km to the south-west. (HAN, **58**, 30; info. P. Remfry)

### Shobdon Court (SO 402 627)

Described in places as a barrow and in others as a Victorian garden mound, this mound adjoins the drive to Shobdon Court some 250m south of the church. It is 18m in diameter and 3m high. There is no sign of an external ditch or a bailey. It is evidently not a natural feature and is of the size and shape of many castle mounds in the area, but its actual purpose is no longer evident or known. (VCH, 230; RCHM, **3**, 182; Treasures, 8; HAN, **24**, 4 + plan; **58**, 30)

### Milton House (SO 385 610)

Milton is some 2km south-west of Shobdon on the road to Staunton-on-Arrow. There is a slight mound on the opposite side of the road to Milton House. It is suggested that the motte, if that is what it was, was succeeded by a later moated site. (HAN, **60**, 8-9 + plan)

### Ledicot (SO 415 623)

The VCH recorded the fragmentary remains of a moated enclosure at Ledicot, about 1.5km east-south-east of Shobdon Church. (VCH, 251; HAN, **58**, 30)

# Sollars Hope

### Mound at Court Farm (SO 613 333)

Sollars Hope is a small parish some 3km west-south-west of Fownhope. The mound, at Court Farm, just to the north of the church, is at the junction of two small streams. It is 33m in diameter with a flat top some 2m above the broad ditch which surrounds it. There are traces of stonework, but this may be because until recently there were pigsties on top. The motte is also damaged on the Court side. It has been suggested that the church could be in a defended enclosure on one side, and the sixteenth century Court Farm in another. (VCH, 251; RCHM, **2**, 170; Treasures, 64; RSB, 18; HAN, **57**, 32; **63**, 52; **65**, 10)

# Stapleton

**Stapleton Castle** (SO 323 656)

> Extensive masonry remains of a seventeenth century
> house incorporating the remains of an earlier castle,
> set on a prominent hill
> Location: 1.5km north-east of Presteigne
> Access: Can be reached by a path from the south-west
> corner of the site, near the road junction

Stapleton is a small parish without a church on the border with
Radnorshire, 1.5km north-east of Presteigne. The castle, on the
summit of a hill in the middle of the parish, was probably founded
some time after 1144. It belonged to the lords of Richard's Castle in
the thirteenth century. At the beginning of the fourteenth century it
passed by marriage to the Cornewalls. Sir Gilbert Cornewall held it
during the Civil War and it was slighted by the Royalist
Commander, Sir Michael Woodhouse, in 1645. In 1706 it passed to
the Harley family.

The earthworks consist of a motte on the southern, higher end of
the knoll with a ditch cut into the hillside on the west and east sides.
On the north side is the main bailey with traces of an entrance and a
slight ditch to the north. There is another enclosure further to the
north. The motte contains the remains of a farmhouse that includes
much of the seventeenth century manor house that was defaced
during the Civil War. It was abandoned at the end of the nineteenth
century. The house consisted of a long central wing with cross
wings at the north and south ends, short of the ends of the main
building. The north end and the north-western projections have both
completely disappeared. The windows on the eastern front have
segmental brick arches of eighteenth century date.

Around the west and south sides of the mound is a wall described
by the RCHM as a retaining wall and assumed to be associated with
the construction of the seventeenth century house. It is now recognised as being part of a polygonal shell keep still standing some
2.5m high in places and including one garderobe shaft on the west
side and another possible one on the east corner. Some walls may
have been utilised in the basement of the seventeenth century
building. A right-angled corner may indicate that the hall was on
the eastern side. On the north side, forming part of the eastern cross
wing of the seventeenth century building, is part of the wall of the

*Stapleton Castle in 1850*

castle gatehouse including a draw-bar slot. The bailey contains
traces of a bridge or drawbridge abutment and a possible barbican.
Foundations of the curtain wall can be seen in places. There are
traces of other enclosures on the north and south that may be associated with the failed borough. Eleventh to twelfth century pottery
has been found in the southern enclosure and around the motte.
(Robinson Cas., 124-25; VCH, 246 + plan; RCHM, **3**, 182 + plan -
xxix; TWNFC, **1898**, 13 Treasures, 6; RSB, 18 + plan opp.; Salter,
42; HAN, **58**, 27-31 + plan; **59**, 7; **61**, 7)

# Staunton-on-Arrow

**Motte & bailey** (SO 369 600)

> A motte set above the River Arrow, with associated baileys
> Location: The motte is immediately south-west of the churchyard
> Access: A public footpath passes between the motte
> and the churchyard

Some 3km north-west of Pembridge, Staunton-on-Arrow is on the north side of the river after which it is named. The motte is circular, with a flat top about 19m across, rising some 8m above the bottom of the dry ditch and could have held a shell keep. There is a ploughed-out ditch and rampart to the north of the motte. The house to the south of the motte appears to be built in the still water-filled moat! The church is apparently in one bailey with other enclosures to the south and west. (VCH, 231; RCHM, **3**, 183; Treasures, 9; RSB, 18; HAN, **50**, 45; info. P. Remfry)

# Stoke Lacy

**Nether Court Moated site** (SO 620 494)
Stoke Lacy is 6km south-west of Bromyard. The RCHM recorded that only two arms of the moat at Nether Court, 120m south-south-west of the church, survived in 1930. Apparently there is little left; according to the HAN report, the mound now seems to contain a tennis court. (RCHM, **2**, 174; HAN, **63**, 59)

**Stoke Cross** (SO 625 505)
About 1.5km north-north-east of Stoke Lacy Church, this mound is on gently sloping ground to the north of the main road and adjoining a minor road leading towards Bredenbury. The motte is oval-shaped, 22m by 17m, and about 2m high, covered in brush and bramble. The road and ploughing has obliterated the moat to the north but there are traces surviving to the south. The slight earthworks of a possible bailey stretch almost as far as the main A465 road. There are traces of former fishponds to the north. (Treasures, 31; HAN, **63**, 56-7 + plan)

**Lower Hopton** (SO 631 493)
Lower Hopton is 1km east of Stoke Lacy. The moat is roughly circular and was described by the VCH as being 'perfect and nearly circular ... with a causeway entrance on the north-west.' However, it has recently been converted into a 'rather pretty Japanese garden with painted wooden bridges and many rare plants.' This has involved clearing out the fill of the moat by machine and spreading the silt on the surrounding garden. The mound is only 1m high above the present water level, and is about 35m across. There are traces of baileys or enclosures on several sides, one at least being covered in a modern mews development utilising the earlier farm buildings. (VCH, 251; RCHM, **2**, 174; Treasures, 31; HAN, **63**, 58-9 + plan)

# Stretford

**Possible castle site** (SO 444 555)
Stretford is 6km west-south-west of Leominster. This possible site is to the south of the church and consists of a hillock on a wide, flat-topped ridge close to where the ground falls steeply to the Stretford Brook. There are traces of a possible bailey rampart adjoining the access road to the church and at one time there was a ditch. The paddock below the hillock is called Castle Green, whilst Chapel Field, between the mound and the A4110, is said to contain much buried stone. (HAN, **60**, 50 + plan - 59)

# Stretton Grandison

**New House moat** (SO 645 445)
New House is about 1km east-north-east of Stretton Grandison Church, on the Roman road 5km north-west of the Trumpet crossroads. New House is basically of sixteenth century date. One arm of the moat survives, to the south-east of the house. (RCHM, **2**, 175)

# Stretton Sugwas

**Moated site** (SO 466 428)
Stretton Sugwas is some 5.5km west-north-west of Hereford. The original village was probably centred on St Mary Magdalene's Church. This building stood near the centre of the parish, just to the north of the Roman road, until it was totally demolished in 1877. The new church was built 1.3km south-west of the old site. The moated site, a short distance to the south-west of the old church site and 130m south-east of Stretton Court, was described as being partly filled in and dry when visited by the Royal Commission about 1930. (RCHM, **2**, 177)

# Sutton

### Offa's Castle (SO 525 464)
The Iron Age hillfort of Sutton Walls is the traditional site of King Offa's Castle or palace, where Ethelbert was killed. Leland noted that: 'At Sutton a palayce of King Offas was King Ethelbright sleyn. Sutton is iii myles fro Heneforth northward apon Lugge. Yt is now cawled Suttun Walles, and now no thing but ruines.' Much of the hillfort has been quarried and then used for dumping waste materials. The precise position of Offa's Castle remains uncertain. (Robinson Cas., 126-7, RCHM, 2, 182)

### Freens Court moat (SO 523 459)
Freens Court was about 0.5km west of Sutton St Nicholas Church and 0.3km from the River Lugg. The house was built in the sixteenth century, probably by the Lingen family, but was demolished in 1957. In 1930 the moat was described as fragmentary, but traces still survive. In addition, recent aerial photographs have shown what appears to be two halls or a hall and a barn close to the site of Freens Court. They have affinities in design to Yeavering, Northumberland, and could well be of Saxon date. It would be surprising, considering the long history of this site, if there were no defensive works whatsoever associated with these early remains. (VCH, 251; RCHM, 2, 179; TWNFC, 1957, 345-6; Treasures 33; HAN, 65, 31)

# Tarrington

### Tarrington Court moat (SO 616 405)
Midway between Hereford and Ledbury on the A438, the late sixteenth century Tarrington Court is on the village road, a little way to the south of the main road. Only one corner of the moat survives, but it appears originally to have enclosed an area of about 0.4 of a hectare. (VCH, 251; RCHM, 2, 183-4; Treasures 54)

# Thornbury

**Netherwood former moat** (SO 634 608)
Netherwood is some 6km north of Bromyard. According to Robinson this farmhouse was formerly a quadrangular mansion enclosed by a moat and surrounded by a park of some 300 acres. The earlier building was demolished in the mid-eighteenth century. The north wing was said to include a chapel with a deep vault underneath containing effigies in stone. (Robinson Man., 267; VCH, 251)

# Thruxton

**Thruxton Court motte** (SO 436 346)
Thruxton is 9km south-west of Hereford. The motte, 100m west of the church, is circular with a slight surrounding ditch. It is about 38m in diameter and stands some 5m above the bottom of the ditch. The top of the motte is now impassable due to brambles, but some time ago there was what appeared to be a stone-lined basement, plastered and used as a water tank. It has also been suggested that foundations seen on the top of the mound could well represent a shell keep. To confuse the matter further, around 120 years ago the mound is said to have been opened and was found to contain a rude chamber of stones. This could well be similar to the mound at St Weonards with an earlier, pre-castle use. There are traces of several baileys or enclosures under the present house and gardens. An exposed section on the east of the motte demonstrated that the top one-third comprised shaly gravel with what appeared to be natural clay underneath. (VCH, 231; RCHM, **1**, 239; RSB, 18; HAN, **50**, 45; **65**, 27-8 + plan)

# Tretire with Michaelchurch

**Tretire Castle** (SO 521 239)
Tretire Castle is immediately south-east of the church of St Mary at Tretire, some 8km west of Ross. The earthwork consists of a rectangular mound, approximately 64m by 50m with the remains of a rampart and a dry ditch to its north-west. The top of the mound was somewhat cut into many years ago to make a tennis court.

When Robinson visited the site during the first half of the nineteenth century he described it as 'a large squarish mound on which several towers appear to have stood, divided from the neighbouring ground on two sides by a fosse. No masonry remains but foundations may still be traced and the internal courtyard is well-defined.' In the thirteenth century, Tretire was part of the possessions of the feudal baron, Fulk Fitzwarine of Whittington in Shropshire. (Robinson Cas., 128; VCH, 255; RCHM, **1**, 240; Treasures, 79)

**Mound** (SO 510 255)
This site was described by the RCHM in the late 1920s as being 1.3km west of St Michael's Church. It was of irregular shape, being segmental on the north and west sides, but possibly cut away on the east during the making of the roadway against which it stood. It rose 1.3m above the surrounding ground on the west and 2.1m above the road. There were two large irregularly-shaped sinkings in the same field. (RCHM, **1**, 240)

# Turnastone

**Cothill Tump** (SO 338 363)
Some 2.2km south-south-west of Peterchurch is a mound about 31m in diameter surrounded by a dry ditch. The mound rises some 3.5m above the ditch with a central sunken area. In 1967 there was some damage caused by tree removal and by the construction of a ramp as access across the ditch on the south. At that time the section along the ramp was cleaned and examined and two large stones in the northern ditch were photographed. The tip lines in the section were seen to fall towards the centre and it was suggested that this was a Bronze Age burial mound rather than a medieval feature. (VCH, 231; RCHM, **1**, 242; TWNFC, **1969**, 475; Treasures, 45; RSB, 19; HAS, **13**, 5 + plan)

**Possible site near church** (SO 357 365)
Close to the church is a possible ringwork, now mainly ploughed out, but some stonework has been noted when ploughing. There is nothing clearly visible on the ground. (RSB, 19)

# Ullingswick

**Moated site** (SO 591 497)
Ullingswick is 8km south-west of Bromyard. This moat, some 0.7m west-south-west of the church and just south of a small stream, encloses a very small square island presently covered in trees and scrub. (RCHM, **2**, 191)

# Upper Sapey

**Yearston Court possible moated site** (SO 694 638)
Upper Sapey is in the north-east of the county and the earthworks are at Yearston Court, 1.2km east of the church. They include a ditch surrounding an oval site on which stands a modern house and outbuildings. There is a low mound to the east and further enclosures possibly associated with water management. (RCHM, **2**, 168; HAN, **59**, 13-14 + plan)

# Upton Bishop

**Motte** (SO 652 281)
This possible motte and bailey is some 7km north-east of Ross-on-Wye and 1km north of Upton Bishop Church. The tithe apportionment produced the names 'Castle Tump Field' and 'Blackwall Field' whilst a neighbouring farm is called Castle Farm. Recent investigations have shown that there is a low motte, about 30m across and rising some 3.5m above the surrounding ditch with traces of an almost ploughed-out bailey. Field walking has produced limestone-tempered pottery of early twelfth century date from Castle Tump Field, and other pottery showing that the site was occupied until the fourteenth century. Iron bloomery slag has also been found. (TWNFC, **1991**, 24-7; RSB, 19; HAN, **55**, 18-20)

# Vowchurch

**Poston Castle** (SO 358 372)

Vowchurch is in the Golden Valley, 2.5km south-east of
Peterchurch. The site at Poston is on the northern side of the valley,
0.8km north-north-west of the church and at the foot of the hill on
which the Iron Age hillfort stands. The scarped, raised platform was
roughly rectangular, being about 37m by 35m. On the north and
east sides there was a broad terrace or berm cut into the slope of the
hillside—it narrowed to the south and west. The summit of the platform had many irregularities but no trace of stonework. The site
was ploughed in the 1970s and many features removed.

Poston, with two hides under cultivation, was held by William de
Écouis at the time of Domesday. Previously it had been waste, but
by then it was worth five shillings. (RSB, 20; TWNFC, **1938**, 151;
**1967**, 42; HAN, **56**, 44; **57**, 13 + plan; **58**, 35)

**Monnington Court motte & bailey** (SO 382 368)

Monnington Court is 2km east of the church of St Bartholomew at
Vowchurch. The oval mound, 55m by 48m, stands about 3.8m
above the partly wet ditch which surrounds it. There is a crescent-
shaped bailey to the west of the motte which had a ditch fed by a
stream. On the eastern side of the motte the defences have been cut
away by farm buildings. To the south there are various earthworks
suggesting additional occupation in that area. They may be associated with Chapel House, a substantial farmhouse used as a farm
store in 1974 but of fifteenth or sixteenth century origin. (VCH,
251; RCHM, **1**, 245; Treasures, 45; RSB, 19; TWNFC, **1938**, 146;
HAN, **29** + plan)

# Chanstone Tump No. 1 (SO 366 359)

0.6km south-east of the church, on the north bank of the River Dore, by the bridge leading to Chanstone Court Farm, is this circular mound. It is some 58m in external diameter and 4m high above the bottom of the external ditch. The ditch could easily have been made to fill with water from the river. There are traces of masonry on the mound suggesting a shell keep. There may have been a bailey to the north.

This, or the following entry, could well be the *Elnodestune* of the Domesday Survey. This 3 hide manor belonged to Walter de Lacy, but the Domesday tenant was William Devereux and it is known that the Devereux family had Chanstone in 1243. (VCH, 231; RCHM, **1**, 245 + plan - xxxv; TWNFC, **1938**, 146; Treasures, 46; RSB, 19; HAN, **50**, 43)

# Chanstone Tump No. 2 (SO 367 358)

On the opposite side of the River Dore to No. 1 and almost adjoining the road is this second motte. It is about 40m in diameter and rises a bare 1.2m above the slight ditch. (VCH, 231; RCHM, **1**, 245 + plan - xxxv; TWNFC, **1938**, 146; Treasures, 46; RSB, 19-20; HAN, **50**, 43)

# Wacton

**Wacton Court moat** (SO 615 575)
Wacton is a small parish 5km north-west of Bromyard. The Court, which is immediately west of the ruined church, is of seventeenth century date and is built in the main bailey of the motte and bailey castle described below, part of the bailey ditch being utilised as a moat around the house. The moat is still visible as a pond on the north and east sides of the Court, separating it from the church ruins. (VCH, 251; RCHM, **2**, 195; RSB, 20)

**Motte & bailey** (SO 614 576)
The motte is about 70m north of the Court. It is oval, about 24m across the main axis and stands about 3.5m above the surrounding ditch. Foundations in the motte point to a probable round keep. A stone scatter, joining the motte to the remaining arm of the moat around the Court, can be seen after ploughing and indicates the line of a probable bailey wall. The Court is within this bailey. It is suggested that the ruined church could be in a second bailey to the east. (RCHM, **2**, 195; Treasures, 27; RSB, 20; HAN, **1**, 1; **50**, 45; **51**, 7; **57**, 16 + plan)

# Walford

**Great Howle Camp** (SO 611 201)
Great Howle is 2.5km east of Walford Church and 4km south of Ross. The Camp, which is on the top of Howle Hill, is described by the RCHM as 'a roughly rectangular enclosure with rounded angles and a rampart with openings, perhaps modern, at the north-west and south-east ends.' The rampart is about 3m high and the internal enclosure, which is about 0.13 of a hectare, is 1-2m above the surrounding ground. There are slight traces of an external ditch. RSB considers it to be a ringwork and notes that Saxo-Norman pottery has been found there along with signs of burning. (RCHM, **2**, 200 + plan - xxvi; RSB, 20)

# Walford, Letton & Newton

**Letton Mound** (SO 381 701)
This site is some 3.5km west-north-west of Wigmore. There are several features here which could, with the eye of faith, represent a castle. They include disturbed areas, a squarish hollow in the ground with 3m sides, and ditches possibly associated with waterworks. It is perhaps more likely that they represent a deserted medieval village rather than a castle site. (HAN, **57**, 26; **60**, 6, 59 + plan - 60)

**Walford motte & bailey** (SO 391 724)
The motte, 0.2km south of the cross-roads at Walford and 2km east of Brampton Bryan, is protected on three sides by streams that flow towards the Teme. The small mound is 29m in diameter at the base, rises about 5m above the encircling ditch, and has a flat top about 11m in diameter with buried foundations that could indicate a stone keep, and traces of stonework on the south-east side. There is a causeway across the ditch on the south-western side. There are traces of a bailey on the north-east side, but the main bailey was on the east, bounded by the stream, remains of a wet moat, and the present farm. Thirteenth to fourteenth century pottery and a piece of bronze have been found on the site. (VCH, 231-2 + plan; RCHM, **3**, 192; RSB, 20 + plan opp.; HAN, **50**, 45; **57**, 24-25 + plan - 27)

**Harris Tump** (SO 386 723)
Harris Tump is 0.6km west-south-west of Walford motte. It rises 1m above the surrounding ground, is 17m in diameter at the base and only 7m across at the top. It is shown on OS maps as a tumulus although the VCH considered it to be defensive. It may have been this mound that contained 'a vase-like yellow-ware vessel of Roman form, with a beaded moulding around the swelling portion and around its base, but otherwise plain and without ornament.' It was found in 1786 and was some 18 inches tall. It was broken in the hope that it contained money, but only human bones mixed with earth were found. It would seem unlikely that this was ever a defensive mound and is more likely to be a round barrow. (VCH, 186, 231-2 + plan; RCHM, **3**, 192; Treasures, 3)

**Walford moated site** (SO 383 723)
0.3km west of Harris Tump, on the edge of Brampton Bryan parish, is an area that has been described as a moated site. It covers a larger area than most such sites, and rises to about 2m above the shallow moat along which willows congregate. It could be the remains of something more substantial. (HAN, **54**, 32A)

**Birtley possible castle site** (SO 368 694)
A low mound on the north side of the minor road to Knighton, in the garden of a stone-built house, may be a former castle. It is scarped on three sides and has pools on the west and south. A curved bank to the south of the road with a former long pool could represent the position of the bailey. The defences could all have been wet. It is perhaps more likely to be a defensive house site.

Adjoining the junction of roads at Newton, 0.3km to the south-east, there are 'many humps and bumps in the field' (SO 371 693). but these may well be associated with a neighbouring mill site.· (HAN, **57**, 22-3 + plan - 27; **58**, 35)

# Walterstone

**Motte & bailey** (SO 339 250)
Walterstone is in the south-west of the county above the River Monnow and 6km south-west of Ewyas Harold Castle. The motte and bailey castle is 100m west of the church. The motte is some 9m high above the ditch which surrounds it, and the flat top is about 10m across. The section of ditch facing the south-eastern bailey is partly wet. This kidney-shaped bailey was surrounded by a slight rampart with traces of a ditch on the southern side although most of this has now been ploughed out. There are also indications of another small bailey to the north. This castle was abandoned by 1137 and stone defences are unlikely. (VCH, 246 + plan; RCHM, **1**, 247 + plan - xxxiv; TWNFC, **1935**, ci-cii; Treasures, 50; RSB, 21; HAN, **40**, 6 + plan opp.9; **50**, 45; **53**, 16; info. P. Remfry)

**Mound** (SO 337 247)

The RCHM mention a mound, some 200m south-south-west of the motte, 6m in diameter and 0.7m high. It is probably a round barrow rather than a castle. (RCHM, **1**, 248)

# Welsh Newton

**Pembridge Castle** (SO 488 193)

*Pembridge Castle in 1846*

An impressive fortified house developed from
a thirteenth century castle
Location: 2km north-west of Welsh Newton
Access: Private, but good views can be had of the
gatehouse from the entrance, and of the whole from the road
to the north-west

Formerly called Newland Castle, the original fortification was built by Matilda de Valery before 1208 when it was passed to the Pembridges. In 1265, the family lost their land at Pembridge in north Herefordshire to Roger Mortimer of Wigmore and continued to live at Newland Castle, though by the mid-fourteenth century they were using Clehonger as their principal residence. Pembridge had a variety of occupiers including Richard de Pembridge, Warden of the Cinque Ports and Knight of the Garter. It subsequently passed to the Burley family and thence to Edmund Tudor, half-brother of Henry VI. It was eventually sold to Sir Walter Pye and became an outpost to royalist Monmouth during the Civil War. It suffered a fortnight's rather phony siege and eventual capture in 1644 and was then garrisoned until 1646 when it was ordered to be slighted.

George Kemble bought it shortly after the war and made it habitable again. At that time St John Kemble (who was executed in Hereford for his faith in 1679 and is buried at Welsh Newton) had an oratory in the house. It continued to be used and had tenant farmers throughout much of the nineteenth century. It was heavily restored at the beginning of the twentieth century when the gatehouse was repaired and the south gatehouse tower rebuilt. The curtain walls were also made complete again.

The castle is roughly rectangular and is surrounded by a moat that is kept wet by a substantial outer bank on the north-east and north-west sides. The entrance was probably by bridge and drawbridge but the moat is now dry at that point. The castle is some 45m long and 30m wide with a central courtyard 36m long and 20m wide. There are buildings along the north-western and south-western sides. The gatehouse, on the south-west side, is impressive, with two semi-circular towers each of two stories and a basement. However, most of the upper work and the ashlar refacing is modern. Even so, the length of the passage, the portcullis slots and the gate positions give an impression of strength. It was probably built in the second half of the thirteenth century.

The earliest part of the castle is probably the circular keep tower at the western angle. It is of four stories with a battered plinth but is only 7.5m in external diameter. The internal rooms are about 5m across and there was no stair within the wall thickness; access at ground and first floor would have been via the adjoining hall block, but above this level it would have probably been by internal wooden stairs or a ladder. Even so, the third floor boasts a fireplace and a corbelled-out latrine. This part of the castle and the hall block next to it (replaced in the seventeenth century) was probably built

*Pembridge Castle in 1846*

by Matilda de Valery. The chapel, which is in the northern corner of the courtyard, has a thirteenth century undercroft; the chapel itself was rebuilt in the sixteenth century. The range between the gatehouse and the circular keep is part of the seventeenth century restoration. The defences that existed in the early thirteenth century are uncertain, though the curtain wall is of the same date as the gatehouse. There are replaced sections on the north-west side (between the hall and the chapel) and on the south-east side (where it is built lower than the original). The castle is still inhabited.

The RCHM noted that to the south-east of the castle there were the remains of gun platforms of Civil War date. However, as they were only a few yards from the moat it was later suggested that they were defensive pits for musketeers as a first line of defence. They are now known to be areas levelled for cattle feeders! The better alternative for a Civil War siege emplacement is about 300m to the south, opposite where most of the damage to the castle occurred and where there is a flattened platform that could well have been the site of the siege cannon. (Robinson Cas., 111-115; VCH, 255; RCHM, **1** 250-252 + plan; TWNFC, **1900**, 20-21 + pre-restoration photo, **1927**, lxxxix-xc, + pre-restoration photo; RSB, 21; Salter, 36-37 + plan; HAN, **62**, 10 & 27-31; **63**, 13-14 + plan; info P. Remfry)

# Weobley

**Weobley Castle** (SO 403 513)

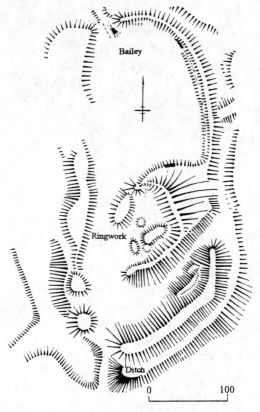

Bailey

Ringwork

Ditch

0          100

Large earthworks and partly water-filled moat
Location: Off the southern end of the village centre
Access: A public footpath crosses the site

The castle was probably built by one of the de Lacys towards the close of the eleventh century. It saw action in the wars between Stephen and Matilda and was occupied by Geoffrey Talbot after he succeeded in escaping from Hereford following the seige by the king. It was from here that Talbot set out to burn Hereford south of the Wye in retaliation for the help that the townsfolk had given the king.

Following the death of its lord, Hugh de Lacy, it temporarily passed into the king's hands and £47 was spent on it, Ewyas Lacy and the New Castle (see Longtown). It eventually passed from the de Lacys, via the de Braoses and the Gamages to the families of Verdon, Crophull, and then, by marriage, to the Devereux. In 1572, Walter Devereux was created Earl of Essex. Shortly after the title became extinct in 1646, the property was bequeathed to Thomas Thynne, Viscount Weymouth. This allowed one or more of the members of the Thynne family to represent the rotten borough of Weobley in Parliament until it was disenfranchised.

Leland, in the early sixteenth century wrote: 'From Herford to Webbeley 7 miles by west northe west, It is a market towne in Hereforde-shire, where is a goodly castell, but somewhat in decay. It was as the chefe lordshipe of the Devereux.' Robinson illustrates a plan of the castle made by Silas Taylor in 1655. It shows a rectangular keep with round corner towers, that is described as having walls 12 feet thick and standing on a hill or bank to the south of the site. The outer walls had six round towers and a gateway to the north. There was a fosse around the whole. The plan also shows two 'dwelling houses' in the bailey area north of the keep.

225

All the masonry has disappeared leaving a complex of earthworks. The main bailey area is oval-shaped, some 75m long and 65m wide, which has a massive rampart and ditch surviving on the east side, but a ditch only on the west. The southern earthwork consists of a ringwork, some 30m across, with a strong outer bank and what appears to be a double ditch. It is likely that all the ditches were originally wet. There are slight traces of stonework buried in the ramparts.

The earthworks are somewhat confused by the use of the site during the Second World War, when huts and an air raid shelter were built there. (Robinson Cas., 131-34 + plan opp. 71; VCH, 246-7; RCHM, **3**, 196 + plan - 198; TWNFC, **1888**, 252-3 + plan opp. 228; Treasures, 20; RSB, 21-22 + plan opp. 22; Salter, 45; HAN, **64**, 23-25 + plan; **65**, 12)

### Garnstone possible motte & bailey (SO 405 501)

Garnstone was the home of the Tomkyns family from the mid-sixteenth century. They probably built their new house on the hill-side on the site of an older one of uncertain date. In 1661 the estate was sold to the Parliamentarian, Colonel Birch, who carried out many alterations. This building was eventually demolished to make way for the Nash-designed castellated mansion built lower down the hill in 1806 for Samuel Peploe. This last Garnstone Castle was demolished in 1958.

The possible motte and bailey castle is close to the site of the later Garnstone Castle. There is a low motte with traces of baileys to east and west. It is on top of a slope so the ditches could never have been wet. The site may have been landscaped as part of the gardens of the last house. (Robinson Man., 291-2; HAN, **64**, 25-6 + plan)

### Little Sarnesfield (Whitehill) moated site (SO 388 522)

About 1.5km west-north-west of Weobley and just to the north-west of the A4112, the moat at Little Sarnesfield, which is now dry, encloses a roughly rectangular island with an entrance on the north. There are traces of a large rectangular enclosure to the south that includes the fourteenth century Little Sarnesfield House and possible fishponds to the east adjoining the main road. (RCHM, **3**, 196; HAN, **64**, 26 + plan)

**Nunsland moated site** (SO 379 538)

Nunsland is 4km north-west of Weobley. The wet moat originally surrounded the house and outbuildings and was almost square. It is still wet on the south-east but has otherwise been obliterated. (VCH, 251; RCHM, **3**, 196; Treasures, 18)

# Westhide

**Westhide Court moat** (SO 587 442)

Westhide is 9km north-east of Hereford. The Court is immediately east of the church and a fragmentary dry moat is apparent north of the house. (VCH, 251; RCHM, **2**, 206)

# Weston Beggard

**Shucknall** (SO 587 424)

Shucknall is the part of Weston Beggard parish adjoining the A4103, some 8km east-north-east of Hereford. Shucknall Court is just to the south of the main road and a fragmentary section of the original moat remains at the south-west corner. (VCH, 251; RCHM, **2**, 208; Treasures, 51)

# Weston-under-Penyard

**Bollitree Castle** (SO 636 240)

Weston is east of Ross-on-Wye on the A40. Bollitree is 1km north-east of the village adjoining the Roman settlement. This is not a castle, the house being of eighteenth century date. However, behind the house is the surprise—two barns of seventeenth century origin that were converted into a sham Gothic castle around 1785, including battlements and angle-turrets. Thomas Hopkins inherited the estate from his uncle and took the name Merrick and it was this Thomas Hopkins Merrick who built the castellated additions. Much of the carved stone used in this conversion probably came from a church that was being demolished in Bristol. The 'towers' are of ashlar blocks, but the 'curtain walls' are of a local rough stone that

could have come from the nearby Roman site of *Ariconium*.
(RCHM, **2**, 211; Pevsner, 317; HAN, **60**, 23)

# Whitbourne

### Whitbourne Court moat (SO 726 568)
Whitbourne Court, some 7km east-north-east of Bromyard and
close to the River Teme, is built on the site of one of the more
important of the palaces of the bishop of Hereford. The present
Court is mainly modern but does include some fifteenth century
work. The original palace may have been on the oval island
surrounded by a wet moat, which is in the garden to the south-east
of the present Court. Robinson noted its capability for defence
during the wars of the Commonwealth. (Robinson Man., 300;
VCH, 256 + plan; RCHM, **2**, 214; TWNFC, **1972**, 333-353; **1976**,
59-60; Treasures, 36)

# Whitchurch

### Lord's Wood, Doward (SO 555 150)
The Doward occupies one of the large bends in the River Wye
between Ross and Monmouth. The moated site at Lord's Wood is
2.4km south of Whitchurch and overlooks the Wye. It is of triangular form with an entrance and an inner bank on the north side.
(RCHM, **1**, 254)

# Whitney

### Whitney Castle (SO 272 465)
Whitney is on the north bank of the Wye close to the border with
Radnorshire. Whitney Castle survived for some 500 years close to
the river, but, when the Wye suddenly changed its course in 1730,
the castle was completely washed away. A tower was described at
the end of the seventeenth century and stone from the castle can be
seen downstream of the site when the river is low. (Robinson Cas.,
135-6; RSB, 22; HAN, **50**, 45)

# Wigmore

**Wigmore Castle** (SO 408 693)

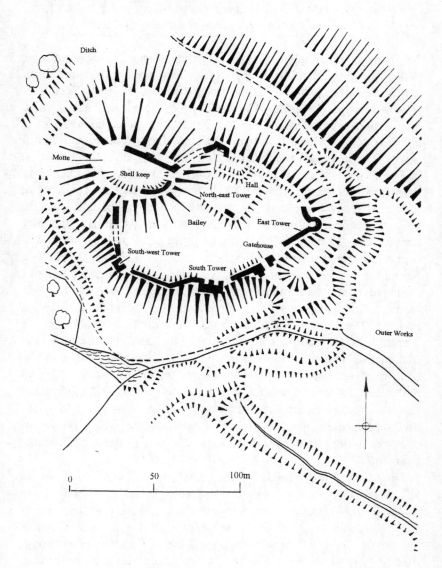

A prominent castle site with many masonry remains
partially buried in their own debris
Location: North-west of the church
Access: The site will not be generally open to the public
until the current works are completed in 1999

The Domesday Survey mentions Wigmore Castle twice, initially as part of the king's land held by Ralph de Mortimer and then in more detail under the land of Ralph. The second entry reads 'Ralph of Mortimer holds Wigmore Castle. Earl William built it on waste land which is called *Merestun*, which Gunfrid held before 1066. 2 hides which pay tax. Ralph has two ploughs in Lordship and 4 slaves. The Borough which is there pays £7.'

The first castle at Wigmore was built by William fitz Osbern in the period between 1068 and 1071. It was granted to Ralph some time after the attempt to unseat the king by Roger, William's son, in 1075. It became Ralph's seat in England and his lands eventually formed the Honour of Wigmore. Initially, Ralph's son Hugh supported the accession of Henry I, but after 1115 he rebelled in favour of the king's son-in-law, Stephen, and it appears that for some years the Mortimers may have been dispossessed of their lands, possibly only regaining them with the accession of Stephen in 1135. His support for Stephen cost him dearly when Henry I's grandson by his daughter Matilda became Henry II, the first of the Plantagenet kings. In 1155, a royal army set out to deal with the Mortimer problem together with others on the Welsh border and laid siege to several castles including Wigmore. An agreement between the parties was eventually reached although there was probably an element of mistrust throughout Henry II's reign and it does not appear that Hugh took much interest in the king's excursions into Wales.

Hugh Mortimer died in 1181, probably, like his father, at an advanced age, shortly after he had transferred his abbey from Shobdon to Wigmore. Some ten years later his son and heir, Roger Mortimer, was forced to leave the country for a while and his lands and castles were left in the hands of Richard I's chancellor. Roger died in 1215, to be succeeded by his eldest son Hugh, who died in 1227, and his second son Ralph who died in 1246. Hugh had been granted 20 marks in 1223 towards strengthening the castle when Llywelyn ab Iorworth was threatening the border.

Ralph's son Roger, who was born in 1231, was a staunch supporter of Henry III in the Baronial and Welsh wars. This period of unrest and civil war, which was greatly to the advantage of the Welsh, is likely to have been a time when the defences of Wigmore Castle were improved. It was this Roger to whom Prince Edward came after escaping from his captivity by Simon de Montfort following the Battle of Lewes in 1264, and who also took part in the decisive Battle of Evesham in the following year. After evading his guards on Widemarsh Common near Hereford, the prince was taken to Roger's stronghold at Wigmore and showed his gratitude before his accession to the throne in 1272, by agreeing to additional powers for the Wigmore lordship.

Roger was succeeded to the lordship of Wigmore in 1282 by his second son, Edmund, who died in 1304 leaving a minor as his heir. This was the Roger who was to become Edward II's lieutenant in Wales, but following his increasing influence on Edward's wife and after an armed rebellion in 1321, he was committed to the Tower, only to escape to France in 1325. A record of the weapons held in the castle in 1322, after Mortimer's rebellion, is curious. 'Three Spryngholds, or machines for casting great stones or metal quarrels; crossbows of horn and wood, some fitted with stirrup irons for the purpose of winding up the bows, others of simple construction; helmets for jousts and for real war, lances and spears, six tents and pavilions, suits of armour and coats of mail, the Irish axe, Saracenic bows and arrows.' Also amongst the effects there were 'a large chess board painted and gilt with chessmen, a board for tables and drafts; and, in the courtyard, five peacocks and a good store of grain and beasts.'

Roger had much influence on Isabella, the wife of the weak king, and was instrumental in Edward being deposed and eventually murdered at Berkeley Castle. Within a year he had been made earl of March and continued his now open relationship with the Queen. However, Edward III, on reaching 18, arranged for Mortimer to be arrested at Nottingham and in 1330 he was hanged at Tyburn.

It was many years before his grandson, Roger, took over the Wigmore estate, to become the second Earl of March, a Knight of

231

the Garter and Warden of the Cinque Ports. By this time the Mortimers were one of the largest landowners in the Marches and had inherited both the de Braose (1235) and the Lacy/Geneville (1312) estates, including some lands in Ireland. When Roger died, his son, Edmund, became the third Earl of March. He had been born in 1351 and, as a result of his marriage to Philippa the only daughter and heiress of the Duke of Clarence (the second son of Edward III), he became Earl of Ulster. He was Richard II's lieutenant in Ireland in 1380, but died the following year.

The considerable Mortimer fortune that he left to his son Roger included 'the cup of gold, and our sword garnished with gold which belonged to the good king Edward ...'. This Roger, fourth Earl of March and second Earl of Ulster, born at Usk in 1374, was left a minor under the guardianship of Richard II. When Roger came of age he found his castles and mansions in good condition. Through his mother he was declared heir presumptive to the throne should Richard die without issue. He was reputed to enjoy a splendid mode of living, but his ambitions were not to be, for Roger was slain in Ireland in 1398 at the age of 24.

His son, Edmund, fifth Earl of March, was eight when Richard II was deposed in 1399 and the new king, Henry IV, rapidly arranged for him to be moved to Windsor. This was a period of strife and rebellion, with various contenders to the throne in England (for Henry's claim to the throne was, to say the least, doubtful), and Owain Glyn Dwr leading an uprising in Wales. Sir Edmund Mortimer, the acting head of the family, went over to Glyn Dwr after his capture by the Welsh at the battle of Pilleth in 1402.

One unsuccessful attempt was made to release Edmund, Earl of March, but he stayed in captivity until Henry died in 1413, whereupon his son, Henry V, released him to help with his battles in France. Later, Edmund was sent to Ireland, where he died without issue at Trim Castle in 1424. This meant that his nephew by a sister, Richard, Duke of York, became the heir to the vast Mortimer estates. Following his death in the Wars of the Roses, his son Edward gathered together a small army from the Wigmore area and, although heavily outnumbered, defeated Owen Tudor at the Battle of Mortimer's Cross, almost within sight of the ancestral home, to become Edward IV.

Wigmore Castle, as crown property, probably had little or no use after this time, Ludlow being the preferred residence. It was apparently repaired by Bishop Lee, President of the Council of the Marches (1534-43), who found it 'utterly decayed in lodging,' and again by Sir Henry Sidney (1559-86) who used it as a prison. In 1586 a survey found that 'Two bridges there leading from the Towne of Wigmore into the Parke and Castle being very much decayed noe carriage can pass with any burden on them into the Castle or Parke. The first bridge, as well as the foundation as in the timber above wholly to be pulled down ... the other bridge partly decayed in the one end as well as in the foundations as above ... the houses, buildings, walls and other edifices in the said Castle being very much ruinous and decayed will not without great charges be repaired.'

In 1601 the castle was purchased by Thomas Harley of Brampton Bryan. Indeed, it appears that his son, Sir Robert Harley was born there. The castle was probably considered difficult to garrison effectively during the Civil War and it was dismantled by the Parliamentarians in 1643 and has remained a ruin since that date. It is suggested that the method used was to dismantle or blow up sections of wall on each side of the gatehouse and towers, thus making the castle indefensible, but allowing some further use of the buildings that remained.

The high ground coming down from Radnorshire between the rivers Lugg and Teme converges and descends towards the east until it forms a spur or ridge, bounded to the south by a steep narrow valley and to the north by the moor after which Wigmore gets part of its name. (The other half comes from the old English *wicga* meaning 'beetle, or something that wriggles'.) The remains of the castle sit astride this ridge and are bounded on the west by a deep, apparently man-made ravine which traverses the ridge and cuts off the eastern portion from the higher, broader ground to the west. The ridge, as it continues to the south-east, includes the church, about 0.5km from the main part of the castle, before dropping down to the present main road. The line of the Roman road, which originally joined Chester to Caerleon, crosses Wigmore Moor about 0.7km east of the present road on its way to the Roman station at Leintwardine, some 5km to the north.

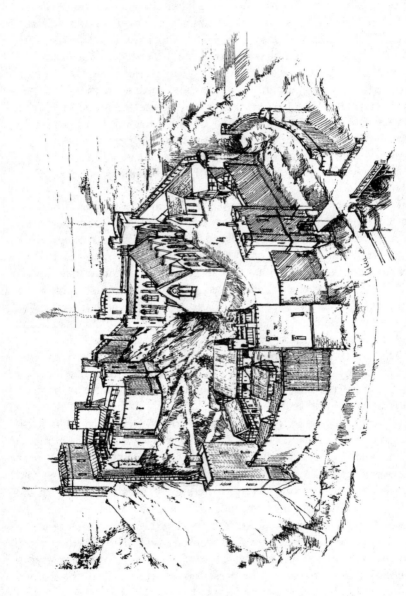

*Reconstruction of Wigmore Castle at the height of its power during the fourteenth and fifteenth centuries*

The castle is essentially of motte and bailey design with the motte to the north-west overlooking the ravine. To the south-east is the main bailey, little larger in ground area than the motte due to the confines of the site, cut off from the rest of the ridge by a 9m deep ditch, counterscarp and outer ditch. The relatively flat area of the ridge to the south-east of the main bailey has little in the way of defence apart from its position, but at the south-eastern end is an embankment, which, although prominent, may be partly natural. Eastwards of this bank is what appears to be a small motte, separated by a ditch from a small bailey between it and the more massive embankment. To the north-west of the main castle, across the ravine, is a small mound separated from the rest of the ridge by two small ditches. It has been suggested that the mound nearest the church could be the original Wigmore Castle or alternatively that both these small mounds are siege castles dating to 1155.

To the north-east, running down the slope towards Wigmore Marsh, was an enclosure formed by two banks with external ditches. These banks were quite prominent in the 1930s, but have since been ploughed out apart from a short section near the main motte. Although they may have had a defensive significance, it is possible that they formed part of Wigmore Park mentioned in the late sixteenth century. The main park, according to an early nineteenth century writer, was on the hills west of the castle but had been 'ploughed up and cultivated.'

There are no indications of stonework associated with the outworks of the castle although it has been suggested that the embankment adjoining the eastern 'castle bailey' conceals a wall and tower and a resistivity survey in the flat area of the ridge to the east of the main bailey has indicated what are considered to be the foundations of two buildings with stone footings.

The counterscarp bank between the two ditches that encircles the main bailey is of some interest. The feature is strongest to the north-east of the castle entry where there is a wide flat area with three almost semi-circular projections into the outer ditch. Although there is no visible masonry a wall with open-backed towers, appearing as an outer defensive work, would seem probable. The Buck engraving suggests that there was an entry from the gatehouse or barbican passage onto this embankment.

*The gateway, looking out, almost blocked with its own debris*

The masonry remains comprise the bailey curtain wall including several towers and a gatehouse; traces of buildings in the bailey; and the remaining buildings and shell keep on the motte.

The gatehouse still stands two storeys high, but the lower 2 to 3m, at least, is buried in debris to the extent that the the arch seems to spring out of the ground. The walls of the external gate passage, apparent on the early prints, have also become largely buried in debris. It has suffered since 1872 when it was described as having 'two chambers above; one for the working of the outer, and one for that of the inner portcullis ... In the inner chamber is seen part of a large fireplace with a good Decorated hood.' Access to the guardrooms was gained in the right tower by a newel staircase. The curtain wall joining the gatehouse to the south tower stands some 3m high above the raised internal ground level and about 6m high on the outer face. The Buck engraving indicates a postern gate and a first-floor window in this section, but these features are no longer apparent.

The south tower was a large, two-storey building that projected out from the curtain wall. Underneath the eastern part is a vaulted basement which, when it was found in 1870, was described as follows: 'The room descends by a great many steps below the level of the adjoining courtyard, to a strong arch or doorway; half-a-yard further on is another strong arch, the bolts, locks, and hinges of massive iron still remain, the doors themselves are decayed. Inside the inner door are two or three very deep steps on descending which the ground floor is reached. On removing the rubbish away, bones, tiles etc were discovered together with two very massive iron staples in the wall. ... The room is arched over and from all appearance was the dungeon of the Castle. By the side of this room was another of the same dimensions, but which had wooden rafters to support the roof. The rafters having decayed, the roof and rubbish above have fallen in.' This three-storied tower had two heated rooms at ground floor level and one larger room, also heated, on the first floor. The internal north wall of this building is missing and may have been of timber.

The south-western tower is reached by following the curtain wall to the west. The inside face of this section of wall cannot be seen from the bailey, being hidden behind a large mound of debris. Part of the outside face of this section of the curtain wall, some 8m in length, collapsed in 1986 exposing a friable wall core. Excavations at this point have shown that the bailey side of the wall is filled over 2.5m deep with debris that has accumulated over the years from the various buildings in the castle.

The south-west tower is projecting and rectangular like the one to the south, but is not as wide and contains only one room on each floor. From here the curtain wall rises up the side of the motte to the keep. At the foot of the motte in the curtain wall is the top of an almost completely hidden doorway—probably a postern gate.

On the eastern side of the gatehouse, the curtain wall continues to the east tower. The east tower is semi-circular, but was apparently not open-backed as traces of a cross-wall can be seen. The upstanding curtain wall continues northwards to a point where it turns abruptly to the north-west. Beyond this point the remains are largely buried, but some 12m from the corner traces of an opening that may have led into a second semi-circular tower similar to that on the east have been recorded. From a defensive point of view this would have been sensible as the two towers would have been able to provide flanking fire for the otherwise undefended and blind corner. Continuing westwards along the line of the curtain wall, and a little way short of the north-east tower, indications of a second buried arch have also been noted. It appears that throughout much of this part of the castle at least a whole storey is buried in debris.

The north-east tower has three separate faces to the outside, being semi-hexagonal. Once again this was a residential tower, probably associated with the adjoining buildings in the courtyard. From this tower, the curtain wall can be followed as a grass-covered mound, up the side of the motte to where it joins the shell keep. There are traces of several buildings in this part of the bailey, where walls appear to be buried in debris up to 3 or 4 metres deep. It is suggested that here are the remains of a vast hall and service complex with the north-east tower acting as a solar. Details from the Buck engraving would seem to add some confirmation to this suggestion. The buried foundations of another building, also shown on Buck, are apparent as grass-covered mounds in the courtyard to the east of the gatehouse. There are indications that there were other buildings in the bailey and it may be that both the south and south-west towers originally acted as solar wings to large hall ranges mainly built of timber on stone foundations.

The motte is large and oval-shaped. The top is about 50m along the ridge and 20m across; the whole being about 20m above the lower part of the bailey. At bailey level the motte occupies an area of about 90 by 60m, almost the same area as the entire lower bailey. The remains of the shell keep are impressive; the buttressed north wall being still 30m long. The south wall is only evident as a series of mounds, but, accepting their height above the central area of the shell keep, they may well conceal the whole of the postern gate(s) and the base of the semi-circular tower shown on the Buck print. Indeed, this opening was described in an article in 1874 as 'in the south wall, much choked with rubbish, is an opening with a low, pointed arch, once the gateway between the inner and the outer ward.' The tower on the south-east, facing the bailey, which is shown with two distinct stories above a buried ground floor on the eighteenth and nineteenth century prints is now reduced to a single storey. This is still the first floor; the ground floor being buried in debris.

However, the greatest recent loss may well be at the western end of the motte, where a single fragment of a stair tower, at least three-stories high, is precariously poised above the ravine. This stair includes doorway and/or window jambs on both the east and the south sides. There is substantial mounding to the north of this fragment. The 1874 article is of some help in resolving these features. The author, whose main description is very reliable, describes the ravine and then goes on to say: 'Upon the eastern verge of this ravine is piled up a mound of earth, in form conical, and about 30ft high, above its rocky base, though 100ft or more above the bottom of the ravine. The mound is about 30ft diameter at its flat top ... Close east of the mound, and about 40ft below its top, is a roughly oval area, about 100ft east and west by 50ft north and south.' It is evident from the description that the 9m high mound that was seen then 'on the edge of, and in part within, an oval area' has largely disappeared—the oval being the area of the present shell keep.

The author goes on to say 'Upon the summit of the mound he built, as the foundations still shew, a circular or polygonal tower as a keep. From thence a curtain-wall sprang from its opposite sides and encircled the small eastern area, forming the inner ward.'

If, as has been suggested, there is a buried opening hidden in the mound of debris to the north of the stair fragment, then there could be a substantial amount of this tower surviving but totally buried. Stirling-Brown, on the basis of observations he made some years ago, also suggests that here was an octagonal tower, at least 14m in diameter, with unequal sides and consisting of three storeys and a basement.

The author of the 1874 report also describes the section of the shell keep opposite the mound. He mentions the north wall, but to the east of it he saw 'what appears to be a round tower, of which only a heap of ruins remains.' He then describes the window embrasure that still exists as being to the south of this tower. He could be describing one side of a gateway.

If it is accepted that there was a mound with a keep upon it at the western edge of the present shell keep, then it can be postulated that the whole of the uppermost levels could represent a small motte and bailey in its own right, with the present shell keep simply reflecting the bailey. This could well be the original eleventh century Wigmore Castle.

The means of access from the lower bailey to the top of the large motte is uncertain. It could have been through the doorway shown on the Buck engraving in the south wall, although it is difficult to see how there could have been any easy access up the side of the motte at that point. The alternative is that the main access was on the eastern side of the motte, close to the curtain wall, and where the round tower also described above stood. Could this tower have been associated with the buildings standing below it at this point? There is no indication of a ditch between the motte and the bailey, so it is quite possible that there was some form of entrance gateway or barbican rising up the side of the motte. The possibility of some form of spiral stair within a high, circular tower is not completely impossible.

When the Department of National Heritage took the monument into guardianship in 1995, English Heritage immediately became responsible for the site and for the safety of visitors and members of the public. This is the largest castle on the Welsh Border and indeed possibly in the country which has been left in its natural state, gradually decaying since it was last in use. Because of this, and because of its importance to the history of England and Wales, it is a site of national or even international importance. The intention is to make the castle safe for visitors, but with the minimum of intervention. English Heritage, appreciating the dangerous condition of much of the masonry, has fenced off the whole of the castle with locked gates and warning notices. (Robinson Cas., 137-142; VCH, 247-8 + plan; RCHM, **3**, 205-8 + plans; Treasures, 5; RSB, 22-24 + plan opp. 24; Salter, 46-7 + plan; HAN, **6**; 48, 30 + plan; **59**, 5; **63**, 15; Remfry, P.M., 1995b; GTC, 1874)

### Possible motte and bailey (SO 411 692)
South-east of the masonry castle, on the ridge towards the church, is a site which, it has been suggested, represents the earlier castle. The ridge is narrow here and steep on the north side, but much of it has been developed for housing making interpretation difficult. The castle, if such it is, consists of a small mound with an equally small bailey on each side along the ridge. It could be a siege castle. (Treasures, 5; RSB, 24; HAN, **61**, 29-30 + plan)

### Mound (SO 405 694)
On the western edge of the great ditch that separates Wigmore Castle from the main ridge is a small mound that could be associated with the defences of the castle or alternatively a second siege castle. (RCHM, **3**, 208; RSB, 24)

### Lodge Farm moated site (SO 387 694)
Lodge Farm, some 2.5 km west of Wigmore, is of early sixteenth century date. The site is about 0.3km north-north-west of the farm and consists of a low circular mound some 24m in diameter surrounded by a moat which is still wet in parts. There are slight traces of a bailey on the east side although it is almost ploughed out. The site is approached from the north-west by a sunken track. (RSB, 25 + plan opp. 20; HAN, **57**, 12 + plan)

# Willey

### Willey Lodge possible castle site (SO 336 692)
Willey is in the west of the county, the seventeenth century Willey Lodge being about 5km north-north-east of Presteigne. The house is towards the end of a small promontory overlooking a narrow valley. There are some foundations which, it has been suggested, represent a keep. There is no indication of a bailey. (RSB, 25)

# Winslow

**Rowden Abbey moat** (SO 632 564)
Winslow is a township to the west of Bromyard. The VCH notes that 'the site of Rowden Abbey retains a large amount of moating on the west, and some portions on other sides.' The Abbey, as the house of the Rowden family was called, was pulled down in the latter part of the eighteenth century, but the moats were left. There is no reason to suppose there was ever an abbey on the site, the more probable derivation of the name being a corruption of Rowden d'Abitot after the family of that name who owned land in the vicinity. (Robinson Man., 50; VCH, 251)

# Yarkhill

**Moated site** (SO 608 426)
Yarkhill is midway between the A4103 Worcester road and the A438 Ledbury road, about 10km east of Hereford. The moat is some 50m south of the church on the north bank of the River Frome, and is rectangular in shape. The island is about 50m across and very overgrown. (VCH, 251; RCHM, **2**, 224; Salter, 52; Treasures, 52; HAN, **24**, 4 + plan)

**Showle Court moat** (SO 612 437)
Showle Court is 1.2m north-north-east of the church. The house is of early seventeenth century date. The moat, which is to the south-east of the house, formerly enclosed a roughly-rectangular island, but is now fragmentary and may have been extended to form a pond. (VCH, 251; RCHM, **2**, 224; Salter, 52)

# Index of Site Names, giving Parishes

| | | | |
|---|---|---|---|
| Ashton Castle | Eye, Moreton & Ashton | Eaton Tregoz | Foy |
| Batch Twt | Almeley | Ecclewall Castle | Linton-by-Ross |
| Birtley | Walford, Letton & Newton | Ellingham Castle | Much Marcle |
| | | Elvastone | Harewood |
| | | Ewyas Lacy Castle | Longtown |
| Bishopstone Court | Bishopstone | Fawley 'Camp' | Brockhampton-by-Ross |
| Bolitree Castle | Weston-u-Penyard | | |
| Bollingham Mound | Eardisley | Fields Place | Dilwyn |
| Bowlston Court | Kentchurch | Ford Abbey | Pudleston |
| Brilley Green | Brilley | Freens Court | Sutton |
| Brinsop Court | Brinsop | Freetown | Ashperton |
| Brockbury | Colwall | Garnstone | Weobley |
| Bronsil Castle | Eastnor | Garway Hill | Garway |
| Bryngwyn | Much Dewchurch | Gatley Farm | Aymestrey |
| Burton Court | Eardisland | Gillow Manor | Hentland |
| Butthouse | King's Pyon | Great Howle | Walford |
| Cabal Tump | Pembridge | Great Hunthouse | Longtown |
| Camp Field | Foy | Hall Court | Much Marcle |
| Camp Wood | Aymestrey | Harris Tump | Walford, Letton & Newton |
| Capel Tump | King's Capel | | |
| Castle Bach | Longtown | Haye Park Wood | Richard's Castle |
| Castle Farm | Madley | Hellens | Much Marcle |
| Castle Farm | Upton Bishop | Hell Moat | Sarnesfield |
| Castle Hill | Kington | Hell Wood | Huntington |
| Castle Twts | Kington Rural | Hemhill | Lugwardine |
| Castleton Farm | Ocle Pychard | Herefs. Beacon | Colwall |
| Chanstone | Vowchurch | Hergest Court | Kington Rural |
| Chapel Tump | Hentland | Hill of Eaton | Foy |
| Checkley | Mordiford | Hinton Farm | Felton |
| Cheyney Court | Bishop's Frome | Hole-in-the-Wall | Foy |
| Chickward | Kington Rural | Hopton | Bishop's Frome |
| Church Farm | Mathon | Howle Hill | Walford |
| Church House Fm. | Moreton on Lugg | Howton Farm | Kenderchurch |
| Clouds | Mordiford | Hunton Tump | Pembridge |
| Colley's Forge | King's Capel | Kentchurch Court | Kentchurch |
| Comfort Castle | Leominster | Knapp Farm | Bridge Sollars |
| Corras | Kentchurch | Knapp Farm | Brilley |
| Cothill Tump | Turnastone | Langstone Court | Llangarron |
| Court Farm | Foy | Lawton's Hope | Canon Pyon |
| Court Farm | Mansell Lacy | Ledicot | Shobdon |
| Court Farm | Sollars Hope | Lemore | Eardisley |
| Court House | Pembridge | Letton Mound | Walford, Letton & Newton |
| Court of Noke | Pembridge | | |
| Court-y-Park | Pixley | Little Dilwyn | Dilwyn |
| Cublington Castle | Madley | Little Hengoed | Huntington |
| Cummins Farm | Colwall | Little Sarnesfield | Weobley |
| Cwmma Farm | Brilley | Llancillo Court | Llancillo |
| Didley Court | St Devereux | Lodge Farm | Wigmore |
| Digget's Wood | Kilpeck | Lord's Wood | Whitchurch |

| | | | |
|---|---|---|---|
| Lower Ashton 'Camp' | Eye, Moreton & Ashton | Rowden Abbey | Winslow |
| Lower Brockhampton | Brockhampton-by-Bromyard | Sawbury Hill | Bredenbury |
| | | Seed Farm | Cradley |
| | | Shobdon Court | Shobdon |
| Lower Court | Kinsham | Showle Court | Yarkhill |
| Lower Court | Munsley | Shucknall | Weston Beggard |
| Lower Hopton | Stoke Lacy | Snodhill Castle | Peterchurch |
| Lower Hyde | Leominster Out | Stoke Cross | Stoke Lacy |
| Lower Lyde Court | Pipe & Lyde | Stretton Court | Stretton Sugwas |
| Lower Pedwardine | Brampton Bryan | Strong House | Canon Frome |
| Mainstone Court | Pixley | Sutton Walls | Sutton |
| Martin's Castle | Collington | Tarrington Court | Tarrington |
| Meer Court | Allensmore | Temple Court | Bosbury |
| Millend Farm | Castle Frome | The Bage | Clifford |
| Milton House | Shobdon | The Camp | Eardisley |
| Moat Farm | Mathon | The Camp | Much Dewchurch |
| Moat Farm | Orcop | The Doward | Whitchurch |
| Moat House | Bodenham | The Gobbets | Peterchurch |
| Moat House | Hope Mansell | The Yeld | Pembridge |
| Monk's Court | Eardisland | Thruxton Court | Thruxton |
| Monnington Court | Vowchurch | Treago Castle | St Weonard's |
| Moor Abbey | Middleton | Tregate Castle | Llanrothal |
| Morehampton Park Farm | Abbey Dore | Trelough | St Devereux |
| | | Tretire Castle | Tretire |
| Mortimer's Castle | Much Marcle | Trilloes Park | Bolstone |
| Mouse Castle | Cusop | Turret Castle | Huntington |
| Mynydd-brith | Dorstone | Turret Tump | Huntington |
| Nant-y-Bar | Dorstone | Twyn-y-Corras | Kentchurch |
| Nether Court | Stoke Lacy | Upleadon Court | Bosbury |
| Netherwood | Thornbury | Upper Buckton | Buckton & Coxall |
| New Birchend | Castle Frome | Upper Hyde | Leominster Out |
| New House | Stretton Grandison | Upper Pedwardine | Brampton Bryan |
| Newcourt Farm | Bacton | Upper Wetton | Pembridge |
| Newland Castle | Welsh Newton | Upper Wintercott | Leominster Out |
| Newton Tump | Clifford | Urishay Castle | Peterchurch |
| Nunsland | Weobley | Wacton Court | Wacton |
| Offa's Castle | Sutton | Walford Motte | Walford, Letton & Newton |
| Old Castleton | Clifford | | |
| Old Court | Bredwardine | Wallingstones | Llangarron |
| Old Court Farm | Bosbury | Walsopthorne | Ashperton |
| Old Longworth | Lugwardine | Wellbrook Manor | Peterchurch |
| Oldcastle Twt | Almeley | Westhide Court | Westhide |
| Oldcastle Wood | Lingen | Wharton Court | Leominster Out |
| Paunceford Court | Munsley | Whitehill | Weobley |
| Pauncefort Court | Much Cowarne | Whitehouse Camp | Michaelchurch Escley |
| Pembridge Castle | Welsh Newton | Whitbourne Court | Whitbourne |
| Penyard Castle | Ross Rural | Willey Lodge | Willey |
| Pixley Court | Pixley | Wilton Castle | Bridstow |
| Pont Hendre | Longtown | Woodsheaves | Eardisley |
| Poston Castle | Vowchurch | Woodville | Kington Rural |
| Quatsford | Ledbury Rural | Yearston Court | Upper Sapey |

# Select Bibliography

Andere, M., 1996, *Arthurian links with Herefordshire*, Logaston, Herefordshire

Anon, nd, *Felsted in Herefordshire*

Anon, 1981, *Herefordshire Countryside Treasures*, 1981

Arch. Camb., 1852, Note referring to Wigmore Castle in *Archaeologia Cambrensis*, Vol III new series, p. 326

Children, G. & Nash, G., 1994, *Prehistoric Sites of Herefordshire*, Monuments in the Landscape - Vol 1, Logaston, Herefordshire

Coplestone-Crow, B., 1989, *Herefordshire Place-Names*, BAR British Series No. 214, Oxford

Cornforth, J., 1973, 'Hampton Court, Herefordshire', *Country Life*, (3 parts in Feb 22, Mar 1 & Mar 8 issues)

Curnow P.E. & Thompson M.W., 1969, Richard's Castle, *J. Brit. Archaeol. Assn.*, 105-27

Davies, W., 1979, *The Llandaff Charters*

Delaney C. J. & Soulsby, I. N., 1975, *Archaeological Implications of redevelopment in the historic towns of Monmouth district*

Fox, C., 1955, *Offa's Dyke - A Field Survey*

Garmonsway, G.N., 1953, (trans), *The Anglo-Saxon Chronicle*

Gelling, M., (ed.), 1983, *Offa's Dyke Reviewed by Frank Noble*, BAR British Series No. 114

Gelling, M., 1992, *The West Midlands in the Early Middle Ages*, Leicester

G.T.C., 'Wigmore', *Archaeologia Cambrensis*, 4th series, XVIII, 1874, 97-109

HAN, various issues, *Herefordshire Archaeological News*

HAS, various reports, *Hereford Archaeology Series*

Heys, F.G., 1963, 'Excavations on a medieval site at Breinton, Herefordshire', *Trans. Woolhope Natur. Fld. Club*, 1963, 272-94

Hillaby, J., 1985, 'Herefordshire Gold: Irish, Welsh and English land. Part 2: The Clients of the Jewish Community at Hereford 1179-1253,' *Trans. Woolhope Natur. Fld. Club*, 1985, 193-270

Hodges, G., 1995, *Owain Glyn Dwr and the war of independence in the Welsh Borders*, Logaston, Herefordshire

Hope-Taylor, B., 'The Norman motte at Abinger, Surrey, and its wooden castle', in Bruce-Mitford, R.L.S., (ed), *Recent archaeological investigations in Britain*, 1956, 223-50

Kenyon, J.R. & Avent, R., (ed.), 1987, *Castles in Wales and the Marches*, Cardiff

Kenyon, J.R., 1990, *Medieval Fortifications*, Leicester

Lamont, A.H., 'Fords and Ferries of the Wye', *Trans. Woolhope Natur. Fld. Club*, 1922, 73-94

Leather , E.M., 1912, *Folklore of Herefordshire*, Hereford (and later reprints)

Lewis, T.T., 1854, *Letters of the Lady Brilliana Harley ...*, Camden Soc., London

Lobel, M.D., 1969, *Historic Towns*, Vol 1 (Hereford offprint)

Margary, 1967, *Roman Roads in Britain*

Marshall, G., 'The Norman Occupation of the Lands in the Golden Valley, Ewyas, and Clifford and their Motte and Bailey Castles', *Trans. Woolhope Natur. Fld. Club*, 1938, 141-58

Pevsner, N., 1963, *The Buildings of England, Herefordshire*

Radford, C.A.R., 1958, *Goodrich Castle*, English Heritage Guidebook

Remfry, P.M., 1995a, *Clifford Castle*, Malvern Link

Remfry, P.M., 1995b, *The Mortimers of Wigmore, 1066 to 1181. Part 1: Wigmore Castle*, Malvern Link

Remfry, P.M., 1996, *Brampton Bryan*, Malvern Link

Renn, D., 1973, *Norman Castles in Britain*, London

RCHM (Vol 1 - 1931; Vol 2 - 1932, Vol 3 - 1934) *An Inventory of the Historical Monuments in Herefordshire*

Robinson, C.J., 1869, *A History of the Castles of Herefordshire and their Lords*

Robinson, C.J., 1872, *A History of the Mansions and Manors of Herefordshire*

Salter, M.,1989, *The Castles of Herefordshire and Worcestershire*

Smith, L.T., 1964, *The itinerary of John Leland*, (5 vols.) Illinois, U.S.

Stanford, S.C., 1991, *The Archaeology of the Welsh Marches*, Leinthall Starkes

Stirling-Brown, R., (RSB), 1989, *Herefordshire Castles*, Privately published

Shoesmith, R., 1980a, *A short history of Castle Green and Hereford Castle*, (pamphlet), Hereford

Shoesmith, R., 1980b, *Excavations at Castle Green*, CBA Research Report No. 36, London

Shoesmith, R., 1987, 'Urishay Chapel', *Trans. Woolhope Natur. Fld. Club*, 1987, 686-720

Shoesmith, R., 1991, *Excavations at Chepstow 1973-1974*, Cambrian Archaeological Monographs No. 4

Shoesmith, R. (ed.), 1992, 'Excavations at Kilpeck, Herefordshire', *Trans. Woolhope Natur. Fld. Club*, 1992, 162-209

Shoesmith, R., 1994, *The Pubs of Hereford City*, Logaston, Herefordshire

Shoesmith, R., 1995, *The Civil War in Hereford*, Logaston, Herefordshire

Shoesmith, R., forthcoming, 'Bronsil Castle', *Trans. Woolhope Natur. Fld. Club*

Slade, H.G., 1981, 'Brampton Bryan Castle', *Archaeological Journal*, 138, 26-29

Thompson, M.W., 1987, *The Decline of the Castle*, Cambridge

Thompson, M.W., 1991, *The Rise of the Castle*, Cambridge

Thorn, F. & Thorn, C., 1983, *Domesday Book - Herefordshire*

TWNFC, various years, *Transactions of the Woolhope Naturalists Field Club*

VCH, 1908, *The Victoria History of the Counties of England - Herefordshire*

Webb, J., (ed) Webb T.W., 1879, *Memorials of the Civil War between King Charles I and the Parliament of England as it affected Herefordshire and the adjacent counties*, 2 Vols, London

Whitehead, D.A., 1982, in Shoesmith, R., *Hereford City Excavations - Excavations on and close to the defences*, CBA Research Report No. 46, London

Wighton, W.E., 1962, *The Palatine Earldom of William fitz Osbern in Gloucestershire and Worcestershire (1066-1071)*, English Historical Review, 77, 1962, 6-17

Williams, A., 1956, *Brampton Bryan 1643-1956*, (pamphlet-privately published)

## Other books in the Monuments in the Landscape series

### Vol. 1 Prehistoric Sites of Herefordshire

by George Children and George Nash, this details our knowledge of the Stone, Bronze and Iron Ages in Herefordshire, using archaeological evidence, comparisons with neighbouring areas and ethnography. The authors advance theories about how early society interacted with the landscape, especially that which they created. Herefordshire is well-known for its array of hillforts, and many of these are detailed in the site descriptions, together with earlier barrows, standing stones and chambered tombs. 144pp with some 50 photographs, plans and maps. £6.95. ISBN 1 873827 09 1

### Vol. III Castles of Radnorshire

by Paul Remfry. The history of the centuries of warfare and changing alliances in Radnorshire is covered in some detail for it provides the background to the construction of the castles; indeed, much of the recorded history is about the regular sieges and their capture. Detailed information is also given about all the castle sites. 160pp with some 35 photographs, plans and maps. £7.95. ISBN 1 873827 54 7

### Vol. IV Prehistoric Sites of Monmouthshire

by George Children and George Nash, this is similar in format to their first volume in the series, *Prehistoric Sites of Herefordshire*. However, they have developed their theories further in the light of additional research in Monmouthshire, an area which has interesting Stone Age finds along the shores of the Severn Estuary, in addition to Bronze Age complexes, standing stones and later hillforts. 144pp with some 40 photographs, plans and maps. £7.95. ISBN 1 873827 49 0